UNLEASHING
the
BEAST

PERRY STONE

UNLEASHING THE BEAST by Perry Stone
Published by FrontLine
Charisma Media/Charisma House
600 Rinehart Road
Lake Mary, Florida 32746
www.charismahouse.com

With warmest regards I dedicate this book to the thousands of partners of our ministry. Without your prayers to strengthen us and your support to send us to the nations, the arms of our outreach would be weaker and shortened. I am thankful that you have caught the vision and importance of the "last day" prophetic message and have stood with us to pull in the net of souls from the sea of humanity. We pray God will bless you in this life, and together we will stand at heaven's gates and watch the souls from the nations that we have won together sit down as a family in the future kingdom of the Messiah.

Your Covenant Partner,
Perry Stone

CONTENTS

INTRODUCTION

THERE IS AN UNSETTLING MOOD HANGING LIKE FOREBODING storm clouds over North America. This restlessness reminds me of the gusting winds that rattle leaves and bend branches prior to a southern April storm sweeping in from the west. From the polished, silver-tongued, ever-promising-the-good-times politicians strutting through the marble halls of Congress to the pin-striped, suit-wearing Wall Street stockbrokers, it seems everyone is concerned about how America will progress going forward. Are the financial good times memories? Are we entering a dark tunnel of moral and spiritual regression?

After all, most prophetic empires continue for two to three hundred years; then they peak and slowly decline. The major empires of history don't necessarily disappear from the scene—many simply no longer have the power, influence, and economic edge that they once had. They become followers instead of leaders, borrowers instead of lenders, the tail and not the head (Deut. 28:43–44).

Americans have pulled up to the gas pump and felt the high price of fuel sucking their expendable income out of their wallet. Some people are digging out a few rusty pennies and change from dresser drawers to help put milk and bread on the table. Nations are anxiously watching as Europe reunites as one borderless coalition into the strong arms of the European Union, and they ask: Will the new

1

euro currency replace the dollar? Will a united Europe rise from the ashes of past wars to emerge as the major, final empire of history?

If Europe will be the final empire, then what about the 1.4 billion Muslims throughout the world who for fourteen hundred years have anticipated the last days and the uniting of a final *Islamic caliphate empire* ruled by their *caliph*? Their "awaited one" will rule the world clutching a sword in one hand and waving a Quran in the other. Will Muslims allow the Western powers of liberal democracy to sweep across Europe and threaten fourteen centuries of Islamic culture, religion, and tradition?

Where is America moving, and where is the world heading? Who will emerge from among the sea of nations as the survivor and the leader? According to the prophets of the Bible, there will arise out of the ocean of humanity a kingdom, described by biblical visionaries as the *kingdom of the beast*. The head of this coalition will unite ten kings and their nations, directing a final assault against Israel, Jerusalem, and the Jews. He will control all buying and selling, and only those who accept his rule, his religion, and his mark will be permitted to purchase and sell goods. (See Revelation 13:16–18.)

Before 9/11, no one could see such a kingdom coming in America except a few high-level officials in federal intelligence agencies. Since 9/11, seldom a day passes without an Islamic nation (such as Iraq, Iran, Afghanistan, and Pakistan) making headline news. Fanatical Islamic regimes such as Hamas and Hezbollah are spewing fiery rhetoric like flaming swords from their mouths in hopes of spreading their message of, "Death to the little Satan, Israel, and death to the great Satan, America." Where are we headed, and what role does America play on this End Time prophetic stage?

This informative and prophetically stirring book, *Unleashing the Beast*, will detail biblical prophecies and Islamic traditions that point to the rise of a coming kingdom and a final global dictator who will seize the world. You will discover that the Bible identifies this man as the *Antichrist*, and Islam calls the leader of the last caliphate the *Mahdi*.

I have had several Muslim friends from the Middle East since 1993 with whom I have shared this information. Although they disagree with my final conclusion, they have told me that they had never seen biblical prophetic information put together in this manner, and it really "made them think" about what the Bible predicts.

There may be some Christians with differing opinions and beliefs from what you will read in this book. However, it is my desire to present fresh insight and to challenge a more traditional mind-set about prophetic events. After all, some prophecies can best be understood as they are being fulfilled in the light of current events.

The Lord Himself said, "Come now, and let us reason together" (Isa. 1:18). Keep reading for a fresh look at the biblical concept of the "time of the end" (Dan. 8:17).

THE EVIDENCE IS IN—WE ARE
IN THE TIME OF THE END

And he said, "Go your way, Daniel, for the words
are closed up and sealed till the time of the end."
—DANIEL 12:9

THE PROPHETIC SEERS ARE AT IT AGAIN. EVERY TIME A MAJOR event such as a Middle East war, a tsunami, a killer earthquake, or a Katrina-style weather phenomenon strikes the planet, the prophetic teachers and secular soothsayers begin chirping their warnings like birds in April announcing spring has arrived. Since Christ rode a cloud to heaven from the top of the Mount of Olives in Jerusalem, centuries of prophetic preachers and teachers have tried to discern every other cloud of global conflict looming over the horizon as the cloud through which Jesus may return. Are we really in the time of the end, and if we are, just what is the time of the end?

First, the time of the end is not the *end of time*—a phrase often repeated when believers speak about the last days. The phrase "end of time" is not found in either of the Testaments. Neither is the time of the end the *end of the world* as some suggest. The concept that the world is going to end is a misunderstanding of a verse in the English translation of Matthew's Gospel. Christ predicted:

> And as he sat upon the mount of Olives, the disciples came unto him privately, saying, Tell us, when shall these things be? and what shall be the sign of thy coming, and of the end of the world?
>
> —MATTHEW 24:3, KJV

The phrase "end of the world" paints a picture on the canvas of the human imagination of a total annihilation of the planet and the complete apocalyptic destruction of mankind. However, since the New Testament was written in Greek, the meanings of certain words differ in Greek from English. For example, there are three different Greek words translated as *world* in Matthew chapter 24, the famous Olivet discourse where Jesus is predicting the signs of Jerusalem's destruction, the future Tribulation, and His return to set up His kingdom. These three Greek words for *world* are:

The Word in Matthew	The Greek Word	The Meaning
The end of the world (Matt. 24:3)	*aion*	An age or a course of time
Gospel preached in all the world (Matt. 24:14)	*oikoumene*	The globe; the earth (Roman Empire)
Tribulation impacting the world (Matt. 24:21)	*kosmos*	The inhabited world

In Matthew 24:3, the disciples were asking Christ to reveal the signs of His return. When Jesus spoke of the "end," He was not alluding to the end of Planet Earth but the "end"—*aion*, or the end of the *age*. These Jewish disciples, raised in synagogues and understanding prophetic writings, were taught that the Hebrew prophets foresaw a coming kingdom in which a Messianic figure would rule the world, Israel's enemies would be defeated, and the Jews would become the leading ethnic group. All nations would amass in Jerusalem once a year to worship (Zech. 14:16). The prophet Daniel made such a prediction:

> I was watching in the night visions,
> And behold, One like the Son of Man,
> Coming with the clouds of heaven!
> He came to the Ancient of Days,
> And they brought Him near before Him.
> Then to Him was given dominion and glory and a
> kingdom,
> That all peoples, nations, and languages should serve
> Him.
> His dominion is an everlasting dominion,
> Which shall not pass away,
> And His kingdom the one
> Which shall not be destroyed.
> —DANIEL 7:13–14

The phrase *son of man* is used 108 times in the King James Version of the Old Testament. God addressed the prophet Ezekiel as "son of man" 93 times. Once, in Daniel's prophecy, the Messiah was identified as, "One like the Son of Man, coming with the clouds…" (Dan. 7:13). In the New Testament, Jesus calls Himself "the Son of Man" on numerous occasions (John 1:51; 3:13; 6:27). Christ came preaching the gospel of the kingdom, performing miracles, and predicting the future of Israel. The disciples discerned He was the Messiah (Son of man) who Daniel prophesied would bring forth the final, victorious kingdom on Earth (Dan. 7:18, 22, 27).

According to Jesus, several key signs would occur before the final

Messianic kingdom would be set up in Jerusalem. He predicted the final age would be preceded by wars and rumors of wars, famines, and pestilences in various places (Matt. 24:6–7). He warned them that enemy armies would surround Jerusalem and eventually level the city and the temple (Matt. 24:2; Luke 21:20). He gave them advanced warning that great persecution would follow, and families would turn on one another, breeding offenses and hatred (Matt. 24:9–12). Christ then revealed the premier indicator that would climax the age of man:

> And this gospel of the kingdom will be preached in all the world as a witness to all the nations, and then the end will come.
>
> —MATTHEW 24:14

The spread of the gospel throughout the Roman Empire in the disciples' day was a sign of the fullness of time for Israel, Jerusalem, the temple, and the Jewish people. From the Day of Pentecost around A.D. 32 when the church was birthed until A.D. 70 when the Roman Tenth Legion invaded Jerusalem and destroyed the city, eventually plowing it under one year later, the gospel of the kingdom had been preached around the Mediterranean Sea in what we call the Middle East, Europe, and Asia Minor. The *end* came for Israel, Jerusalem, and the temple just as Christ predicted in Matthew 24:1–2.

Today, some well-meaning but theologically lame individuals attempt to *prove* that all of the prophecies related to the time of the end and the return of Christ were fulfilled between A.D. 66 and 70. They quote the historian Flavius Josephus, saying that the events of which he speaks give evidence that all the cosmic signs predicted by Christ have been fulfilled. These events recorded by Josephus included strange cosmic activity—a star shaped like a sword hanging over the city and a comet that appeared over Jerusalem—for one year prior to the destruction. He also told of a supernatural light that was seen at night, and the eastern gate of the inner court, "shut by twenty men, and rested upon a basis armed with iron, and had bolts fastened very deep into the firm floor, which was there made of one entire stone, was seen to be opened of its own accord about the sixth hour of the night."[1]

When I'm told that Matthew 24 was fulfilled in A.D. 70, I remind the person to keep reading *all* of Matthew 24, which predicts the destruction of the temple, the signs of Christ's coming, *and* the end of the age. The latter part of Matthew 24, verses 15–21, did not occur in A.D. 70, or for that matter at any other time in past history. These signs include:

- The abomination that makes Jerusalem desolate by standing in the holy place (Matt. 24:15)

- A Great Tribulation such as has never been seen in world history or shall ever be (Matt. 24:21)

- The shortening of the days of the Tribulation for the elect's sake (Matt. 24:22)

- The sun being darkened, the moon not giving light, and stars falling (Matt. 24:29)

- The Son of man appearing in the heavens for all to see (Matt. 24:30)

- Angels gathering His elect from the four areas of the earth (Matt. 24:31)

The above events have not yet happened but will unfold at the time of the end. This small three-letter English word *end* is also used several times in Matthew's Gospel and is important to understand when answering the question: Are we really in the time of the end?

The disciples asked for the signs of the *end* of the age. This word in Greek means "the completion, or the consummation of a thing." *W. E. Vine's Expository Dictionary of Old and New Testament Words* says the word *end* "does not denote a termination, but the heading up of events to the appointed climax."[2] The disciples were requesting certain indicators of the completion and consummation of the age. The word *end* is used in Matthew 24 when Jesus warned of wars, famines, and pestilences, saying that when these things were seen happening on Earth, they were "the beginning of sorrows" (v. 8), but "the end is not yet" (v. 6). The Greek word *end* (*telos*) in this passage is a common word also used in Matthew 24:13 when Jesus said, "…endure unto the end" (KJV), and in Matthew 24:14, which says that after the gospel is preached around the world, "then shall the end come" (KJV).

In these references the Greek word is *telos*, which has a variety of meanings, including, "to set out, to reach a final goal, the uttermost and the conclusion of a thing." According to *Thayer's Greek Lexicon*, *telos* alludes to a "termination, the limit at which a thing ceases to be."[3] In Greek writings, *telos* always indicates the end of some act or state, but not the end of a period of time, which they call (in Greek) *teletutte*.

Notice this word indicates the termination of something but not the end of a time period. In other words, Christ is revealing that certain signs will indicate the termination of one age and the beginning of another. It does not refer to "the end of time," a term that some use but that is not found in Scripture. The concept of the *end of time* possibly comes from Revelation 10:6, in which during the future Tribulation an angel states, "There should be time no longer" (KJV). A clearer translation is, "Time will no longer be delayed."[4]

This verse in Revelation alludes to how the prophetic events surrounding the Great Tribulation, which occurs at the time of the end, will suddenly accelerate like an eighteen-wheeler going downhill without any brakes. Once the final time is set in motion, the prophecies will come to pass faster than one can keep up with! There will be no restraining of events, as the restraining power will be removed.[5] (See 2 Thessalonians 2:1–8.) The actual meaning of "the time of the end" refers to when certain prophetic signs related to the return of Christ begin to merge in one season and during one generation.

Jesus warned His generation that they would see the destruction of Jerusalem because their forefathers were guilty of killing the prophets:

> Therefore, indeed, I send you prophets, wise men, and scribes: some of them you will kill and crucify, and some of them you will scourge in your synagogues and persecute from city to city, that on you may come all the righteous blood shed on the earth, from the blood of righteous Abel to the blood of Zechariah, son of Berechiah, whom you murdered between the temple and the altar. Assuredly, I say to you, all these things will come upon this generation.
>
> —MATTHEW 23:34–36

Just as Christ predicted a final season (end) would come for Israel, Jerusalem, and the temple (fulfilled in A.D. 70), the prophets of Scripture also predicted a future generation that would witness the return of the Jews to Israel from the Gentile nations, the rebuilding and expansion of Jerusalem under Jewish control, the blossoming of the land, and a restoration and rebuilding of the temple.

There was a living generation that remembered the predictions of Jesus and saw Jerusalem surrounded by armies between A.D. 66 and A.D. 70 and witnessed the destruction of the Holy City. Most traditional prophetic scholars believe that the generation that witnesses the restoration of Israel and Jerusalem and the return of the Jews will be the generation of the time of the end. The apostle Peter gave a dynamic revelation of the link between these future restorations and the return of Christ.

The Prophecy: Times of Restitution

> Repent ye therefore, and be converted, that your sins may be blotted out, when the times of refreshing shall come from the presence of the Lord; and he shall send Jesus Christ, which before was preached unto you: whom the heaven must receive until the times of restitution of all things, which God hath spoken by the mouth of all his holy prophets since the world began.
> —Acts 3:19–21, kjv

The return of Christ is contingent upon "the times of restitution of all things." The word *times* is in the plural form, meaning "a series of events" linked to restitution. The word *restitution* is similar to the word *restoration*. The Greek word for *restitution* (*apokatastasis*) was used to describe the Jews' return to Israel from Egypt with Moses and their return to Israel after the Babylonian captivity. In both cases the Hebrew nation was released from bondage, returned to their land, and brought restoration to the land through agriculture and farming (Jer. 27:22; Joel 2:25). Christ will return after an order of restoration occurs.

The biblical prophets also predicted a series of restorations that will unfold prior to the return of the Messiah. When these predictions begin to come to pass, it is a major witness that the closing out of the end of the age is at hand and the kingdom of the Messiah is over the horizon.

The first major event would be the reestablishing of Israel as a nation. Over a hundred years before Israel was reborn on May 14–15, 1948, Bible scholars who accepted the literal interpretation of the restoration prophecies began writing and teaching that the Jews must return to a restored nation called Israel prior to the Lord's return.

One such man was Professor S. W. Watson, who in 1888 taught that three things must occur before Christ could return. First, Israel would again be a nation. Second, Jerusalem must be in the hands and control of the Jews, and, finally, the Jews would be returning from all nations back to the Promised Land. In 1912, A. B. Simpson wrote a book titled *The Coming One*, in which he stated:

> Then there is the promise of their [Israel's] restoration. This is to be in two stages: first, national, and then, spiritual. The two stages are represented by Ezekiel in the vision of the valley of dry bones.[6]

In 1940 Harry Rimmer wrote a prophetic book titled *The Coming War and the Rise of Russia*.[7] In it he mentions fourteen things that must occur prior to the coming of Christ. He stated that the Jews would be back in Palestine and will have Jerusalem back. He predicted that there would be a great war that would drive the Jews back to Palestine. He also spoke of Hitler dividing Germany and how Germany would later be united again.

In the 1930s and 1940s, a great Bible scholar, Finis Dake, author of the *Dake's Annotated Bible*, spent thousands of hours researching the Scriptures and writing personal notes and commentaries on each verse. In Isaiah 35, the prophet Isaiah predicted a time when the barren deserts of Israel would blossom as a rose and fill the world with fruit (Isa. 35:1; see also Isa. 27:6). At the time of Mr. Dake's research, most of Palestine was either a swamp or a desolate, dry wilderness with little or no vegetation. In this setting, Dake commented on the twenty-five-hundred-year-old prediction by Isaiah that Israel's deserts would blossom and fill the world with fruit:

> A complete restoration or reestablishment. It refers to the Millennium when Christ will reign 1,000 years. No prophecy about the coming of the Lord can be fulfilled until the Jews are back in their land.[8]

In the 1930s and early 1940s, Dake understood two facts: that no prophecy about the coming of the Lord could be fulfilled until the Jews were back in their land (Israel), and that the blossoming of the desert was to be taken literally and not as some spiritual allegory. In other words, the dry land would one day become fruitful. He only missed one part of his interpretation. He placed the timing of this fulfillment during the thousand-year reign of Christ (Rev. 20:4), not during the time of the end. When his Bible notes were written, the Jews were still scattered among the nations and were being persecuted by the Nazis. The nation of Israel was nonexistent, and the land was called *Palestine* and was under British mandate.

When examining prophetic Scripture, these men and others like them took the prophecies about Israel's restoration literally and not spiritually or allegorically. They predicted a day when the Jews would return and rebuild the places of old. Several understood there were seven signs of the time of the end.

THE SEVEN SIGNS OF THE TIME OF THE END

Not all signs related to the return of Christ are negative (wars, famines, earthquakes, and so on) in nature. Many are very encouraging and exciting. There are seven events that have transpired and are continuing to unfold that are a part of the restitution and give evidence of the coming of Christ. They are:

1. Israel would be restored as a nation in one day (Isa. 66:7–8; Zech. 3:9; Hos. 3:4–5).

2. The land would begin to blossom and be fruitful (Isa. 35:1–8; 27:6).

3. Water would break out in the desert for irrigation (Isa. 35:6–7; 41:18).

4. Jerusalem would be in Jewish hands and expand its borders (Ps. 102:16).

5. Jews from Gentile nations outside Palestine would return back to Israel (Isa. 43:5–6; Jer. 16:14–16).

6. The early and latter rains would return in the last days (Hos. 6:3; Joel 2:23; Amos 4:7).

7. The walls of Jerusalem would be rebuilt by strangers and the gates open continually (Isa. 60:1–11).

Israel's restoration process began during the 1800s with the birth of the Zionist Movement, but it was manifested to the world on May 14–15, 1948, when David Ben-Gurion made a proclamation declaring a new state for Jews called *Israel*. Part of the proclamation read: "The State of Israel will be open for immigration of Jews from all countries of their dispersion."[9] Within hours, Arab armies advanced toward the infant nation to abort the plan. Just as ancient Israel had to deal with seven nations living around them in Joshua's time (Deut. 7:1), in 1948 the Jews had to deal with troops from seven surrounding Arab nations who announced the Jews would be "thrown into the sea."[10] A war of independence was waged in which Israel survived against amazing odds. Today they boast one of the most advanced militaries in the world.

One of Ben-Gurion's goals was to fulfill the prophecy of Isaiah and make the desert blossom with vegetation. In 1953, at age sixty-seven,

Ben-Gurion resigned as prime minister of Israel to pursue his dream. This former Israeli leader and his wife, Paula, moved into a three-room wooden prefab hut at Sde Boker in the desolate Negev Desert. It was a dry, empty, sun-baked landscape. Years later, Beersheba, the hometown of Abraham, became a large town, and today more than fifty-four farms are scattered throughout a region called the *Arabah*—the Negev and the southern part of Israel—producing tomatoes, peppers, melons, and a host of fruits and vegetables. Today, the desert is blossoming.[11]

Ben-Gurion and other early Israeli settlers were also responsible for laying water pipelines to assist in irrigation. Years later, US satellites discovered a huge reservoir of water under the desert, which today is pumped out and is the lifeblood used in the drip irrigation process, enabling the desert to blossom with agricultural life.[12]

In 1967, Egyptian military forces, headed by Egyptian president Gamal Abdel Nasser, threatened Israel and were planning an attack. Israel preempted the assault with an air campaign, destroying Egypt's air force while the planes were still on the runway.[13] During this Six-Day War involving Egypt, Jordan, and Syria, Israeli paratroopers seized the eastern (Arab) half of Jerusalem. At this time, this section was known as the country of Transjordan. At the conclusion of the war, Israel annexed both East and West Jerusalem together, forming a united Jerusalem under Israeli control. At that moment Jerusalem was united as one city without walls and became the long-promised capital of Israel.

Although from 1948 to 1967 Jews continually immigrated to Israel from surrounding nations, the Russian Jews living behind the iron curtain were forbidden visas to exit the communist stronghold. In the latter part of the 1980s, with the approval of Mikhail Gorbachev, Jews received visas to return from the north country of the Soviet Union back to Israel, thus fulfilling the promises God gave them through Jeremiah and Isaiah thousands of years ago.[14]

Years later, in the early 1990s, there was a sudden return of the physical rains that soaked the soil of Israel, thus replenishing and nourishing the farmland, the deserts, and the Upper Golan Heights. As the windows of heaven were opened, once-dry riverbeds were flowing with fresh water. It was a sign of the return of the latter rains upon the land.

Today, the old city of Jerusalem is shared by the world's three monotheistic religions: Islam, Judaism, and Christianity. Out of the eight gates built in the walls of the old city, only one, the Eastern Gate, remains sealed with large stones. All other gates are opened to citizens and visitors. Children are seen strolling along the streets continually amidst noisy buses and cars, occasionally darting in and out of the crowd that fills avenues throughout the day.

THE STAGE IS READY

This seven-phase restoration that is now occurring is a sign of the time of the end and evidence that the Messiah will soon return. We are the generation that has witnessed the culmination of these events during one specific time period, and I believe we are witnessing many other prophetic stepping-stones as the stage is set and the curtain is about to rise for another act of the drama of the End Times.

Not everyone, however, is happy about Israel's return or the nation's development. In fact, a large majority of the approximate 1.4 billion Muslims are very unsettled or unhappy about Israel. To them, Israel is a modern nation forced upon the world by the Americans and British, and the Jews occupy Islamic lands, illegitimately surrounding two famous Islamic mosques in Jerusalem. This is why Islamic nations or radical Islamic groups have six times initiated a war with Israel. They want to defeat the Jews and drive them from the land that Muslims believe originally belonged to Islam.

The Rise of the Prince of Persia

> I will turn you around, put hooks into your jaws, and
> lead you out, with all your army, horses, and horsemen,
> all splendidly clothed, a great company with bucklers
> and shields, all of them handling swords. Persia, Ethi-
> opia, and Libya are with them, all of them with shield
> and helmet; Gomer and all its troops; the house of Tog-
> armah from the far north and all its troops—many
> people are with you.
>
> —Ezekiel 38:4–6

History appears to be repeating itself. Ancient Israel dealt with six major world empires, and since their reformation as a nation, we are seeing the same leading nations battle the new Jewish state in modern time.

In their past, Israel has dealt with Egypt, Assyria, Babylon, Media-Persia, Greece, and Rome. Since Israel was re-formed as a nation in 1948, it has entered conflicts with the first three prophetic nations from the past. The next nation on the war list will be the Persians, or the Iranians. The following chart shows how these conflicts in the present are paralleling conflicts in ancient Israel's past:

The Nation	The Wars Fought With Israel
Egypt	Egypt fought Israel in 1948, 1956, and 1967
Assyria	Syria fought Israel in 1948, 1967, and 1973
Babylon	Babylon (Iraq) in 1991
Media-Persia	The coming conflict
Greece	
Roman Empire	

Israel's advanced military technology, coupled with five victories in five major conflicts since 1948 (in 1948, 1956, 1967, 1973, and 1991), has prevented a coalition of surrounding Islamic nations from annihilating the Jewish state. Israel's secret arsenal of advanced bombs and laser weapons has deterred fanatical regimes from launching a massive invasion of the nation. However, that is about to change in the coming days. Islamists have several agendas, including a long-term military strategy inspired by what I term *apocalyptic Islam.*

This End Time, last days, Islamic theology is inbred into Islamic minds from the birth of a child forward. The ultimate goal of Islam is to form a global empire one day and to convert the world to its religion, eventually defeating both Jews and Christians. This is not just a tradition handed down among a few *fanatics.* The ideas of Islamic global domination and the defeat of the Jews are taught continually in Islamic schools around the world.

According to Daniel and John, two apocalyptic prophets whose biblical predictions have fascinated, inspired, and, yes, at times bewildered generations of Christians, a final empire will form that will control all buying and selling and will behead those who resist (Rev. 13:17; 20:4). I believe this final prophetic empire is an Islamic coalition of nations whose influence will overshadow the Middle East and much of Europe, and whose heart will beat the strongest in the regions of Syria, Iraq, and Iran. Its command center will be in Iraq and will be eventually moved to Jerusalem. The man who will direct this final showdown among the nations will be the Antichrist of biblical prophecy.

The countdown to the showdown has begun. The final act of the apocalyptic play is about to begin. Let's go behind the curtain, backstage, and get a major preview of the script written for the time of the end. The final act is titled, "Seven Down and One More to Go."

SEVEN DOWN AND ONE MORE TO GO

There are also seven kings. Five have fallen, one is, and the other has not yet come. And when he comes, he must continue a short time. And the beast that was, and is not, is himself also the eighth, and is of the seven, and is going to perdition.
—REVELATION 17:10–11

F ROM A BIBLICAL/PROPHETIC PERSPECTIVE, SIX MAJOR empires have risen on the world scene and faded into the fog of history, with the seventh empire still to arise. It will exist for a short period and will be followed by an eighth and final empire, identified as the *kingdom of the beast.* The beast's kingdom will form a ten-nation coalition that will wreak havoc on opposing nations, beheading all its enemies (Rev. 20:4).

Both past and future biblical prophecy is always linked to Israel and the Jewish people. Of the seven prophetic kings, John, when writing the Book of Revelation, indicated that five had already fallen and no longer existed in John's time. These kingdoms began with the

Egyptian Empire, which was the first major empire in the Bible to impact the Hebrew people for more than four hundred years (Gen. 15:13). These five kingdoms included:

1. *The Egyptian Empire*—their history is recorded in the Book of Exodus.

2. *The Assyrian Empire*—their history is recorded in 1 and 2 Kings and 1 and 2 Chronicles.

3. *The Babylonian Empire*—their history is recorded in Daniel, Ezra, and Nehemiah.

4. *The Media-Persian Empire*—their history is recorded in Daniel.

5. *The Greek Empire*—their history is found in symbolism in the Book of Daniel.

When John wrote the Book of Revelation in approximately A.D. 95, these five major empires had fallen from the charts of history and were no longer in global control. However, John identified an empire in existence in his day, calling it "one is." The only global empire in John's day was the Roman Empire, whose armies were occupying Israel in Christ's time. In A.D. 70, the Roman Tenth Legion had used battering rams to beat down the walls of Jerusalem, torching the temple and leading Jews in chains onto ships taking them back to Rome. By A.D. 95, a great persecution was sweeping the Christian church, and Christians in Rome were hiding in miles of underground caves called *catacombs*. At the time of John's apocalyptic vision in Revelation, Rome was in complete control of all political, military, and economic affairs in the nations surrounding the Mediterranean Sea.

In Revelation 17:10, John identifies the seventh empire as, "...and the other has not yet come. And when he comes, he must continue a short time." The identity of this kingdom has differed among Bible scholars. Every empire from the past was succeeded by a stronger empire, and this succession has never been broken. If the Roman Empire was the sixth prophetic empire that eventually faded, and the succession would continue until the end of days, then who or what was the *seventh* empire that continues for "a short space" (KJV)? The question actually is, Who or what *followed* the Roman Empire? This is difficult to answer, because the Roman Empire was never defeated politically or militarily by a single empire. Rome simply deteriorated morally, politically, and spiritually and faded from power. The Roman Empire was eventually overrun by numerous Germanic tribes.

Some historians point out that when Imperial Rome declined, Germanic tribes from the east seized much of the land once ruled by Rome. They identify this period as the dark time of the barbarian age for the former Imperial Rome. Scholars note that there were ten groups that eventually took over the land once ruled by Rome. These ten groups are identified by most researchers as:

- The Huns
- The Visigoths
- The Vandals
- The Ostrogoths
- The Franks
- The Anglo-Saxons
- The Suevi
- The Burgundians
- The Heruli
- The Lombards[1]

Such groups as the Seventh-Day Adventists believe that the prophecy of the ten horns of Daniel (Dan. 7:24) and John's ten-horned beast (Rev. 17:12), along with the ten toes on the metallic image (Dan. 2:42), were fulfilled when these ten groups eventually settled throughout the countries that Rome once ruled. This, however, cannot be the final literal fulfillment.

The Bible teaches: "And in the days of these kings the God of heaven will set up a kingdom which shall never be destroyed; and the kingdom shall not be left to other people; it shall break in pieces and consume all these kingdoms, and it shall stand forever" (Dan. 2:44). In the days of the ten kings, thrones will be cast down and the judgment will be set (Dan. 7:7–10).

These ten groups listed above eventually took over the land of Imperial Rome. However, the future ten prophetic kings receive their power and authority in the span of *one hour* when the beast (Antichrist) forms his eighth kingdom (Rev. 17:12). I have read the many beliefs that the ten kings of prophecy were these ten groups that have already come and gone, but this is not the fulfillment of the many End Time predictions in Daniel and Revelation.

Christ will return in the days of the ten kings, and He did not return after the demise of the ten tribes who seized the Roman regions in ancient history. (See Revelation 17:12–14.)

THE FALL OF ROME

After three centuries of persecution, Constantine became emperor of Rome in A.D. 312, legalizing Christianity by proclaiming it one of the official religions of the Roman Empire. The imperial Roman Empire was then split between Rome in the west and Constantinople in the east, a city built by Constantine in Turkey, which today is known as Istanbul. As *Imperial* Rome fell, a new *spiritual* Rome emerged that combined the power of *church* and *state* under one entity—the pope and the Roman Church in the west. A new political/spiritual empire came into existence in the east, which was called the Byzantine Empire.

When answering the question, Who or what took the place of the Roman Empire? there are several suggestions.

Some suggest that the seventh empire was the Holy Roman Empire, which consisted of a coalition of territories located in Central Europe during the Middle Ages and continued through early modern history. Otto the Great, crowned as emperor in A.D. 962, is considered the first of the Holy Roman emperors. During the war with Napoleon in 1806, Francis II, the last Holy Roman emperor, dissolved the empire.

In the late fifteenth century, the empire was termed the Holy Roman Empire of the German Nation. Although the empire dissolved in the seventeenth century, the power of Germany was evident in World Wars I and II. Only after the defeat of Hitler in 1945 was the power of Germany broken and replaced with a movement to unite Europe into a new coalition, later identified as the European Union.

This brings us to the second theory, which connects the modern European Union (EU) with the seventh empire of prophecy, continuing a "short space." It is noted that many of the EU's membership nations were historically a part of the ancient Roman Empire, and since the seventh empire is a continual succession of the other, then the seventh, or the EU, is linked with the sixth (Imperial Rome). Since the Holy Roman Empire existed for more than 840 years, this empire cannot be the empire continuing a "short space," as mentioned by John. The EU, originally called the European Economic Community, was built on the foundation of the European coal and steel communities and was set up to help unite Europe, to prevent the many wars in Europe, and to establish peace. The Union began with six nations and has grown to twenty-seven nations.

Since John says the seventh will continue a "short space," some suggest that the EU's currency, the euro, and the leaders of the EU nations will rule and control the economic strategies of Europe for a short time but eventually be swallowed up by the eighth and final kingdom of the Antichrist.

There is also a third theory. Some westerners are unaware that in the past, Islam forged a major empire in the Middle East. The Ottoman Turks conquered the Byzantines in a battle in Constantinople in 1299 and seized the largest Christian church in the empire, turning it into a mosque. The Turks spread their influence and dominion through northern Africa, the Middle East, Turkey, and southern Russia. At one time, the Ottoman Turkish Empire was as large as the ancient Roman Empire. From 1299 to 1923, the world—especially the Middle East, northern Africa, and southeastern Europe—dealt with the Turks.

Just after World War I, the Turks invaded Armenia, killing at least 1.5 million Armenians, many of whom were Christians. In 1917, the grip of the Ottoman Turkish Empire began to slip, as evidenced when British commander General Allenby conquered Palestine in 1917.[2] Eventually, the Americans, French, and British became the main players in dominating the politics and economies of northern Africa and much of the Middle East. The discovery of oil in 1908 in Persia was the beginning of Western influence. The West needed oil, and the Arab nations of the Middle East needed the money to become more than a tribe of nomads living in the desert. Prosperity was hidden in the liquid black gold of the desert, and Western oil companies drilled in the sand dunes, turning oil into a cash flow. The Gulf States befriended the West for bringing them needed technology that created untold wealth.

Oil wealth linked the Islamic Gulf States in the East to Western nations, and relations focused on prosperity and growth. The West was appreciated and admired by the Islamic kings and princes of the Middle Eastern Gulf States. However, the clear skies turned ominously dark in 1948 when Britain and America participated in re-forming the nation of Israel and handing a partitioned Palestine back to the Jews. Since the demise of the Ottoman Empire, Islamic eyes have scanned the global horizon looking for an expected "white horse rider" who will unite the Muslims under a new Islamic caliph.

Since the Ottoman Turkish Empire began in 1299 and continued until 1923 (624 years), it is unlikely that it is the seventh prophetic empire, which continues for only "a short space." We know that Rome was divided between East and West, with Rome leading the West and Turkey leading the East. However, the ten kings are leaders in the *future* and not leaders from the *past*.

Please notice that although Imperial Rome collapsed, the Roman Church united the church with the state and maintained spiritual and political dominion throughout areas of Europe. The Byzantine Empire ruled from the east and continued its dominion for over a thousand years. Then the Holy Roman Empire was forged. Thus, in some form or another, a Roman form of government and system has continued throughout history since the time of Christ.

I believe the best choice for the seventh empire that forms in the last days prior to the rise of the Antichrist is linked to the European Union, since most of the present EU nations were a part of the imperial Roman Empire. For the first time since the Roman Empire was divided under Constantine, Europe has been united under one banner, with one currency, and with one open border. The EU is heavily influenced by the West and will eventually be overrun by forces from the East.

THE RISE OF THE EIGHTH KINGDOM

Following the "short-spaced" seventh empire, an eighth and final prophetic empire will emerge during the latter time called the Great Tribulation (Matt. 24:21). This eighth and final empire consists of a coalition of ten kings who will hand over their authority to one man, identified by scholars as the Antichrist. This eight-kingdom coalition will dominate world affairs for forty-two months, as Daniel predicted: "...and they shall be given into his hand until a time [one year] and times [two years] and the dividing of time [six months]" (Dan. 7:25, KJV; see also Dan. 12:7). This final forty-two months is set to occur at the conclusion of a seven-year time frame identified as the Great Tribulation (Matt. 24:21). It will include a time of trouble for Israel such as the nation has never experienced (Dan. 12:1).

When carefully examining all of the details given in the Bible and in the commentaries of the early fathers concerning the rise of the Antichrist and his "beast kingdom" and by comparing them with certain Islamic apocalyptic expectations of their final awaited one, it is obvious that the biblical description of this final dictator is eerily similar to an anticipated Islamic man that Muslims believe will arise at the end of days. Identified by Muslims as the *Mahdi*, according to Islamic traditions and beliefs handed down concerning this future leader, this man will unite Islam under one empire, which parallels prophecies about the biblical Antichrist.

In the next chapter we will look closely at biblical prophecies about the Antichrist—the man who would be the beast of prophecy.

THE MAN WHO
WOULD BE THE BEAST

*Then I stood on the sand of the sea. And I saw a beast
rising up out of the sea, having seven heads and ten
horns, and on his horns ten crowns, and on his heads
a blasphemous name. Now the beast which I saw was
like a leopard, his feet were like the feet of a bear, and
his mouth like the mouth of a lion. The dragon gave
him his power, his throne, and great authority.*

—REVELATION 13:1–2

AMONG THE WRITINGS OF THE OLD TESTAMENT PROPHETS,
Moses is named in Scripture 768 times, while Abram
or Abraham's name is mentioned 303 times. The one individual
who holds more predictions about his appearance and ministry
throughout the Scriptures is the promised Messiah. There are hundreds of prophecies that refer to the Messiah, many of which were
fulfilled though Christ, and many others will be fulfilled in the
future. The only other person who receives such attention in the

biblical prophetic Scriptures is a person identified as the final *prince of darkness*, called the Antichrist.

There are few Christians living today who have not heard the term *the Antichrist*. The average Christian in the Western Hemisphere who has read prophecy books, watched End Time DVDs, or viewed apocalyptic-oriented television specials understands four basic facts revealed in Scripture about the coming Antichrist. They are:

1. The Antichrist is a man who will form a final empire at the end of the age.

2. The Antichrist will make a treaty with Israel for seven years.

3. The Antichrist will eventually set up his kingdom in Jerusalem.

4. The Antichrist will be involved in the final battle, called Armageddon.

Two biblical prophets, Daniel and the apostle John, give numerous details in their writings and prophetic visions concerning this man's rise to power, his realm of influence, and his violent reaction to those who reject his mission. Much of the church's historical understanding of this man comes from these two prophetic books, Daniel and Revelation.

COMPARING DANIEL WITH THE BOOK OF REVELATION

The prophet Daniel and the apostle John lived more than six hundred years apart. Yet, when comparing their visions, it is amazing how the Book of Daniel complements the Book of Revelation. Revelation is a continuation of, and includes deeper explanation of, the apocalyptic visions found in Daniel. Below is a list of what both visionaries saw.

1. Both saw a final period of seven years. Daniel identified the time frame as one prophetic week (seven years) in Daniel 9:27. John divided the seven years into two forty-two-month periods (Rev. 11:2; 13:5).

2. Both saw forty-two final months of world history. Daniel gave the time frame as time (one year), times (two years), and dividing of time (half of a year) (Dan. 12:7). John said the final time frame would be 1,260 days—three and a half years (Rev. 12:6).

3. Both identified the Antichrist as a "beast." Daniel saw the Antichrist as the fourth beast that would arise (Dan. 7:7). John saw the Antichrist as the beast rising up from the sea (Rev. 13:1).

4. Both reveal a time of great trouble on Earth. Daniel said it was a time such as never was or ever shall be (Dan. 12:1). John described a time of wrath and trouble (Rev. 12:7–12).

5. Both prophets saw Michael the archangel. Daniel saw Michael standing up at the time of trouble (Dan. 12:1). John saw Michael warring with Satan in heaven (Rev. 12:7).

6. Both prophets saw ten kings that would arise at the end of days. Daniel said the ten horns were ten kings (Dan. 7:24). John saw ten horns with ten crowns that were ten kings (Rev. 13:1).

7. Both saw the resurrection of the dead. Daniel recorded a resurrection after the Tribulation (Dan. 12:2). John saw a resurrection of those who were beheaded in the Tribulation (Rev. 7:9–17).

8. Both prophets saw the return of the Lord to set up His kingdom. Daniel saw an everlasting kingdom of the Messiah (Dan. 7:13–14). John saw Christ returning to make war (Rev. 19:11).

After studying this subject for more than thirty-four years, I have discovered many facts about this topic that are very clear in prophetic scriptures. I have also concluded that some church teachings from the past were based more on men's traditions or on *private interpretations* handed down from generation to generation, either of which are often built more on assumptions than on biblical or historical foundations.

For example, have you ever attended a prophetic conference, read a prophetic book, or came across research that taught the following?

◆ The Antichrist will be a Jew from the tribe of Dan.

◆ The Antichrist will rebuild a temple for the Jews on the Temple Mount in Jerusalem.

◆ The Antichrist will be a man of *peace* and will oversee the Common Market.

These three theories are based on individual interpretations or traditional theological ideas handed down for generations from a few early church fathers' specific interpretations, and they are not necessarily based upon specific biblical scriptures. In fact, as I will explain, there is much more information alluding to the Antichrist that has *not* been taught or understood than what has been taught or written. After thirty-four years and more than forty thousand hours of biblical study and research, I firmly believe the following is an accurate description of coming events related to the Antichrist:

- ◆ The Antichrist will be a Gentile (from an Islamic background) and not a Jew from Israel.

- ◆ The Antichrist will not rebuild the Jewish temple—the prophet Elijah will initiate that process.

- ◆ The Antichrist will control the oil-rich Gulf States and will control much of Europe.

- ◆ The Antichrist brings peace only to his followers and death to those who resist him.

I realize these four statements may cut against the grain of some traditional interpretations of prophetic teaching. However, when we move from *assumptions* to direct biblical *interpretation* and insight, the fog clears.

THE ANTICHRIST—A GENTILE, NOT A JEW

First, let's examine my belief that the Antichrist will be a Gentile leader and not a Jew. During the second and third centuries, many early church fathers became quite anti-Semitic in their theological interpretations. Several early fathers like Irenaeus (*Heresies*, vol. 302) and Hippolytus (*De Christo et Antichristo*, pp. 14–15) taught that the Antichrist would be a Jew rising from the tribe of Dan, a teaching based on their interpretation of Jeremiah 8:15–16 and three passages in the Scriptures.

Two of these passages mentioned the Jewish tribe of Dan and horses:

> Dan shall be a serpent by the way, an adder in the path, that biteth the horse heels, so that his rider shall fall backward.
>
> —Genesis 49:17, kjv

> The snorting of his horses was heard from Dan: the whole land trembled at the sound of the neighing of his strong ones; for they are come, and have devoured the land, and all that is in it; the city, and those that dwell therein.
>
> —Jeremiah 8:16, kjv

The *assumption* links the tribe of Dan to the four horsemen of the Apocalypse, mentioned in Revelation 6:1–8, whose appearance introduces the beginning of the Tribulation and the rise of the Antichrist.

A third passage is found in the register of the tribes of Israel, listed in Revelation 7. Scholars note that the tribe of Dan is missing from among the list of the tribes of Israel that receive a protective seal from God during the Tribulation. Thus, since Dan is missing, it is assumed that the Antichrist must arise from the tribe of Dan, inside of Israel.

Why is Dan missing? Today in modern Israel, many of the Jewish people living in the contemporary cities of Israel identified as part of Dan's ancient territory either are agnostics, atheists, or very non-religious secular Jews. In the other areas of Israel there are many religious Jews, including reformed, orthodox, and, in Jerusalem, ultraorthodox Jews. It may be that Dan is missing because the Jewish men living in the area of Dan are simply unbelievers and therefore are not sealed as others who "[have kept] the commandments..."

(Rev. 12:17). It is actually a biblical mystery why Dan is missing, and to suggest why is entirely speculative.

For many years I heard prophetic teachers proclaim that the Antichrist would be a Jewish political/military leader from Israel. This theory puzzled me, because I knew the world's 1.4 billion Muslims would never follow a Jew who, while living in Israel, would rule and control surrounding Middle East nations, all which are Islamic. After many trips to Israel, I began asking noted prophetic teachers, "Why is no one explaining the role that Muslims will play in End Time prophecy?" Teachers were teaching the significance of Israel and the Jews, along with a Gentile-ruled Common Market, but consistently writers and researchers of eschatology seemed to ignore the importance of the Islamic religion and the Muslims living in the Middle East and Europe.

One explanation was that Islam would be defeated in the war of Gog and Magog. This cannot be true, since there are presently fifty-two nations whose population is predominantly Islamic, and in the war of Gog and Magog, only five major Islamic nations are listed as taking part in the battle. When God said He would defeat all but one-sixth of Gog's army, it did not mean that one-sixth of the Islamic nations would remain, but that five-sixths of the invading armies would be destroyed (Ezek. 39:2, KJV).

After much research and study, I believe the prophecies point out that the Antichrist will be a Gentile and not a Jew. I base this on several important prophecies and apocalyptic dreams and visions.

First, in Daniel chapter 2, King Nebuchadnezzar had a dream of a metallic image that prophetically identifies the world empires from the time of Babylon, the empire symbolized by the image's head of gold, down through the final kingdom, symbolized by the ten toes of the image. All of the empires represented by the image are Gentile—not one is Jewish. In reality, each of the empires symbolized by the image has impacted or affected the Jewish people and

Israel in some manner. This image, and the empires represented, will be discussed in detail in the next chapter.

The concept that the final prophetic empire will be Gentile, not Jewish, is also referred to by Christ in Luke 21:24:

> And they will fall by the edge of the sword, and be led away captive into all nations. And Jerusalem will be trampled by Gentiles until the times of the Gentiles are fulfilled.

In the context of this prophecy in Luke, Jesus was speaking of "the days of vengeance" (v. 22), a word used by Old Testament prophets to allude to the coming time of God's wrath or Tribulation (Isa. 34:8; 35:4; 61:2; 63:4). Other signs Christ also mentioned include cosmic signs, men's hearts failing them, and His return (Luke 21:22–27). The point is that this prophecy alluding to the fall of Jerusalem to the Gentiles was not just fulfilled in A.D. 70 when the Romans destroyed the city. It will occur once more in the future when the Gentile Antichrist will invade Jerusalem, divide the city (Zech. 14:2), and set up an image of himself at the Temple Mount in Jerusalem (Rev. 13:14–15).

Revelation 11:1–2 also alludes to the Gentile control of Jerusalem. John states:

> Then I was given a reed like a measuring rod. And the angel stood, saying, "Rise and measure the temple of God, the altar, and those who worship there. But leave out the court which is outside the temple, and do not measure it, for it has been given to the Gentiles. And they will tread the holy city underfoot for forty-two months."

Most scholars believe the Book of Revelation was written around A.D. 95 in the time of the emperor Domitian. The temple in Jerusalem had already been destroyed in the year A.D. 70. Twenty-five years later, John was told to "…measure the temple." How could John measure the temple and the outer court, which we are told the Gentiles would "trample underfoot for forty-two months," if the temple was already in ruins? The most common answer is that there will be a rebuilt temple in Jerusalem during the Tribulation. (See information on this subject in a later chapter.) It will be at this temple where the Gentile Antichrist will place his abominable image and be worshiped by masses of his followers, causing Jews to flee from Jerusalem into the wilderness (Rev. 12:6).

THE ANTICHRIST—A RADICAL MUSLIM?

The Middle East is the heart of Islam, and Israel is the thorn in the side of Islamic leaders who desire to form an Islamic crescent. What role will Islam play in future apocalyptic events? In early 1992, I met a young woman from Iran who shared with me the detailed apocalyptic beliefs of Shi'ite Muslims, who make up the majority of Iran's population. Few Americans, including myself, had ever heard these beliefs. When I compared her information with the prophecies of the Bible, I became convinced that the Antichrist will claim the Islamic religion as his religion and will proclaim himself—and be received as—Islam's final awaited "messiah." He will be a master of war, using weapons of mass destruction to hold entire nations hostage (Rev. 13:4). Those who do not convert to his religion will be beheaded, and others will be forced into starvation (Rev. 13:17; 20:4). Before thinking this is mere prophetic fiction, take a journey with me into the Scriptures to receive a clearer picture of the Antichrist of prophecy.

THE WORD *ANTICHRIST* IN SCRIPTURE

The word *Antichrist* was coined by the apostle John and is found only in the epistles of John. It can mean "against Christ" or "instead of Christ." W. E. Vine comments on this word, saying that by combining the two words *anti* and *Christ*, it can mean "one who assumes the guise of Christ, or opposes Christ."[1] In approximately A.D. 90, John penned the epistles that carry his name—1, 2, and 3 John. There are four passages where John used the word *Antichrist*.

> Little children, it is the last hour; and as you have heard that the Antichrist is coming, even now many antichrists have come, by which we know that it is the last hour.
> —1 JOHN 2:18

> Who is a liar but he who denies that Jesus is the Christ? He is antichrist who denies the Father and the Son.
> —1 JOHN 2:22

> And every spirit that does not confess that Jesus Christ has come in the flesh is not of God. And this is the spirit of the Antichrist, which you have heard was coming, and is now already in the world.
> —1 JOHN 4:3

> For many deceivers have gone out into the world who do not confess Jesus Christ as coming in the flesh. This is a deceiver and an antichrist.
> —2 JOHN 7

Because John said, "Many antichrists are already in the world," some teach there is not a future person called the *Antichrist*, but that the Antichrist is only a spirit that throughout history has rejected the divinity of Christ. I submit to you that the Antichrist is both a spirit and a person. The "Antichrist spirit" certainly existed in the time of the apostolic church, as some heretical teachers were already denying the divinity of Christ and His position as the Son of God. Yet, at the end of days one man will appear who will be a prince of darkness, a son of perdition, who is identified as *the* Antichrist. In these four passages in his epistles, John elaborates on the three key elements linked to Christ that the spirit of Antichrist and the Antichrist deny:

1. He will deny the deity of Jesus Christ (1 John 2:22).

2. He will deny Jesus Christ is the Son of God (1 John 2:22).

3. He will deny the unique relationship between the Father and the Son (1 John 2:22).

Just as the future land of conflict will be Israel and the future city of conflict Jerusalem, the present and future spiritual conflict will center around the question: *Who is* or *who was* Jesus Christ? Was He a mere man, a prophet among prophets, or was He the Son of God? To many religious Jews, Jesus Christ was a mortal man of ancient history who formed a new religion. To devout Muslims, Jesus Christ was one of the great prophets of Allah (God). But to the true Christian, Jesus Christ was and is the Son of the living God (Matt. 16:16).

Further evidence that the Antichrist is a mortal man and not just some evil spirit or theological belief is revealed in other New Testament passages through the use of personal pronouns. Evangelical scholars point to the following passages, which reveal significant details about this future world dictator. In each case he is identified with the use of a masculine noun or pronoun:

◆   *Man*—"The *man* of sin...the son of perdition..." (2 Thess. 2:3).

◆   *He*—"*He* sits as God in the temple of God, showing *himself* that *he* is God....*He* may be revealed in his own time..." (2 Thess. 2:4, 6).

♦ *Him/his*—"The dragon gave *him his* power, *his*
throne, and great authority.... 'Who is able to
make war with him?' And he was given a mouth
speaking great things and blasphemies, and he
was given authority to continue for forty-two
months.... It was granted to *him* to make war..."
(Rev. 13:2, 4–5, 7).

Even in John's writings, he distinguished the spirit of Antichrist
from the person of the Antichrist. In 1 John 2:22, the Greek Interlinear reads: "Who is the liar if it is not the one that denies that
Jesus is Christ? This is the Antichrist..."[2] The phrase "the Antichrist" in Greek is *ho antichristos,* or "the Antichrist," alluding to
a specific person. While some suggest that the Greek definite article
(*ho*), translated *the,* should not be translated as "the Antichrist," but
simply a general term, "antichrist," this does not change the fact that
Daniel and John saw a man and not some spirit ruling the world!

The *spirit* (or the attitude) of Antichrist was working in John's
day. Even then there were heretics who wrote denying Christ's deity.
But the Antichrist, the man of End Time prophecy, is yet to come.
It was this man whom Daniel identified as the "little horn" rising
among ten kings and to whom John refers as *the apocalyptic beast.*

In the Book of Revelation, he is identified as the symbol of a
"beast" (Rev. 13:1). The word *beast* is also found in the King James
Version of Revelation 4:6, used to identify the living creatures around
God's throne who continually worship God. The Greek word used to
describe these angelic creatures is *zoon,* which is a living creature.
The word used to describe the beast system of the Antichrist is *the-
rion,* alluding to a "wild beast, or a dangerous animal."[3] The character of this wild man is thus compared by John to a wild beast that
tramples, devours, and kills.

Names Given to the Antichrist

For centuries, Bible scholars have pored over the ancient prophecies to identify numerous passages that speak of this final world leader. The following scriptures reveal the character and nature of the world's final dictator:

- The "little horn" (Dan. 7:8, KJV)

- A "king of fierce countenance" (Dan. 8:23, KJV)

- The "prince who is to come" (Dan. 9:26)

- The "one who makes desolate" (Dan. 9:27)

- The "king" who "shall do according to his own will" (Dan. 11:36)

- The "man of sin" (2 Thess. 2:3)

- The "son of perdition" (2 Thess. 2:3)

- The "lawless one" (2 Thess. 2:8)

- The "antichrist" (1 John 2:22)

- The "beast" (Rev. 11:7)

What the Early Fathers Believed

When mentioning the writings of the early church fathers, they were categorized in three groups, as follows:

1. The apostolic fathers

2. The ante-Nicene fathers

3. The post-Nicene fathers

The *apostolic fathers* were bishops and ministers who were taught and instructed directly under the tutorship of the apostles or under men who were trained by the early leaders in the first-century church. The *ante-Nicene fathers* are identified as the bishops and leaders after the apostolic fathers and until the time of the Council of Nicea in A.D. 325. Some noted ante-Nicene fathers were Justin Martyr, Irenaeus, and Ignatius. The *post-Nicene fathers* were bishops and leaders after the 325 council, such as Augustine of Hippo (who wrote on church doctrine), Chrysostom, and Eusebius.

There are numerous written statements made by the early fathers concerning the rise and dominion of the Antichrist. At one point, some felt that the wicked Roman emperor Nero, a severe persecutor of the Christians, had faked his death and would rise once again from the East as the Antichrist.

> He [the Antichrist] himself shall divide the globe into three ruling powers, when, moreover, Nero shall be raised up from hell, Elias shall first come to seal the beloved ones; at which things the region of Africa and the northern nation, the whole earth from all sides, for seven years shall tremble.[4]

> But Elias [Elijah] shall occupy the half of the time, Nero shall occupy half.[5]

Nero came to power in A.D. 54, at age sixteen. He desired to rebuild Rome and to construct a series of palaces known as *Neropolis*.[6] His senate rejected the idea. On July 19, A.D. 64, a major fire broke out in Rome that continued for six days, reigniting for two more days. As the smoke cleared, two-thirds of Rome was destroyed. It is believed by many that Nero started the fire to clear land for his Neropolis. Because some Christians of that time believed prophetically that Rome would be destroyed by fire, Nero found his scapegoat for setting the city on fire—the Christians. He announced that Christians had set Rome on fire.

This lie created an eruption of violence against Christians throughout the Roman Empire, but especially in Rome. Nero eventually committed suicide; however, some believed he would come back from the dead in the form of the dreaded Antichrist. I am sure the early fathers had read Revelation 17:11, where it is predicted that the beast that "was, and is not," along with Isaiah 24:18, which states, "he who comes up from the midst of the pit," to apply the prophecies to Nero. This is an incorrect interpretation of Scripture and tradition.

There are also those who believe that Judas will once again come back from his confinement in hell and become the Antichrist, basing the belief on passages in John and 2 Thessalonians that call both Judas Iscariot and the coming Antichrist "the son of perdition" (John 17:12; 2 Thess. 2:3).

Another passage in Revelation 17:7–8, along with an unusual reference in Acts 1, has led several contemporary scholars to form a theory that Judas, the betrayer of Christ, would actually be the future Antichrist. Greek scholars, such as Kenneth Wuest in his book *Prophetic Light in Present Darkness*, have taken certain scriptures as a cryptic clue identifying Judas Iscariot as the son of perdition who will return from the "pit" of hell during the Tribulation, taking possession of a human body (the embodiment of evil), thus becoming the Antichrist. We are told that Satan entered Judas's heart, and he became obsessed with turning Christ over to the Roman soldiers and priests (John 13:27). Afterward, Judas realized his error and, just as Nero committed suicide, fled to a hill outside the city walls of Jerusalem and hung himself. It appears the rope broke, and he fell headlong (Acts 1:18).

Peter, when recounting the death of Judas in an apostolic meeting, said, "Judas by transgression fell, that he might go to his own place" (v. 25). The phrase "his own place" has created interesting discussion.

Some say Peter was simply saying he died and was now in hell, a place reserved for him because of his transgression. Others teach this "place" is a special compartment of confinement in hell, separate from the other souls and chambers of the underworld. The theory adds that Judas will be the one whose deadly wound will be healed, and he will return from the abyss at the end of days and become the Antichrist of Bible prophecy.

The theories of Nero rising again and the return of Judas have one major biblical roadblock: Both of these individuals committed suicide and have already died. Their physical bodies have returned to the dust of the earth. It would require a physical resurrection of either person to fulfill the literal prediction concerning the Antichrist. If the spirits of Judas or Nero only returned from the abyss, then none of mankind would be able to physically see either one with natural eyes, just as we cannot see angels and demons with our physical eyes. Angels and demons are spirit beings and are invisible in the natural realm, unless they appear in the forms of humans, which occurred occasionally (Gen. 19:1–5).

One argument often espoused for the return of Judas from his confined compartment in hell is that when Christ was praying for His disciples, He identified Judas as the "son of perdition" (John 17:12). The word *perdition* means "destruction." Judas was doomed for destruction for directing the betrayal of the Savior. Jesus said it would have been better for Judas never to have been born than to betray the Son of man (Matt. 26:24). Years later, when Paul began to identify the activity of the coming Antichrist, he calls the Antichrist "the man of sin...the son of perdition" (2 Thess. 2:3). The word link between what Christ said of Judas and what Paul wrote of the future Antichrist is the phrase "perdition." Many years after Paul called the future man of sin "the son of perdition," John used the same word in describing the apocalyptic End Time beast and his kingdom of ten kings:

> The beast that you saw was, and is not, and will ascend
> out of the bottomless pit and go to perdition. And those
> who dwell on the earth will marvel, whose names are
> not written in the Book of Life from the foundation of
> the world, when they see the beast that was, and is not,
> and yet is.
>
> —Revelation 17:8

> And the beast that was, and is not, is himself also the
> eighth, and is of the seven, and is going to perdition.
>
> —Revelation 17:11

To further *confirm* the Judas-as-the-Antichrist theory, some point out that the demonic power controlling the Antichrist will "go into perdition," or enter the "son of perdition," in the same manner that Satan entered the heart of Judas at the Last Supper. Thus the Antichrist will become possessed with one of the strongest evil spirits to be released in world history.

In one passage, John describes the releasing of large numbers of creatures from the bottomless pit (the abyss) and names the demonic king directing them:

> And they had as king over them the angel of the bottomless pit, whose name in Hebrew is Abaddon, but in Greek he has the name Apollyon.
>
> —Revelation 9:11

This Greek and Hebrew name of this angel means "a destroyer." For example, during the time when the Hebrew nation was preparing to depart from Egypt, God sent a "death angel" to slay the firstborn in the homes of the Egyptians. This angel was called "the destroyer" (Exod. 12:23).

My point is this: When John was stating that the beast would "go into perdition," he was not necessarily alluding to a spirit possessing the Antichrist but to the fact that the conclusion of the beast and his kingdom would be "perdition," or destruction. At the conclusion of the Tribulation the Antichrist will be removed from the earth and be "given to the burning flame" (Dan. 7:11).

I believe that Judas sealed his doom at his death and will remain confined in "his place" for eternity. Likewise, Nero has never re-appeared as anticipated, as he too met his eternal fate and is confined forever. There is no biblical record of the Lord allowing a disobedient person to leave hell after years of death and return to live on Earth for any reason. In fact, the opposite is true. In Luke 16, a rich man died, and his soul and spirit were taken to hell. He desired to return to Earth from that terrible place and warn his five brothers about the dangers of the fiery chamber of eternal confinement. In the dis-course, he was told he could not leave where he was, neither could he be permitted to return to Earth and warn his family members (Luke 16:19–31).

From all biblical evidence, the Antichrist is a mortal man with an "antichrist spirit" that motivates his teaching, his kingdom, and his authority. He will arise at the end of the age and will unite an army of followers that make war against all who oppose him.

As we will discuss later, this beast is more than a person. It is an *empire* from the past that will resurrect in the future.

As far back as the time of the destruction of the temple there was an understanding of a final world dictator who would control the world and wreak havoc on the nations. There are several interesting statements made about the Antichrist in early church writings:

> When the close of time draws near, a great prophet shall be sent from God to turn men to the knowledge of God, and he shall receive power of doing wonderful things....And when his works shall be accomplished, another king shall arise out of Syria, born from an evil spirit, the overthrower and destroyer of the human

race, who shall destroy that which is left by the former evil, together with himself...[7]

Another commentary reads:

Now this is he who is called Antichrist; but he shall falsely call himself Christ, and shall fight against the truth, and being overcome shall flee; and shall renew the war, and often be conquered, until in the fourth battle, all the wicked shall be slain, subdued and captured, he shall at length pay the penalty of his crimes...[8]

In a section called the "Scholia on Daniel," commenting on Daniel, we read:

"And I inquired about the fourth beast." It is to the fourth kingdom, of which we have already spoken, that he refers: that kingdom, than which no greater kingdom of like nature has arisen upon the earth; from which also ten horns are to spring, and to be apportioned among ten crowns. And amid these another little horn shall rise, which is that of Antichrist. And it shall pluck by the roots the three others before it; that is to say, he shall subvert the three kings of Egypt, Libya, and Ethiopia, with the view of acquiring for himself universal dominion. And after conquering the remaining seven horns, he will at last begin, inflated by a strange and wicked spirit, to stir up war against the saints, and to persecute all everywhere, with the aim of being glorified by all, and being worshiped as God.[9]

There are many more *church traditions* concerning the Antichrist. Bishop Hippolytus said:

...in the same manner also will the accuser come forth from an impure woman upon the earth, but shall be born of a virgin spuriously.[10]

These early traditions are interesting and can, at times, shed light upon the subject. Yet, the Bible gives ample revelation and understanding concerning the Antichrist and his kingdom, which I call *the kingdom of the beast,* seen over twenty-six hundred years ago by a Hebrew prophet named Daniel who was living at the time in Babylon—the very area where the beast of prophecy would one day set up his command center.

Two Feet, Ten Toes,
and a Little Horn
With a Big Mouth

Whereas you saw the feet and toes, partly of potter's clay and partly of iron, the kingdom shall be divided; yet the strength of the iron shall be in it, just as you saw the iron mixed with ceramic clay. And as the toes of the feet were partly of iron and partly of clay, so the kingdom shall be partly strong and partly fragile.
—Daniel 2:41–42

I was considering the horns, and there was another horn, a little one, coming up among them, before whom three of the first horns were plucked out by the roots. And there, in this horn, were eyes like the eyes of a man, and a mouth speaking pompous words.
—Daniel 7:8

Daniel was the first major Old Testament prophet to actually unveil details of the final empire that would arise at the time of the end. This revelation of the kingdom of the beast is revealed in several major prophetic dreams and visions recorded in the Book of Daniel. This Hebrew prophet was living in Babylon at the time the first dream was revealed to Nebuchadnezzar, the king of Babylon. The three main dreams/visions are:

- ◆ Daniel 2—the dream of a metallic image given to King Nebuchadnezzar

- ◆ Daniel 7—the vision of a beast with ten horns

- ◆ Daniel 8—the vision of a ten-horned beast and little horn (final leader) speaking great things

First, let's carefully examine the Daniel 2 account of Nebuchadnezzar's dream. During the night, the Babylonian king saw a large image of a man, which consisted of various grades of metal, beginning with gold at the head and concluding with a mix of iron and clay feet with ten toes (Dan. 2:31–35). The image had:

- ◆ A head of gold

- ◆ A chest and two arms of silver

- ◆ Thighs made of brass

- ◆ Two legs of iron

- ◆ Two feet that were a mixture of iron and clay

- ◆ Ten toes that were a mixture of iron and clay

The ancient Persians had a strange belief in seven levels of heaven. The first level was made of lead, the second of tin, the third of copper, the fourth of iron, the fifth was a mix, the sixth was of silver, and the seventh was made of gold. The Persian belief started with the lesser metal and went up to the most precious metal last.[1] In

Nebuchadnezzar's dream, the image begins with the most precious metal at the top and concludes with the least valuable at the bottom.

Around 700 B.C., the Greek poet Hesiod divided humanity into five different ages—consisting of gold, silver, bronze, heroic (the only nonmetal age), and iron.[2] In other writings, the world's spiritual history is divided into gold, silver, steel, and *mixed iron* ages, moving it from the age of *revelation* to the age of *apostasy*!

THE METALLIC IMAGE IN DANIEL 2

Nebuchadnezzar's vision is a mix of both world history and spiritual history and moves from gold to iron and clay. This image with its metals represented the major empires of prophecy that would begin in Daniel's day with Babylon and conclude with a ten-king coalition that would be ruling the world at the return of the Messiah. History has interpreted the meaning.

The head of gold

The head of gold represented Babylon, the empire responsible for destroying the temple and taking the Jews captive. The Babylonians were known for their gold wealth. One hundred years after the death of King Nebuchadnezzar, an ancient historian wrote that he had never seen so much gold as was in Babylon. One temple, the Temple of Belus, had an eighteen-foot human statue of solid gold. There were also statues of two golden lions and one golden image of Ishtar. Inside the temple, there was a forty-foot-long golden table, on which were placed three golden religious objects weighing a total of five thousand pounds. No wonder Babylon was called *the golden city*.

The chest and arms of silver

The second empire, following Babylon, was Media-Persia. They are represented on the image by the chest and arms of silver. It was the Media-Persian Empire that allowed the Jews to return to Israel and rebuild their homes and temple. Silver was an important metal to the Persians, since their taxes were to be paid in silver. It is said that the Persians also placed silver harnesses on their horses.

The thighs of brass

The third empire was Greece, under the command of the military genius Alexander the Great. The Grecians were typified by the imagery of thighs of brass on the image. The armies of the Greeks used brass helmets and weaponry in their conflicts.

It was the Grecian ruler Antiochus Epiphanes who defiled the temple, filling it with pagan idols, placing a Hellenistic priest in the temple, and requiring the sacrifice of pigs on the altar.

The legs of iron

The Roman Empire, identified by the legs of iron, followed the Grecians. Iron has a twofold meaning: it was a metal the Romans mastered for use in their chariots and weapons, and it also typifies war and fighting, which was a central feature when the Romans set out to conquer new territory. The Romans destroyed the temple for a second time and took the Jews captive.

The metallic image in the king's dream stands on *two* iron legs, which predicted a two-division split in the Roman Empire. The process began in A.D. 395 when the Roman Empire was divided between the East (one leg) and the West (the other leg). In A.D. 476 the West (Rome) fell to the Germanic tribes, but the eastern leg became the Byzantine Empire. The Byzantines ruled out of Constantinople, Turkey, and built churches in Palestine commemorating many of the Christian holy sites. While the Roman Church maintained dominion through much of Western Europe through the influence of the popes and cardinals of the Roman Church, the Byzantines exercised influence over much of the East, including Palestine and Jerusalem, during a period of one thousand years.

Eventually the eastern (Byzantine) branch of the leg of Rome fell into the hands of Muslim Turks in 1453. An Islamic empire called the *Ottoman Turkish Empire* ruled from Palestine from 1517 to 1917. After seizing control of Palestine and Jerusalem in 1517, the Turks began rebuilding the upper walls on the old city of Jerusalem. The Turkish power continued until the early twentieth century. During the peak of its authority, this empire stretched over three continents and contained twenty-nine provinces. This empire succeeded both the Roman and Byzantine legs of the Roman Empire. Eventually, Palestine and Jerusalem were occupied by the British, who crushed the Turkish rule after four hundred years.

The Ottoman Empire was the seat of the Islamic caliphate until 1923 when it was abandoned and replaced by the Republic of Turkey, today known as the country of Turkey. Since 1923, Muslims worldwide have dreamed of the time when a *holy man* will arise and restore Islam to its glory days of influence, experienced during the days following Muhammad and the times of the Ottoman Empire.

The feet, a mixture of iron and clay

As time and history move forward, the metals become less in value and weaker in strength. The king saw two legs of iron that eventually turned into two feet of iron and clay, representing Rome and Turkey and the final East-West division.

The division of the iron and clay

Iron is mentioned ninety-five times in the Old Testament and is used when referring to weapons. Thus, iron is a picture of war, strength, and fighting. The word *clay* is used twenty-six times in the English translation, identifying a clay jar, a clay seal, a clay house, and, in this reference, clay feet.

If we examine history, we can begin to see the possible interpretation of the iron and the clay mixture of the Roman Empire, divided into two divisions—the East and the West. These divisions can be observed in:

1. The Roman Empire division

2. The Roman religious division

3. The Roman political division

4. The Roman spiritual divisions

The Roman split placed Rome on one leg and Constantinople on the other. Both Rome and Constantinople came into play when Constantine legalized Christianity in the Roman Empire. Both Rome and Constantinople were built on seven hills, and Constantinople was called the *new Rome.*

There was both a political and a religious split in the empire. The Catholic Church was the main force from Rome, and the Orthodox branch of the church eventually evolved after a split in the eleventh century.

In contemporary times, the iron and the clay also became visible through communism and democracy. In fact, communism was known as *the iron curtain.* With the decline of Russia, in so many nations today we can now see the iron of Islam clashing with the clay of democracy.

> And as the toes of the feet were partly of iron and partly of clay, so the kingdom shall be partly strong and partly fragile. As you saw iron mixed with ceramic clay, they will mingle with the seed of men; but they will not adhere to one another, just as iron does not mix with clay.
> —DANIEL 2:42–43

Contemporary history has become the interpreter of the two feet. The clay represents democracy, and the iron is a part of a kingdom that uses war, fighting, and its strength to control. Beginning with the decline of the Ottoman Empire, another political/ military force entered the world stage at the conclusion of World

War I—communism. This movement out of Russia eventually grew into an atheistic, anti-God, anti-Christian belief system that rules its people with an iron fist. Their national symbol was the (iron) hammer and the sickle, and those living in its bondage were said to be behind the *iron curtain*. For seventy years, from 1917 to 1987, the iron fist of communism clashed with the clay of democracy, crushing any democratic opposition. Iron ruled in the East, and clay (democracy) in the West.

In the late 1980s with the fall of Poland, the Berlin wall, and, eventually, the breakup of the Soviet Union, another *iron kingdom* that was scattered across the Middle East began to pull together like metal attracted to a magnet. Their common vision was to defeat Israel and remove the Jews from *Palestinian lands*. This new iron was the fanatical branch of the Islamic religion, which preached a call to jihad (a holy war for the Islamic cause). These radicals wanted to unite Islam and strategically defeat Israel and her Western allies. Once again, we see where the clay of democracy is strong in the West and the iron is rising out of the (Middle) East.

The *clay democracies* of America and Britain have led the charge to reform Afghanistan, Pakistan, and nations in the Middle East into flourishing democracies. However, the iron and the clay are not mingling well. Islamic militants and strict followers of Islamic law will not permit liberal democratic ideas to mingle with the strict observance of Islamic law and tradition. To devout Islam, democracy is *too soft*. Secular democracies allow alcohol, something forbidden among Muslims. Women in democratic nations often expose their body in an immodest fashion, something again forbidden in a strict Islamic culture. As the West attempts to *liberate Islamic nations* using democracy as the weapon, the clay is not mixing with the strict *iron* of Islam. I believe this is why Daniel said that the iron and the clay will not mix (Dan. 2:43).

The ten toes, made of a mixture of iron and clay

At the conclusion of the age at the time of the end, the image is standing on two feet with ten toes. These two feet are a mixture of iron and clay. Therefore, in prophetic symbolism, one foot is East and one foot is West. The early father Hippolytus comments on these:

> As these things, then, are in the future, and as the toes of the image are equivalent to (so many) democracies, and the ten horns of the fourth beast are distributed over ten kingdoms...[3]

The ten toes are ten future kings. It appears that five will emerge from the West and five from the East, since the two legs and two feet identify the East and West. Scholars have long debated the identity of the ten kings the ten toes represent. They are certainly a coalition of End Time nations prior to the return of Christ. Many prophecy teachers have taught that the Common Market (now the European Union) would be the fulfillment of this prophecy. In 1951, the Treaty of Paris was signed, creating the European Coal and Steel Community (ECSC). This stirred prophetic interest, since coal came out of the *clay* of the earth, and *steel* was made from iron ore (thus the iron and the clay).

One purpose for the creation of the ECSC was to unify nations in Europe to prevent further war. Eventually, the Treaty of Rome was signed in 1957, creating the European Economic Community and the European Atomic Energy Community. Eventually, a common economic market was set up in Europe. There were six original member countries: France, West Germany, Italy, Belgium, Netherlands, and Luxembourg.

In the 1980s Greece became the tenth member to join, and prophetic teachers began sounding the trumpet, warning North America that the ten kings of prophecy had formed. However, the trumpet became a more muffled sound as more than ten nations have since united with the EU coalition. By 2008 there were twenty-seven nations in the coalition, with more waiting in wings to join.

I believe the EU is part of the seventh empire that continues a short space, but I do not agree that it is the eighth empire with the final ten kings. There are three facts that present a challenge in making the EU the final ten kings of prophecy. First, as stated, there are more than ten nations in the EU, with many others planning to join in the future. Second, the present nations in the EU are predominately Western nations from the Western side of the Roman Empire. The two toes and ten kings must be both East and West. It is pointed out that the EU is a continuation of the old Roman Empire. Third, take a look at the other nations that were a part of the old Roman Empire and which are NOT presently a part of the EU:

1. Egypt
2. Ethiopia
3. Israel
4. Lebanon
5. Syria
6. Parts of Iraq
7. Turkey
8. Jordan
9. Morocco

These nations were all part of the Roman territory when John wrote the Apocalypse (the Book of Revelation) and, with the exception of Israel, are all Islamic nations today; yet eighteen hundred years ago these regions were all under the occupation, control, or influence of the emperors of Rome. I have often said, "Some prophecy teachers have all ten toes growing out of one foot—the Western one," which would be the case if we force a belief that the EU is the sole fulfill-ment of Daniel's ten toes.

One explanation is that most of the above nations will eventually join the EU and use the euro currency, which may be possible with the demise or decline of the US dollar. Or the ten kings may actu-ally be a combination of Islamic nations (some listed above) that will form a ten-nation coalition and give their Islamic nations over to the Antichrist to form one unit of ten kings.

The rising of the ten kings

Some prophets identify the leaders of this ten-nation coalition as the ten kings mentioned in Daniel 7:24 and Revelation 17:12. Demo-cratic nations like America elect one person as *president*. The Romans gave their leader the title of *emperor*. Britain and Israel speak of their leaders as *prime minister*. The only area in the world where the gov-ernmental leaders are still identified as *kings* is in the Islamic Per-sian Gulf, with such leaders as the king of Saudi Arabia. Seven of the Gulf nations are called *emirates*. Several have a *prince* who oversees their nation. The kingdom of Jordan also has a *king* and a monarchy form of government. This may be another clue as to the identity of the Antichrist, as he is called "the prince who is to come…" (Dan. 9:26).

The Persian Gulf is a major sea through which much of the world's oil travels on oil tankers. This prophetic beast could rise up not only out of the *sea* of nations but also from the literal nations that are sur-rounded by the Persian Gulf.

It is during the days of these ten kings when "the God of heaven will set up a kingdom which shall never be destroyed" (Dan. 2:44).

THE VISIONS OF THE FOUR BEASTS

The second prophetic vision is recorded in Daniel 7. This vision describes four animals, each representing a different prophetic empire. Daniel saw, "…the four winds of heaven were stirring up the Great Sea" (v. 2). The "Great Sea" is identified as an early name for what is today the Mediterranean Sea—the great ocean linking northern Africa, Israel, Turkey, Italy, and Spain.

The four beasts in the vision represent empires that would have dominion over the nations surrounding the sea.

The first beast was a lion with two wings, which is traditionally identified as Babylon (v. 4). In the time of ancient Babylon, there were carved statues of creatures with human heads and the bodies of winged lions called *lamassu*, which were positioned at the entrances of temples and gates. Two winged lions are carved at the corners of the gates of Xerxes at Persepolis in Iran. When a winged lion was carved with an open book it meant peace, but one with a closed book meant war.

The second beast in succession was a bear and is historically linked to the second empire of biblical prophecy—the Persian Empire (v. 5). History reveals that some of the largest bears in the world came from the mountains of Persia. The bear in Nebuchadnezzar's vision had three ribs in its mouth (v. 5), representing the three nations the Persians overthrew—Lydia, Babylon, and Egypt. The Book of Daniel mentions the Persian king Cyrus's victory over the Babylonians.

The third apocalyptic creature is identified as a leopard with four wings (v. 6). The leopard is known for its speed. This accurately describes the swiftness with which the third empire—Greece, led by Alexander the Great—defeated the Persians and moved its headquarters to Babylon. Alexander expanded his empire from Egypt to India.

The fourth and final beast is the most important to us and the most interesting. There is no physical description of a specific animal given by Daniel, other than this: "…a fourth beast, dreadful and terrible, exceedingly strong. It had huge iron teeth; it was devouring, breaking in pieces, and trampling the residue with its feet. It was different from all the beasts that were before it, and it had ten horns" (v. 7). This fourth beast fits the imagery of the imperial Roman Empire.

Some may suggest that the interpretation of these beasts is a more contemporary interpretation, written long after the fact. However, one of the earliest Christian theologians, Hippolytus (A.D. 170–236), pastor of the church at Rome and familiar with the prophetic interpretations, taught that the meanings of these animals were:

◆ The lion was Babylon, and Nebuchadnezzar was the head on the image. The two wings on the lion represented the glory that was taken from Nebuchadnezzar but restored after his breakdown.

◆ The bear was the Medes and Persians, and the three ribs in the mouth of the bear represented Media, Persia, and Babylon.

◆ The leopard was Alexander the Great, and the four wings represented the four divisions of the empire after his death.

◆ The nondescriptive beast was Rome. The ten toes are ten kings that arise out of the Roman area.[4]

This interpretation has remained the primary interpretation by traditional Christian prophetic teachers for centuries. These four beasts are the four successive empires of Babylon, Media-Persia, Greece, and Rome.

THE LITTLE HORN

The apocalyptic literature of both Daniel and Revelation allude to a beast that had ten horns on the head (Dan. 7:7–8, 20, 24; Rev. 13:1; 17:3, 12). Horns can represent a kingdom, a king, or a superior authority. The horns on the head of the apocalyptic beast are identified as ten kingdoms ruled by ten kings.

> And the ten horns out of this kingdom are ten kings
> that shall arise: and another shall rise after them; and
> he shall be diverse from the first, and he shall subdue
> three kings.
>
> —DANIEL 7:24, KJV

> The ten horns which you saw are ten kings who have
> received no kingdom as yet, but they receive authority
> for one hour as kings with the beast.
>
> —REVELATION 17:12

Daniel saw one man identified as a "little horn" (leader) who will arise in the midst of the ten. He is described in Daniel's vision.

> I was considering the horns, and there was another
> horn, a little one, coming up among them, before whom
> three of the first horns were plucked out by the roots.
> And there, in this horn, were eyes like the eyes of a
> man, and a mouth speaking pompous words.
>
> —DANIEL 7:8

> And out of one of them came a little horn which grew
> exceedingly great toward the south, toward the east,
> and toward the Glorious Land.
>
> —DANIEL 8:9

This little horn, which has "eyes like the eyes of a man," is symbolic of a person who will become the final world dictator. The term "little horn" is unique. It could allude to his physical size as being small in stature. It may also refer to his authority being diminished and small, and yet, through his "big mouth," he will gain authority and influence. He will have a "mouth speaking great things" (Dan. 7:8, KJV) and shall "speak great words against the most High" (v. 25, KJV). This little horn will also uproot or take over three of the ten kings

(v. 8). Daniel mentions that Egypt, Libya, and Ethiopia will be the three nations that he will overthrow (Dan. 11:43). Several early fathers also identify these three nations in northern Africa as being the three nations that the Antichrist will root up when he rises to power. All three of these nations are presently Islamic in nature, with all three having a small Christian population.

The Command Center of the Beast

With many nations involved, where will the beast set up his command center headquarters? Daniel was the first biblical prophet to see three empires compared to the beast resembling a lion, a bear, and a leopard. More than six hundred years later, John saw the final beast's empire, which was the same *nondescriptive beast* Daniel saw, which had ten horns on its head. John gave a very graphic description and revealed that the last beast's kingdom is a combination of the beast empires revealed by Daniel!

> Now the beast which I saw was like a leopard, his feet were like the feet of a bear, and his mouth like the mouth of a lion. The dragon gave him his power, his throne, and great authority.
> —Revelation 13:2

The lion of Daniel was ancient Babylon (Dan. 7:4). Today, this area consists of Iraq, Syria, and Lebanon. The bear of Persia (v. 5) today includes the nations of Iran, Iraq, Afghanistan, and Pakistan. The ancient Greek Empire, symbolized by the leopard (v. 6), would today include all of the above, including Macedonia and Turkey. With the exception of Greece, all the nations listed above have one common thread—they are Islamic nations, controlled by Islamic governments. It is clear that this End Time beast's kingdom is a united coalition of Islamic nations or the formation of a long-awaited Islamic crescent that will stretch from Pakistan in the east all the way to Egypt in the northern horn of Africa. The nations would include but not be limited to:

- Afghanistan
- Pakistan
- Iran
- Iraq
- Syria
- Lebanon
- Egypt
- Libya
- Ethiopia
- Greece
- Macedonia

FURTHER EVIDENCE OF ISLAMIC CONTROL

The body of the beast was a leopard, the imagery identifying the kingdom of Greece. After the death of Alexander the Great, his (Grecian) empire was divided among his four main generals (Dan. 11:4). Each of Alexander's four generals received a portion of the massive landmass that had been conquered and controlled by the Greek Empire. The four generals and the areas they ruled from are:

The General	The Region	The Present Area
Ptolemy	Egypt and northern Africa	Egypt, Libya, and North Africa
Seleucus	Assyria and Babylon	Lebanon, Syria, and Iraq

The General	The Region	The Present Area
Lysimachus	Turkey	Turkey and southern Russia
Cassander	Greece and Macedonia	Greece, Bulgaria, and Romania

After seeing this four-part division of the Greek Empire, Daniel gives a clue as to the area from which the coming Antichrist would arise:

> And out of one of them came forth a little horn, which waxed exceeding great, toward the south, and toward the east, and toward the pleasant land.
> —Daniel 8:9, kjv

The Antichrist arises from one of the following four divisions of the former Greek Empire:

1. Egypt—home of the ancient Egyptian Empire

2. Turkey—home of the one-thousand-year Turkish Empire

3. Greece and Macedonia—home of the ancient Greek Empire

4. Syria and Iraq— home of the ancient Babylonian Empire

We are informed that the Antichrist will invade northern Africa, seizing Egypt, Libya, and Ethiopia (Dan. 11:43). We read that, during a series of wars: "News from the east and the north shall trouble him" (v. 44). During this time in prophetic history, the northern king will be Turkey, one of the strongest Islamic nations in the Middle East. If Turkey comes against the Antichrist, then he obviously is not head-quartered in Turkey. If he invades from the outside and takes over northern Africa, then neither is his headquarters centered there. That leaves the region of Greece or Syria-Babylon.

The best choice among the four locations from a biblical and historical viewpoint is the Syria-Babylon territory. For centuries, scholars have observed numerous prophecies indicating the rise of a leader from the Assyrian territory. Biblical prophecy also links him to Babylon.

THE DEADLY WOUND

John's last prophetic beast was a seven-headed creature with ten horns. These seven heads allude to the seven empires of past and future Bible prophecy. (Remember, five empires had already fallen in John's day, and one was—but John was also seeing a future king—the seventh head.) Out of these seven major prophetic empires, one of the "heads" was wounded to the point of death, but he would revive.

> And I saw one of his heads as if it had been mortally wounded, and his deadly wound was healed. And all the world marveled and followed the beast.
> —REVELATION 13:3

I have heard ministers explain this prediction to mean that the Antichrist will be shot in the head and be raised from the dead to the amazement of the masses. The big challenge with this interpretation is the text itself, which reads "one of his heads," not "his head." Any man has just one head, but a kingdom has many heads, or leaders, within that kingdom.

There are three possible meanings as to the interpretation of one of the seven heads being wounded. The word *wound* here means "to maim or slay violently, like an animal." It implies a sudden blow that defeats one of the heads on the beast. Some use this passage to teach that the Antichrist will receive a physical wound to his head and die, but he will supernaturally be resurrected from the dead as a *demonic resurrection* to imitate the resurrection of Christ.

Another school of thought believes that the Antichrist will take a major military defeat at the midway point in the Tribulation, then suddenly, near the point of complete defeat, he will be reenergized and will seize opposing nations, annexing them into his kingdom. One reason to suggest this interpretation is in Revelation 13:4, where the world "wonders after the beast" and says, "Who can make war against the beast?" The Antichrist will amaze the world with his ability to fight and conquer nations.

The third and most plausible meaning is that one of the previous seven kingdoms (one of the beast's heads) was mortally wounded. Notice, one of the *heads*, and not one of the *horns*, is wounded. The horns represent the individual kings, and the heads allude to earthly prophetic kingdoms. The emphasis is not on the Antichrist as such, but upon one of the beast's heads or one of the seven empires of prophecy. As previously stated, the seven empires are as follows:

- Egypt
- Assyria
- Babylon
- Media-Persia
- Greece
- Rome
- The East-West Division

Out of the above list, which empire or nation no longer exists? The Egyptian empire faded in glory after the departure of the Hebrews, but the nation of Egypt still exists. The Assyrians, presently called Syria, exist but with little to no influence on the global scene. The Persians are today called the Iranians, and the Iranian people still consider themselves to be Persians, not Arabs. Greece is a contemporary nation and part of the EU. Italy, whose capital is Rome, is a nation among world nations and the headquarters for the Roman Catholic Church, centered in the Vatican City in Rome. Even Turkey continues to exist with the same name of its former empire. Only one of the previous empires of the ancient world no longer exists in name, and that is Babylon.

BABYLON—BACK FROM THE DEAD

The Tower of Babel built by Nimrod, mentioned in Genesis 11, is the beginning of the kingdom of Babel (Gen. 10:10). Centuries later, Nebuchadnezzar constructed one of the world's most elaborate cities off the Tigris River in Mesopotamia. This is the Babylon where Daniel penned the Book of Daniel during his time as a Jewish captive.

Although the name *Babylon* is the ancient name of an empire of prophecy, the area of Babylon was called by that name five hundred years after the Jews returned from captivity. In 1 Peter 5:13, Peter addressed "the church that is in Babylon…" (KJV). The name *Babylon* is mentioned six times from Matthew's Gospel to 1 Peter 5:13, and in each reference it alludes to Babylon, the capital of Chaldea. John in Revelation mentions the name of Babylon six times, referring to a spiritual Babylon (Mystery Babylon—Rev. 17:5), and predicts the economic collapse of Babylon. Why does John use the name Babylon when alluding to the future destruction of a city built on seven hills (Rev. 17:9)?

The present territory of Iraq is the same region of the ancient political Babylon of the Bible. The early name was the land of Shinar, the site of the first megastructure called the Tower of Babel (Gen. 11). Centuries later, the prophet Zechariah saw and was given dimensions of a flying scroll. Using the measure of one cubit to equal twenty-five inches, the scroll was forty-one feet eight inches long and twenty feet ten inches in diameter.

This scroll recorded a curse that consumed the timbers and the stones of a house. The prophet peered into the future and saw an *ephah* (basket) with a lead lid covering it, weighing one talent (122 pounds). Inside the basket was a woman who was called "Wickedness." She was being carried by two angelic-like beings with wings to a foundation located in the plains of Shinar (Zech. 5:1–11). Today there is a section of flat land near Baghdad called *Shinar*. This is the area referred to in the vision of Zechariah.

When commenting on this strange prediction in the 1940s, biblical scholar Finis Dake, in the side notes in his *Annotated Bible*, commented:

> One thing is certain—Babylon will be the center of activities in the East during the last days, in commerce, religion, and politics. It will be rebuilt and become the capital of the Antichrist. He will come from Syria, which will take in Babylon in those days, for the Syrian division of the old Grecian empire included all the countries of Syria and Iraq.[5]

Babylon is also a theme in the prophecy of Isaiah. Isaiah exposed the fall of Lucifer (Satan) from heaven in Isaiah 14:12–15. God then predicts the defeat of Babylon and how He will break the rod of Assyria out of the land of Israel (Isa. 14:22, 25). The prophecy suddenly takes an abrupt turn from an Assyrian prophecy to a prophecy against Palestina:

> Do not rejoice, all you of Philistia,
> Because the rod that struck you is broken;
> For out of the serpent's roots will come forth a viper,
> And its offspring will be a fiery flying serpent.
> —ISAIAH 14:29

Palestina is the ancient name of the area where the Philistines once ruled in Israel. One of the theological definitions identifies "the general territory on the West coast of Canaan, or the entire country of Palestine."[6] In the prophetic future, the leaders of both Assyria and Babylon will be deeply involved with people living in *Palestine*. Out of this Palestinian conflict will come forth a "fiery flying serpent." The only place in Scripture where the symbolism of a fire-colored serpent is found is in Revelation 12 where John saw: "And another sign appeared in heaven: behold, a great, fiery red dragon having seven heads and ten horns, and seven diadems on his heads" (Rev. 12:3). This dragon is Satan, and the seven heads are the seven empires of prophecy, each of which had a strong demonic *prince* spirit attempting to control the spiritual atmosphere and governmental leaders of these empires (Dan. 10:20).

I believe the event of the Palestinians forging a Palestinian state, and the resulting conflict surrounding this event, will initiate many of the wars between Israel and her Muslim neighbors.

ISLAM 101—
WHAT YOU SHOULD KNOW

...which things are symbolic. For these are the two cov-
enants: the one from Mount Sinai which gives birth
to bondage, which is Hagar—for this Hagar is Mount
Sinai in Arabia, and corresponds to Jerusalem which
now is, and is in bondage with her children—but the
Jerusalem above is free, which is the mother of us all.
—GALATIANS 4:24–26

T HOSE LIVING IN THE WEST OFTEN STRUGGLE TO UNDERSTAND why millions of Muslims have such hatred for the Jewish people. Until 9/11, many Americans knew nothing about Muslims or the Islamic religion. The founder of the Islamic religion, Muhammad, whose name means "the praised one," was born in 570 and was from Arabia.

Muhammad claimed he received a series of visions and revelations from Allah, which became the basis of the Islamic holy book called the *Quran.* Muhammad was from the Quraysh tribe, which claimed to be direct descendants from Abraham through his son

Ishmael. Muhammad's father, Abdullah, died before Muhammad was born. His mother, Amina, died when Muhammad was six. He was raised by his uncle and traveled with caravans throughout Syria and Arabia. At age twenty-five, he married a wealthy widow named Khadija and had six children through her.

Muhammad lived near Mecca, a settlement in Arabia. It was a community situated at the center of the north/south and east/west caravan routes. Arabian merchants covered the area with beds, food, stables for camels, and other services. Mecca also contained a 140-foot-deep well with crystal clear water. Called *Zam Zam*, the well was believed to cure illnesses. This well drew people from far and near to Mecca.

The other distinguishing mark of Mecca was a large black rock, different from all others in the area. No one knew how it got there, and the caravans were afraid of it. (It was probably a meteorite.) Those living in Mecca built a large cube-shaped stone building over the rock called the *Ka'ba* (meaning "cube" in Arabic). On the stone the local inhabitants of Mecca had placed statues of different gods and goddesses. Muhammad's grandfather was the keeper of the keys to the Ka'ba.

Before Muhammad's time, Mecca had become a tourist attraction for the caravans. Each year, pilgrims traveled to Mecca to drink of the special springs and kiss the black stone. The local people charged money for visitors who wanted to kiss the rock for good luck.

By the fifth century, the tribe members of Quraysh were the guardians of the Ka'ba and were the dominant tribe in Mecca. This tribe provided the arrangements for all pilgrims visiting the Ka'ba, and the senior members of the group collected the income from the pilgrims. At the time of Muhammad, there were 360 different idols sitting on the black stone in the Ka'ba. It was in this spiritual setting that Muhammad began praying and fasting at age forty.

As Muhammad grew, he spent time on the hills outside the city of

Mecca, in Arabia. Beginning in the year 610, at age forty, he claimed to have heard a voice speaking to him while praying in a cave above Mecca. Fearful, he ran home, where his wife wrapped him in a blanket. Then he heard the voice again, telling him that he was the chosen messenger of God to bring his people, the Arabs, the message of one God who controlled all things. He alleged to hear the voice saying, "You, wrapped in your mantle, arise and warn."

According to Muslim belief, Muhammad received a series of visions from an angel who he claimed was Gabriel. His early messages spoke of God's goodness and power, the need to return to God, and the final judgment that was coming. He declared that there was only one God, and his name (in Arabic) was *Allah*. It was taught that Allah was the same God worshiped by both Jews and Christians. As Muhammad preached his messages among the Arabs, those who chose to follow his teachings became known as *Muslims*, and the religion was called *Islam,* meaning "submission."

During Muhammad's time, there was much idol worship throughout Arabia. There were theological divisions among Christians, and the Jews and Christians were at odds. In the Arabian city of Mecca, a conflict arose among the merchants at the Ka'ba. If the people believed there was only one God, it would destroy the pilgrimages and the income from visitors who came to pray before their gods sitting on the stone. Many Arabs called Muhammad a liar, a fraud, and a false prophet. Eventually, Muhammad and his new followers were forced from Mecca, and they moved to a new city where they were received. Muhammad named the city *Madinat al Nabi*, meaning, "City of the Prophet," today called *Medina* in Saudi Arabia.

Soon conflicts arose between followers of Muhammad in Medina and the people of Mecca. Muslim groups began raiding the caravans. Muhammad began teaching that if his followers died fighting, they would go straight to paradise. The eight-year war finally ceased when the people in Mecca gave in to the Muslims. Muhammad declared

Allah to be the true God, removed the idols, and made Mecca the center for the Islamic religion. The pilgrimages to the Ka'ba remained a central feature of his teachings, and today one of the five pillars of Islam requires a Muslim follower to pray at the Ka'ba in Mecca at least one time before death. This is called the *hajj*. The Islamic religion began to sweep through Arabia, as every day more Arabs continued joining the religion.

At age sixty-two, Muhammad began complaining of severe headaches and fever. Some Muslims believe he was poisoned by one of his wives, who was Jewish. He never recovered, and one day, after saying a few prayers, he passed away.

During his lifetime, the followers of Muhammad claimed him to be a prophet. He brought forth a series of what believers called *revelations*. After the death of Muhammad, his sayings were collected and placed in a book called the Quran. The Quran is considered to be the sacred revelations of Islam, just as the Bible is considered God's sacred revelation to Jews and Christians. The Quran contains 114 surahs, or chapters, starting with the longest surah and ending with the shortest. The surahs were the alleged revelations given to Muhammad over a twenty-two-year period. Muhammad was believed to be illiterate; therefore, the revelations were written down by his followers as they heard him recite it. The words were written on leaves, pieces of parchment, and even dried bones. The Quran was compiled after Muhammad's death and written in the Arabic language.

Muslims believe that one hundred four sacred books were given by God to mankind. However, one hundred of these were given to Adam, Seth, Enoch, and Abraham and have been lost. The four remaining books are the books of Moses (or the Torah), the psalms of David, the Gospels of Christ, and the Quran. Other books contain the *hadith* (traditions), which are the teachings of Muhammad that were put together by his followers who knew him personally. Fourteen hundred years later, Islam claims an estimated 1.4 billion followers and is said to be the fastest growing religion in the world.

While Muslims claim to accept the Torah, Psalms, and the four Gospels, they also claim the Bible has been *tahrif,* meaning, "corrupted" or "altered." Muslims believe that since Jesus did not write the Bible Himself, it is not accurate. Many stories in the Quran are very different from the stories in the Bible. For example, the Bible teaches that Abraham dwelt by the *trees of Mamre* and built an altar there to the Lord (Gen. 13:18). The Quran teaches that Abraham said, "O our Lord! I have made some of my offspring to dwell in a valley without cultivation, by Your Sacred House [Ka'ba]; in order, O our Lord, that they may establish regular Prayer…" (Surah 14:37). When asking a Muslim about the contradiction that Mamre is in Hebron and the Ka'ba is in Arabia, a Muslim said, "The Quran is infallible. The Jews and Christians changed the Bible to make it fit for them." This is why witnessing to Muslims by simply quoting Scripture seldom wins them to Christ. It is love and the presence of the Holy Spirit that can impact their hearts.

Let me point out that this book is not intended to form a debate on the doctrines of Islam and Christianity. However, one will not understand how Islam will fulfill many of the Bible's predictions of an eighth kingdom that seeks to destroy Israel and the Jews unless one understands certain Islamic beliefs and traditions.

After Muhammad's Death— Two Branches of Islam

The death of Muhammad left a void in the leadership of the Islamic religion. He announced no successor; therefore, the battle for the *prophet's successor* began immediately. The Muslim elders elected Muhammad's second convert and the oldest man in the group, Abu Bakr. Abu's title was *caliph*. Most Muslims accepted this decision, but a small minority did not. The smaller group believed that

Ali, Muhammad's adopted son and the father of Muhammad's two grandsons, Hassan and Hussein, should replace Muhammad. A struggle began that led to the deaths of many of Islam's first caliphs. As a result, two branches of Islam developed—the *Sunnis* and the *Shi'ites*. The Sunnis accepted Abu as successor, and the Shi'ites believed the heir to Muhammad was Ali.

Abu Bakr, the first caliph, brought the tribes of Arabia under Islamic rule. The second caliph, Omar (634–644), began an expansion that lasted for one hundred years. It was under Omar that the mosque in Jerusalem was built on the Temple Mount. During these hundred years, Muslim armies extended the empire into Iraq, Iran, and parts of central Asia. As Syria came under Islamic control, the headquarters of the Umayyad Dynasty (661–750) was Damascus, Syria.

The third caliph, Othman, was assassinated, thus causing a war between the Sunnis and the Shi'ites that continues off and on to this day. As the years progressed, several different Islamic dynasties arose, and the headquarters of the Shi'ites eventually became Baghdad, Iraq. It was in Karbala, Iraq, that Hussein, the son of Ali, was murdered along with seventy followers. Each year during the Islamic month of Muharram the Shi'ites commemorate the death of Ali.

The division not only split the religion into two branches, but it also caused a split in opinions as to where the headquarters of Islam should be. While all Muslims consider Mecca and Medina to be sacred places, the Sunnis claimed Mecca as their headquarters, and the Shi'ites moved from Damascus to Baghdad. Today Tehran, Iran, has become the strength of the Shi'ite branch, and 93 percent of the Muslim population are Shi'ite Muslims.

THE SHI'ITES

The desire for the Iranians to take over Iraq may be based on more than a need to acquire oil or a desire to control a land closer to Israel.

It appears to be rooted in the concept that the Mahdi will reappear in present-day Iraq. To Shi'ite Muslims, Iraq held an important role in its past history and will do so in its future.

For many years the countries of Iraq, Syria, and Lebanon have been inhabited predominantly by members of the Sunni Muslim sect. The more radical Shi'ite Muslims have been centered in the country of Iran. It has been a plan of the radical Muslims to overthrow the governments of Iraq, Lebanon, and Syria and form a huge Islamic crescent under the control of the Shi'ite group. Eventually, Iraq will fall to radical Islam. Once radical Islamists control Iraq, they will have Syria in their back pocket! Lebanon was once an Arab Christian nation, but when radical Muslims took over the nation during the civil war of 1975–1990, many Arab Christians were forced to flee the country. Some were permitted into Israel, and others had to face severe persecution and even death at the hands of the fanatics. Today in Lebanon, two radical Shi'ite groups—Hezbollah and Amal—are gaining ground in their desire to control the nation, populated by a larger majority of Shi'ite Muslims than Sunni Muslims.

The Shi'ite Muslims are quite different from the Sunni Muslims for several reasons:

1. Many Shi'ite Muslims are involved heavily in occult activities. They practice palm reading and the reading of tea leaves. Many Shi'ites celebrate Ashura, the anniversary of the murder of Muhammad's grandson Hussein thirteen hundred years ago, by beating themselves, slashing their back with knives or their heads with nails, or piercing their bodies with a sword.[1]

2. The Shi'ite Muslims often display pictures of their imams, which is normally not done by the Sunnis. It would not be difficult to imagine seeing a group

of Shi'ite Muslims, along with a group of apostate Christians, worshiping the image of the beast that will be brought to life through the demonic powers of the false prophet (Rev. 13:11–15).

3. Shi'ites have a strong desire to take Jerusalem and destroy Israel. They are constantly calling for jihad, which is a holy war against Israel and any other groups or religions opposing radical Islam.

For the following simple reasons, I believe that out of a strong fanatical branch of Islam will come a man who will hold the world hostage with nuclear, chemical, and biological weapons. It appears likely he will come from the Shi'ite branch of Islam.

1. The world's final dictator will, according to Daniel, "become strong with a small number of people" (Dan. 11:23). The Shi'ites only make up about 15 percent of the Muslim population.[2]

2. Daniel also indicates that the Antichrist will be "great...toward the east" (Dan. 8:9). East of Jerusalem, Israel, are the countries of Iraq, Iran, Afghanistan, and Pakistan, along with the southern Russian states. These territories are strongholds for the more radical Muslims. An estimated 93 percent of Muslims in Iran are Shi'ite Muslims.[3]

3. While many Sunni Muslims have Jewish friends and get along with Christians from the West, the Middle East Shi'ite Muslims have a tendency to be overtly anti-Semitic and consider America "the

Great Satan." (It should be noted, however, that many members of al Qaeda are Sunni Muslims.)

I have heard Sunni Muslims in Israel and America say that the actions and thinking of radical Islamists are not truly representative of Islamic teachings and are perversions of the traditions. One Sunni in Israel said, "I hate the Shi'ites. They give everyone a bad name."

Today, the thread that ties the fabric of Islam together is the belief that Israel and Jerusalem will once again be in the total control of Muslims, with the Jews and Christians expelled permanently from the Holy Land.

6

ISLAM AND THE LAST DAYS

Fight those who do not believe in Allah nor the Last Day,
nor hold that forbidden which has been forbidden by Allah
and His Messenger, nor acknowledge the Religion of Truth,
(even if they are) of the People of the Book, until they pay the
Jizya with willing submission, and feel themselves subdued.
                                                    —SURAH 9:29

And when the Word is fulfilled against them (the
unjust), We shall produce from the earth a Beast
to (face) them: he will speak to them for that man-
kind did not believe with assurance in Our Signs.
                                                    —SURAH 27:82

IT COMES AS A SURPRISE TO MANY TO LEARN THAT MUSLIMS have strong traditions concerning the last days. Their expectations of what is coming in the future is eerily parallel to the biblical predictions of a final world empire controlled by a warlike military leader. In Israel I have met with both former Muslims and practicing Muslims to compile many of their beliefs relating to the last days. In the Quran, the last days are noted by several terms:

- ◆ Day of uprising

- ◆ Day of separation

- ◆ Day of reckoning

- ◆ Day of awakening and sending forth

- ◆ The last day

- ◆ The encompassing day

- ◆ The hour

Many Muslims teach that the last days will be preceded by three trumpet blasts. At the first blast, all creatures in heaven and the earth will be struck by terror. At the second blast, all creatures in heaven and the earth will die. At the last blast, forty years after the first two blasts, all will be raised again for the judgment. The length of judgment will be one thousand years. (Some Islamic scholars say it will be fifty thousand years.)

ISLAM'S FINAL PROPHET—THE MAHDI

Years ago I was amazed to discover that Muslims believe they will one day control the entire world and everyone will convert to their religion. I was also disturbed to learn how most Muslims actually feel about Jews and the state of Israel, especially the strong feelings among Muslims living in the Middle East.

The split between the two divisions of Islam—Sunni and Shi'ite—eventually became so great that eleven of the twelve early leaders of Islam from the Shi'ite branch were poisoned or killed by their opposition. According to Shi'ite belief, it is this twelfth leader who will play a role at the end of days.

Many Shi'ites in Iran have a teaching called the *Doctrine of the Twelver*. The twelfth imam was the twelve-year-old son of the eleventh imam. At age twelve, this young boy, destined to be a chosen imam of the Shi'ite branch, disappeared off the street in his city and was never heard from again.

Since the graves of the other eleven are known and the grave of the twelfth has never been discovered, the tradition states that the twelfth caliph has been supernaturally protected by God for the past twelve hundred years. Most say he is in a desert in Arabia. Still others believe he is in Iraq. Since the disappearance of the twelfth imam in A.D. 878, the Shi'ite sect has been expecting this twelfth prophet to reappear at the end of days and become the final unifier of Islam. Called the *Mahdi*, this man, according to Islamic tradition, will be a military expert who will bring the world under the control of Islamic law and justice.

THE MYSTERIOUS COMING OF IMAM AL-MAHDI

The word *Mahdi* translates as "the guided one." The Shi'ites believe the Mahdi will be guided so directly by God that he will be divinely protected by God from all error and sin in all he does. He will interpret Islam to all men and lead the final Islamic revolution that will convert the world to the Islamic faith. Shi'ites believe the Mahdi will be both a political and military leader of great conquest.

There are numerous traditions concerning this mysterious person. The Islamic holy book, the Quran, has little to say concerning this person. Most traditions about the Mahdi developed in the eighth century or later. While both the Sunni and the Shi'ite branches have a teaching on the Mahdi, the Shi'ites have the strongest teaching, believing he will appear toward the end of the world. Below are a list of teachings from Islamic tradition concerning the Mahdi and the end of days.

- ◆ His name will be Muhammad, and he will trace his lineage as a direct descendant through Fatima, the daughter of Muhammad.

- ◆ The name of his father and Muhammad's father will be the same.

- ◆ He will have the disposition of Muhammad.

- ◆ He will have a bald forehead and a high, hooked nose.

- ◆ He will have a distinctive mole (the "mark of a prophet") and a V-shaped aperture between his front teeth.

- ◆ He will appear just before the end of the world, during a time of great difficulty.

- ◆ He will convert the world to the Islamic faith.

Most Muslims believe the Mahdi will arise from the East. Other traditions state that this man will unite Muslims into a single united kingdom. If men do not submit to his teaching and instruction, he will *beat* them into submission until they return to Allah. Of course, those who rebel against him will meet a swift death by the sword of Islam. Many Islamic nations still behead people for certain crimes. Several years ago, a former CIA agent who attended my father's church was in Saudi Arabia when a group of men were buried in the sand with their heads protruding from the ground. Using a bulldozer with blades, the heads of the offenders were literally snapped from their bodies and covered with sand.[1]

ANOTHER SET OF TRADITIONS

Other Islamic traditions further enlighten us concerning the expectations of Muslims about the coming Mahdi:

- ◆ The Syrian army will attack him but will be destroyed in the desert. When this happens, both Iran and Syria will unite to pledge their allegiance to him.

- ◆ He will take Turkey through force.

- ◆ After uniting all of Islam, he will then take over the entire world in the name of Islam. Muhammad predicted the conquest of Spain, which some believe will occur under the Mahdi.

- ◆ Under the Mahdi's leadership, there will be great prosperity, including gold and silver for his faithful followers.

- ◆ After all of this is accomplished, the Mahdi will rule for five, seven, or nine years (depending upon which tradition is followed), and then the end of the world will come, followed by the judgment of Allah.

When one studies the expectations of Muslims, there are amazing links between their traditions of the Mahdi and the prophecies given by biblical prophets. For example, I have compared Islamic traditions about the Mahdi to biblical references regarding the Antichrist—the world's final world dictator. Some Muslims would not appreciate such a comparison, but other Muslims with whom I have shared this comparison were almost shocked by the parallels between the twelve-hundred-year-old Islamic beliefs and the ancient prophecies of the Bible concerning the world's last dictator:

Muslim Belief	Bible Prophecy
The Mahdi will unite the Muslim world.	The Antichrist will bring ten kings under his subjection (Rev. 17:12).
The Mahdi will bring gold and silver to his followers.	The prophet Daniel predicted that the coming Antichrist "shall honor a god…which his fathers did not know…with gold and silver" (Dan. 11:38).
The Mahdi, according to some traditions, will rule for seven years.	The Antichrist will come to his position early during the seven-year Tribulation (Dan. 9:27).
According to Islamic beliefs, the Mahdi will take over Turkey.	Daniel states that the "king of the North shall come against him like a whirlwind, with chariots, horsemen, and with many ships" (Dan. 11:40). The "king of the north" during the Tribulation will be the nation of Turkey. Turkey will be in conflict with the Antichrist.
Syria and Iraq will submit to the Mahdi.	I believe there is biblical evidence that the Antichrist will come out of the area of Syria and Iraq, which is the territory of ancient Babylon.
Most Muslims believe the Mahdi will appear from the *east.*	Daniel states the coming Antichrist "grew exceedingly great…toward the east" (Dan. 8:9).
Muslims believe that after the appearing of the Mahdi, Jesus will reappear and will march into Jerusalem following this Islamic leader. Jesus will then announce He is a Muslim and not the Son of God and will convert the people to Islam. This is when the Mahdi will kill the *swine* (Jews) and remove the *cross* (alluding to killing Christians).	The Bible indicates a false prophet will arise following the Antichrist's taking Jerusalem captive, and both the Antichrist and false prophet will form a large religious following (Rev. 13:11–15).

THE SIGN OF WAR

The theme of war is predicted and anticipated in Islamic apocalyptic belief. It is predicted that a war will occur between the Eastern powers and the Western powers. Two European countries will also be attacked. Some Muslims note that Osama bin Laden initiated the beginning of the war between the East and the West with the 9/11 attacks on America. Since 9/11, both Spain and Britain have been attacked by terrorists, which some saw as the beginning of the attacks on the two European countries. Sheikh Nazim Adil al-Haqqani, world leader of the Naqshbandhia Order, said the following about the coming Mahdi:

> As believers of the traditions, we believe in a savior who will come first, before Jesus Christ. We have in our traditions his name, which is Muhammad d'ul Mahdi. He is coming, but his arrival will be after a great war. It will be the fight of the big powers with each other. And in that war the savior will come like a divine hand from heavens to the earth and stop the war.[2]

One of the important signs will be when an Islamic army is prepared for the arrival of the Mahdi. In Iraq, the al Qaeda army has been replaced by the *Mahdi Army*, called "the country's most dangerous accelerant of potentially self-sustaining sectarian violence" by the Pentagon.[3] Prior to the recent war in Iraq, I was eating lunch with a friend who serves as an officer in the United States military. At that time he mentioned a cleric in Iraq who had approximately five hundred seminary students serving as an armed militia. Their leader, a black-turban-wearing religious cleric named Muqtada al-Sadr, is a Shi'ite Muslim with close ties to Iran. He is also a close friend with the leader of Hezbollah in Lebanon. Since the beginning of the recent war, al-Sadr's small army grew from five hundred to more than sixty thousand radical militia members.

Why would this cleric form a Mahdi army? The Shi'ite Muslims believe the Mahdi will appear in Iraq. Al-Sadr is simply preparing the minds and hearts of his followers for the arrival of this man, and he is preparing the army that will march to Jerusalem to liberate the city from the Jews and Christians.

Fearing his own assassination, al-Sadr has fled back and forth from Iraq to Iran many times. He believes the time will come when Iran will move into Iraq and take over at least the southern half of Iraq, including the half of Baghdad where he and his militia will be waiting to join Iran's army.

Al-Sadr's mark is the large black turban he wears. While black turbans are common among the Shi'ite branch of Muslims living in Iran and parts of Iraq, a quote from the Muslim hadith will explain the power of the back turban: "On the authority of Thawbaan, the Messenger of Allah said: 'If you see the Black Banners coming from Khurasan go to them immediately, even if you must crawl over ice, because indeed amongst them is the Caliph, Al Mahdi.'"[4] It is also reported that the Messenger of Allah, Muhammad, said: "The black banners will come from the east and their hearts will be as firm as iron."[5]

The Iranian Shi'ites believe they are the fulfillment of this prediction. Since they are situated in the east of Palestine, many Shi'ites believe they are the black-turbaned people.

THE ATTACK IN MECCA IN 1979

On November 20, 1979, some fifty thousand Muslims were celebrating the Islamic New Year in the Islamic year 1400. As the crowds were assembling for morning prayers, a group of about two hundred armed men and their followers suddenly burst into the al-Haram Mosque that encloses the Ka'ba, the large black stone at Islam's holiest site. They demanded that one of their holy men, Mohammed

Abdullah al-'Utaibah, be declared the Mahdi. When the chief imam refused their demands and pronounced them as heretics, fighting suddenly broke out, trapping fifty thousand worshipers in the conflict.[6]

The command was given to close and lock the gates of the mosque. Snipers rushed atop seven minarets (prayer towers). The battle lasted nearly two weeks. This was due to certain Islamic laws relating to damaging the mosque. Also, the hostages were not to be injured; the Saudi government wanted to take the hostages alive.

It would be discovered the *heretics* believed the time had come to cleanse Islam of the influences that were corrupting it. They wanted a ban on soccer, television, and higher education. After the assault ended, sixty-three of the rebels were beheaded, including the leader, Juhayman al-'Utaybi.[7]

At the same time, a group of Shi'ites began rioting in the eastern section of the country. These were followers of Ayatollah Khomeini, the new leader of Iran. The riot ended with the death of fifteen people.

It was during the fourteen-hundred-year anniversary of Islam that an Iranian exile named Ayatollah Khomeini managed to return to his country, remove the moderate shah of Iran (a friend of the West), and seize control of the nation, instituting a very radical form of Islam. Americans were shocked and amazed that the US embassy and personnel were held hostage for 444 days. During his exile, Ayatollah Khomeini smuggled thousands of cassette-tape messages to his followers in Iran. These messages inspired the people of Iran to be ready to accept this radical leader's return as ruler.

The timing of Ayatollah Khomeini's return on the anniversary of the founding of Islam was suspect. There were high expectations among many Muslims that the Mahdi would rise out of Iran or a neighboring nation. Some believe Khomeini timed his return on the fourteen-hundred-year anniversary of the founding of Islam in hopes that the people of Iran would declare him the final prophet and expected one.

In 1991, prior to the Gulf War, Yasser Arafat contacted the president of Iraq, Saddam Hussein, and congratulated him for waging war on the United States. He then spoke of the glorious time when he, Arafat, would wave the Palestinian flag over Jerusalem, the capital of the new Palestinian state, and Saddam would ride his white stallion across the Mount of Olives into Jerusalem toward the Temple Mount! Many Islamic leaders own a white stallion or horse in case Allah should choose one of them to be the Mahdi.

A RELIGION OF PEACE?

The first murder in the Bible was done *in the name of religion*, as Cain slew his brother Abel. Both men brought an offering before the Lord, but the Lord favored Abel's sacrifice. In a jealous rage, Cain murdered his brother (Gen. 4:5–8). Since that time, men have killed one another "in the name of God."

Jesus warned of a time when His people would die as martyrs, and the murderers would believe they were doing God a favor.

> They will put you out of the synagogues; yes, the time is coming that whoever kills you will think that he offers God service.
>
> —John 16:2

During the past two thousand years, the world has been drenched in the blood of innocent people who were victims of religious conflict. From the Roman Empire, the Roman Church, and the Inquisition to the Islamic call for jihad, men are dying in the name of religion.

Some politicians and American Muslims have pointed out that Islam is "a religion of peace." I have certainly met and personally know

Muslims in Israel and Jordan—both desert dwellers and secularists—who want to live in peace. The early history of the religion, however, is one of fighting, conquering, and conflict. While most Muslims are not looking for an actual combat, dedicated and practicing radical Islamists believe the world needs to be converted to Islam, just as true Christians wish to spread the gospel around the world.

One of the tenets of Islam is that of jihad, or a holy war. Few Americans had heard the term *jihad* before the attack on America on September 11, 2001. Even then, for fear of anti-Islamic backlash, secular newscasters were reminding Americans that Islam is a peaceful religion. Yet, few commentators were familiar with the Islamic scriptures that allow for war and death to the infidel.

Since there are two different branches in Islam with a mixture of End Time theology, a spiritual and military conflict is occurring between the Sunnis and the Shi'ites as to in which region of Iraq the future Mahdi will appear. The two specified locations are the cities of Samarra, a holy site for Shi'ite Muslims, and Karbala, a holy site for Sunni Muslims.

The Great Mosque of Samarra, one of Shi'ite Muslim's holiest sites, was constructed in the ninth century in Samarra. Samarra also holds the shrine where the tenth and eleventh caliphs, Ali al-Hadi and Hassan al-Askari, were buried. It was at a well in Samarra where the twelfth imam, Muhammad Al-Mahdi, the son of the eleventh, disappeared. Some suggest the young boy was hidden in the well and will reemerge from that well to announce the new Islamic caliphate at the end of days.[8]

The apocalyptic struggle between these two locations was evident on February 22, 2006, when bombs were set off in the Golden Mosque, a Shi'ite mosque that sits adjacent to the Mosque of the Twelfth Imam in Samarra. Americans could not comprehend why Muslims would destroy one of their own mosques. However, it was a group of Sunni Muslims who posed as police officers who blew up the famous Shi'ite mosque. It was an attempt by the opposing group to destroy the mosque where the last (twelfth) imam was allegedly to appear. The bombing was a division over the apocalyptic beliefs of two opposing groups within the Islamic religion. Months later, the Shi'ites retaliated against the Sunnis by bombing an important mosque in Karbala, which the Sunnis believe would be the site of the appearance of the Mahdi.

Both Sunnis and Shi'ites have extensive End Time beliefs, many of which agree, and others that differ between the sects. The battle for Iraq was more than "sectarian violence" and a struggle to remove Western forces from the land of Allah. It was the rebirth of an ancient religious conflict that dates to the earliest times of Islam. Most informed Muslims believe in prophetic events with the same passion as Jews who believe in the Scriptures and Christians who believe in Christ's return. It is interesting to understand how these beliefs crisscross and form an End Time theology with the world's 1.4 billion Muslims.

A Crescent Revolution
Rises Over the Middle East

THE THREE MAJOR MONOTHEISTIC RELIGIONS ALL HAVE symbols representing their faith. Christians have the cross, Jews have the Star of David, and Muslims have the crescent moon.

The crescent moon and star symbol actually predates Islam by several thousand years. The crescent moon became a symbol of Islam in the time of the Ottoman Empire, after the Turks conquered Constantinople in 1453. It had been the symbol of the city (previously called Byzantium) as far back as before Christ's birth. According to legend, Osman, the founder of the Ottoman/Turkish Empire, dreamed that the crescent moon stretched from one end of the earth to another. Thus he kept the crescent as the emblem of his dynasty.[1]

An emblem of a crescent moon, usually constructed out of metal, sits perched atop many mosques and minarets (prayer towers) worldwide. The emblem of the crescent moon is also found on the flags of numerous Muslim countries, including Turkey. However, on the famed Dome of the Rock, the Muslim shrine built on the Temple Mount in Jerusalem, the emblem on top is not a partial crescent, similar to other mosques and minarets—it is a full circle, or a full moon. It is aligned so that if you look through it, you would be looking directly toward Mecca in Saudi Arabia. An Israeli friend living in Jerusalem pointed this out to me and said that he had been told by a Palestinian that the full moon is a picture of a completion—a full circle that begins and ends in Jerusalem. Biblically, all prophetic events surrounding the Messiah's return began in Jerusalem and will climax there. According to Islamic belief, the crescent of Islam will eventually come full circle and return for the battle of Jerusalem, Islam's third holiest site where the two Islamic mosques are surrounded by Christians and Jews.

The prophet Joel spoke of a day when the moon would turn to blood (Joel 2:31), a common rabbinical metaphor for full lunar eclipses when the moon turns a reddish orange color.[2] In Scripture, blood can allude to:

- The literal blood of a sacrifice—Exodus 12:7

- The blood of humans being shed—Matthew 27:4

- A metaphor for war and fighting—Ezekiel 38:22

Events in the Middle East—the Islamic Revolution and multiple uprisings throughout the Middle Eastern Arab countries—are today striking the world suddenly and unexpectedly. Current events are colliding with biblical prophecies with ever-increasing frequency. When such a collision of prophetic forewarnings and world events takes place, the outcome is usually a prophetic *stepping-stone* or a major prophetic *milestone*. I define a *stepping-stone* as an event or series of events that are not a direct fulfillment of prophecy but that eventually lead to a prophetic fulfillment. A *milestone*, on the other hand, is when the birth pangs of world events actually signal the birth of fulfilled biblical prophecy.

One example of such a collision can be seen in the events that led to World War II. The vision of the valley of dry bones in the Book of Ezekiel (chapter 37) describes the prophetic symbolism of a grave-yard of human bones—which became physically apparent as a *mile-stone* in the appearance of those who survived the horrors of the Holocaust. The Holocaust was a tragic event, and the blood of suf-fering Jews paved a road into Palestine, leading to the reestablishing of Israel as a nation.

Following Ezekiel's prophetic vision in chapter 37, where God raises up Israel from her grave, the Almighty restores Israel as a nation and causes the people of Israel to dwell safely in unwalled villages (Ezek. 38:8–11). As we know, the prophetic fulfillment of this happened with the restoration of the nation of Israel in 1948. As prophecy and world events again collided, we can see that the Holo-caust was the stepping-stone that led to the milestone of the reestab-lishing of Israel as a nation!

THE MIDDLE EAST REVOLT

I believe the Middle East revolt of today is evolving as the early formation of the kingdom of the beast. Not only are the uprisings involving the nations of biblical prophecy, but they also are occur-ring in the region of the world where the Antichrist will set up his final empire as prophesied.

The first trigger of the resistance movement began with the Tunisia Revolution, which began on December 17, 2010, when twenty-six-year-old Tunisian Mohamed Bouazizi set himself on fire in protest of the treatment he had received at the hands of local authorities. His tragic circumstances sparked protests, which turned into riots and quickly spread throughout the Islamic country of Tunisia. These events led to the overthrow of the country's long-term president, Zine el-Abidine Ben Ali.[3]

Following the success of the Tunisians, civil protestors, using modern social media—primarily Facebook and Twitter—began organizing in Cairo and Alexandria, Egypt. They demanded the resignation of Egyptian president Hosni Mubarak. As I watched each day, the protests built, the crowds swelled, and the pressure mounted for Mubarak, Egypt's president, to resign. Based on key prophetic passages in the Book of Daniel, I knew that Egypt would eventually fall into the hands of the Antichrist. However, I never expected to see this moderate Islamic nation change governments in such a manner and this soon! Just eighteen days passed from the beginning of the protests until Hosni Mubarak had resigned as president, with the crowds of protestors pouring into the streets of Tahrir with cries of "Egypt is free! Egypt is free!"[4]

When the announcement was made that President Mubarak had stepped down, I began to state to my listeners in regional meetings that if we were truly in the time of the end, the next nation to encounter a major revolution leading to the overthrow of their dictator would be the country of Libya. On February 15, just days after the resignation of Mubarak, rebels in Benghazi began rioting against the bloody dictatorship of Colonel Muammar Gaddafi. Gaddafi vows to die "a martyr" in Libya and refuses to resign, saying he will crush the revolt.[5] As of the writing of this chapter, Gaddafi is still in power, but many leaders of his regime and of his Libyan army have defected and left the country or joined the rebel forces. Other countries have become involved, including the United States and the United Nations. Gaddafi has vowed to unleash a wave of retaliatory attacks if he is forced from the presidency.[6]

As soon as the conflict began, I began receiving e-mails and questions asking me how I knew this would occur and where it was found in the Bible. Before I share the amazing prediction, let me point out some important things to note about the intersection of prophecy and current events in the Middle East. If the Antichrist reigns with ten kings, all of whom receive power and authority as kings in "one hour as kings with the beast" (Rev. 17:12), then all ten kings will have their own nation, and the Antichrist is simply the leader of this ten-nation confederacy.

However, when Daniel saw these ten kings, identified as ten horns on the final beast kingdom, he also saw a little horn (the Antichrist) rising among the ten and uprooting three of the ten horns (kings). (See Daniel 7.) According to Daniel and the early church fathers, the three nations (horns) that the Antichrist uproots are the nations of Egypt, Libya, and Ethiopia. Daniel reveals this in Daniel 11:

> He shall also enter the Glorious Land, and many countries shall be overthrown; but these shall escape from his hand: Edom, Moab, and the prominent people of Ammon. He shall stretch out his hand against the countries, and the land of Egypt shall not escape. He shall have power over the treasures of gold and silver, and over all the precious things of Egypt; also the Libyans and Ethiopians shall follow at his heels.
>
> —Daniel 11:41–43

The belief that these three nations—Egypt, Libya, and Ethiopia—are the three uprooted horns is also alluded to in the writings of the early fathers. In a section called the "Fragments From Commentaries," contained in the writings of the Ante-Nicene fathers, we read this comment about Daniel's vision:

> "And I inquired about the fourth beast." It is the fourth kingdom, of which we have already spoken, that he here refers: that kingdom, than which no greater kingdom of like nature has arisen upon the earth; from which also

ten horns are to spring, and to be apportioned among ten crowns. And amid these another little horn shall rise, which is that of Antichrist. And it shall pluck by the roots the three others before it; that is to say, he shall subvert the three kings of Egypt, Libya, and Ethiopia, with the view of acquiring for himself universal domain. And after conquering the remaining seven horns, he will at last begin, inflated by a strange and wicked spirit, to stir up war against the saints, and to persecute all everywhere, with the aim of being glorified by all, and being worshiped as God.[7]

Egypt's Coming Trouble

The prophet Isaiah also gave a rather unique prediction concerning a civil war type of conflict that will occur in Egypt:

"I will set Egyptians against Egyptians;
Everyone will fight against his brother,
And everyone against his neighbor,
City against city, kingdom against kingdom.
The spirit of Egypt will fail in its midst;
I will destroy their counsel,
And they will consult the idols and the charmers,
The mediums and the sorcerers.
And the Egyptians I will give
Into the hand of a cruel master,
And a fierce king will rule over them,"
Says the Lord, the Lord of hosts.
—Isaiah 19:2–4

The "cruel master" and "fierce king" in this passage, according to many scholars, is the biblical Antichrist who will rule Egypt during the final forty-two months of the Great Tribulation. Notice that a civil war emerges at this time. This war could be the result of a struggle between Sunni and Shi'ite Muslims, between the radical elements and the more moderate elements of Islam, and between the armies of the Antichrist and the common Egyptians who desire freedom from the bondage of the Antichrist's rule. In the future, there will be a major shaking in the land of Egypt that will cause the entire northern horn of Africa to fall into the hands of a cruel ruler.

It is important to pay attention to events in Egypt for the following reasons:

1. Egypt is a major and respected voice in the Arab world. Egypt's long ancient history and the fact it was once a major empire give the Egyptians an edge on being a respected voice among the Arabs in the Middle East. The Egyptians can boast that their empire was the first major empire of world history and lasted longer and was stronger than the early region of the tower of Babel, recorded in Genesis 11.

2. Egypt controls 40 percent of the world's oil through the Suez Canal, the shipping lane where oil tankers coming from the Persian Gulf exit the Red Sea into the Mediterranean to carry their "black gold" to the world markets.[8] The Suez gives Egypt a special *authority* for possible control of ships transporting oil to the West and to European nations.

3. Egypt is one of the two main Arab nations (Jordan being the other) that has a *peace treaty* with Israel, which was signed in Washington DC on March 26, 1979, during the Carter administration. The

agreement was signed by then-Israeli Prime Minister Menachem Begin and former Egyptian President Anwar al-Sadat. This agreement with Israel may have actually cost the life of Sadat, who, on October 6, 1981, was assassinated, along with at least eight others, during a victory parade held in Cairo. His replacement was Egypt's vice president Hosni Mubarak, who upheld the peace agreements with Israel for thirty-one years.

4. Egypt has also provided *natural gas* through a major pipeline that runs from Egypt to both Israel and Jordan. In fact, Jordan generates 80 percent of its power and Israel 40 percent of its electricity using Egyptian oil.[9] Shortly after the Egyptian revolution, the pipeline was sabotaged twice in less than three months, disrupting the supply and causing Israel to consider alternative sources of energy.

5. Egypt's future is important, for biblical prophecy indicates that it will be the first Islamic nation to be seized by the future Antichrist.

Referring back to Daniel 11:41, the phrase "Glorious Land" is a reference to the land of Israel. The one nation in the Middle East that is mentioned as *escaping* the control of the Antichrist is the region of Edom, Moab, and Ammon—the nation of Jordan, whose capitol is Ammon! It has been suggested that the reason Jordan will not be overrun by the Antichrist is because the mountains of Edom and Moab are where the remnant of Jews will flee from Jerusalem and will be protected from the assaults of the Antichrist for 1,260 days. More specifically, this site of protection will be the natural fortification of Petra, the red-rose city carved in the rock in the mountains of Jordan (Ps. 108:9; Rev. 12:6). The prophecy indicates that when the Antichrist seizes control of Egypt, Libya and Ethiopia will follow on his heels and in his steps. According to *Barnes' Notes:* "Gesenius renders this, 'in his company.' The word means properly step, or walk. Compare Psalm 37:23; Proverbs 20:24. The Vulgate renders this: 'And he shall pass also through Libya and Ethiopia.'"[10] Egypt falls first, and the other two nations mentioned will simply capitulate and follow the Antichrist's leadership.

SUDAN IS INCLUDED IN THIS SIEGE

When looking at a map of Africa, one will note that there is a large nation that lies between Egypt and Ethiopia: the nation of Sudan. Throughout its ancient history, the nation of Sudan has been intertwined with the Egyptians. It was in 1956 that Sudan gained its independence from Egypt and the United Kingdom. Sudan has been a nation that in recent years has been torn by civil war (first in 1955–1972, then 1983) and conflicts with its neighbors. Because Sudan is pinned between Egypt and Ethiopia, is a radical Islamic nation, and its history in the time of Daniel would have been linked with the Egyptians, it can be suggested that the Antichrist will also include Sudan in the packet of nations he controls.

One of Ethiopia's eastern-border neighbors is Somalia, a small African nation noted for its pirates who have frequently hijacked large tankers and ships in the waters near it. Since the mid-1990s, Somali pirates have hijacked and held for ransom numerous ships. In 2010 alone, fifty-three ships were hijacked, with nearly twelve hundred seafarers and others killed.[11] Experts believe that pirates in Somalia, which is the most dangerous point in the rising tide of piracy at sea, earn up to $79,000 a year—a stark contrast to the average annual income of $500 for other Somalians. Somali piracy was worth $238 million in 2010 and is set to rise to as much as $400 million by 2015.[12] This entire region, known as the *Horn of Africa*, is the home of three nations that will fall into the hands of the future beast: Egypt, Libya, and Ethiopia. (The beast in Daniel 7 had three horns that fell when "the other horn" came up [v. 20], and it states further in verse 24 that this other horn "shall subdue three kings.")

THE VOID CREATES THE DICTATOR

Since the founding of Israel in 1948, Egypt has already engaged Israel in five different wars:[13]

1. The Israeli War of Independence—1948–1949

2. The Sinai War—1956

3. The Six-Day War—1967

4. The War of Attrition—1968–1970

5. The Yom Kippur War—1973

In the future wars of prophecy, Egypt is not mentioned in the conflicts. We do read where the city of Damascus will be destroyed and will become a ruinous heap (Isa. 17:1). This city is one of the oldest cities on the earth and has never been destroyed in a war or conflict. Damascus is the capital of Syria. The nation of Syria will eventually engage in a military conflict with Israel, to its own demise. We know from Ezekiel's prophecy that both Libya and Ethiopia will be in the coalition joining Persia (Iran) in the Gog of Magog War (Ezek. 38). Egypt is missing from the Ezekiel 38 listing of all the nations joining the Persian coalition of attack against Israel.

Perhaps one of the main reasons that in the future Egypt does not engage Israel in a major conflict (this does not include smaller border conflicts) is that war costs huge amounts of money, and for Egypt, the terrifying reality is that the country does not have the necessary hundreds of millions of dollars it would take in military equipment (losses), troop costs, and the shutting down of their tourist economy for another conflict. The prophet Isaiah may be alluding to this frightening reality when he writes: "And the land of Judah will be a terror to Egypt; everyone who makes mention of it will be afraid in himself, because of the counsel of the LORD of hosts which He has determined against it" (Isa. 19:17).

A second reason may be that Egypt has traditionally been a more moderate Islamic nation and has a large Coptic Christian population. Of the more than 82 million Egyptians, there is an estimated 9 percent of the population that are Coptic Christians.[14] The Christian population is by no means *pro-Israel*, but they are at least more moderate and open in their historical/biblical understanding of Israel and the Hebrew people.

Third, for many years Egypt has had direct dealings with Western powers—America, Britain, and France—and has a more Western mind-set than some of its neighbors, including the Iranian leadership and others. While some Islamic nations are anti-Western and resist negotiating with Western leaders, the nations with strong tourist businesses, primarily Egypt and Jordan, are more friendly toward the West as they enjoy millions of dollars in tourism yearly, much of that coming directly from Western countries. Egypt's tourism industry was already reeling from much of the political unheavals in the country, but the US killing of al Qaeda's leader Osama bin Laden will cause the situation to worsen, as people in Western countries begin to think twice before traveling to Arab countries, including Egypt.[15]

When any leader who has been in charge for twenty or thirty years—as is the case with many of the presidents and kings of the Middle East and Persian Gulf States—is removed, it creates a major void in the nation. This void often creates an internal struggle or a clash between tribal leaders or religious imams who seek to fill the empty seat of a former leader or dictator. Many of the uprisings are a result of the poverty within the nation and a lack of jobs for the youth. However, when the Egyptian revolution concluded, there were no more jobs that had been created than there were prior to the revolution, and tourism was dead. The wages for the common man basically remained unchanged, as the entire world at the time was experiencing an economic recession with job losses in every country. With this in mind, consider the prediction made by Isaiah concerning Egypt:

> The LORD has mingled a perverse spirit in her midst;
> And they have caused Egypt to err in all her work,
> As a drunken man staggers in his vomit.
> Neither will there be any work for Egypt,
> Which the head or tail,
> Palm branch or bulrush, may do.
>
> In that day Egypt will be like women, and will be afraid and fear because of the waving of the hand of the LORD of hosts, which He waves over it. And the land of Judah will be a terror to Egypt; everyone who makes mention of it will be afraid in himself, because of the counsel of the LORD of hosts which He has determined against it.
> —ISAIAH 19:14–17

The Amplified Bible, in verse 14, alludes to a "spirit of perverseness, error, and confusion" upon Egypt. Another translation uses this phrase: "The LORD has poured into them a spirit of dizziness" (v. 14, NIV). The intent here is to show that confusion will overcome the Egyptians, and there will be no work among them! The lack of jobs always creates unrest, and it opens the door to anyone who can promise prosperity and work to the masses. In recent days many Arab nations have experienced protests that have brought change. In some of these nations the efforts of the protestors were squelched by the iron hand of the country's rulers, or in other cases protestors were paid off to simply go away and not draw attention to the leadership. Unrest and protests have risen recently in each of the following countries:

- Tunisia
- Egypt
- Libya
- Syria
- Yemen
- Morocco
- Algeria
- Bahrain
- Iran
- Jordan
- Saudi Arabia (brief protests)

Notice that all of the above nations are located near or around the Mediterranean Sea, the Persian Gulf, or the Euphrates River. All three of these regions are prophesied to be regions where demonic activity will increase at the time of the rise of the beast's kingdom. Daniel saw the beast's empires of prophecy rising up out of the Great Sea (Dan. 7:2–3), which was an early name for the Mediterranean. Not only does the Euphrates River dry up in the latter part of the future tribulation (Rev. 16:12), but also it is from under the river bed of the Euphrates that four of the strongest, most evil angels will be released during the middle part of the Great Tribulation (Rev. 9:14). We can assume that the Persian Gulf, although not mentioned directly in Scripture, will also be a focal point of prophetic conflict, because a large percentage of oil travels the gulf through the Strait of Hormuz.

The Strait of Hormuz is the waterway that separates Iran from the Arabian peninsula and connects the Persian Gulf with the Gulf of Oman. The strait is only twenty-one miles across at its narrowest point and is made up of two-mile-wide channels for tanker traffic. Roughly 40 percent of all seaborne oil traded in the world passes through this strait, with an average of fifteen oil tankers a day traveling through the strait.[16]

Iran has the third largest oil reserves in the world and the second largest natural gas reserves, and it produces 4 million barrels of oil a day that is delivered to China and Russia.[17] This Strait of Hormuz is controlled by Iran. Tankers in the Persian Gulf must also pass through the narrow strait of Bab-el Mandeb, or the "gate of tears," a strait located between Yemen and the Arabia Peninsula. There are 3.3 million barrels a day that travels through the strait.

The table below will show the nations that are strongly connected to prophetic events in the time of the end:

NATIONS OF PROPHETIC SIGNIFICANCE FOR THE END TIMES		
Biblical Name	**Modern Nation**	**Nation's Religion**
Israel (Dan. 12:1)	Israel	Jewish/Islamic/Christian
Edom, Moab, and Ammon (Dan. 11:41)	Jordan	Islamic/small Christian groups
Egypt (Dan. 11:42)	Egypt	Islamic/small Christian groups
Libya (Dan. 11:43)	Libya	Islamic
Ethiopia (Dan. 11:43)	Ethiopia	Islamic/small Christian groups
King of the North (Dan. 11:40)	Turkey	Islamic/small Christian population

Biblical Name	Modern Nation	Nation's Religion
Lebanon (Zech. 11:1)	Lebanon	Islamic/small Christian population
Damascus (Isa. 17:1)	Syria	Islamic/small Christian population
Persia (Ezek. 38:5)	Iran	Islamic
Gomer (Ezek. 38:6)	Turkey/ Armenia	Islamic/Christian
Togarmah (Ezek. 38:6)	Turkey/near Syrian border	Islamic
Sheba and Dedan (Ezek. 38:13)	Arabian Gulf states	Islamic
Gaza (Amos 1:6)	Gaza Strip	Islamic

You will notice that all of the above nations are either entirely Muslim- or Islamic-controlled governments with just small Christian minorities. Islamic nations such as Iran have severely persecuted Christians. Saudi Arabia forbids Christians to enter the country with Bibles and forbids the wearing of crosses or other Christian emblems.

The current uprisings are said to be taking place in the name of democracy. However, the concept of democracy among Muslims is not the same type of democracy that we understand in the West. Our democratic government guarantees the freedom of speech and religion. Western democracy differs greatly with the Islamic/Muslim concept of democracy, because Islamic democracy *does not* grant the freedom of religion—the religion of Islam is strictly enforced. For Muslim youth, *democracy* means only the freedom to dress in "Western-style" clothes, to use cosmetics (if they are girls), to listen to more *contemporary* music, watch Western movies, and have the opportunity for a secular education.

If true democracy blanketed the Islamic nations, it would require complete freedom for every individual in the nation to accept whatever religion he or she desired—including the possibly of Muslims turning to the Christian faith. This is strictly forbidden—if a Muslim turns from his or her Islamic beliefs to another religion, that individual can be (and is) expelled from the family and threatened with death for dishonoring the family traditions and the family name.

As the revolutions have spread, there is one important point that is often overlooked: if current leadership is overthrown, who will take charge of the nation—including control of the military and control of the country's economy and resources? In most cases, when Middle Eastern leaders or dictators are removed, a tribal clash arises between the tribal leaders of the government or ruling family that dominated in the previous government and the tribes in other regions of the country. With the fall of Saddam Hussein in Iraq, we have seen the ensuing clash between the Sunni and Shi'ite tribes of the country. Other tribal and ethnic clashes have created problems in both Afghanistan and Pakistan, and these same clashes are already evident in many of the Arab countries currently experiencing protests and uprisings.

When a corrupt dictator is overthrown and leaves the country, the corruption usually continues. I believe the current revolutions of the Islamic world are creating a massive void and opportunity for one man who can arise from the sea of nations and unite the Arab countries under a new Islamic caliph under his authority. With such a diversity of tribal leaders—Sunni vs. Shi'ites, rich vs. poor, traditional, *old* power dynasties vs. *young* student revolutionaries—it will not be an easy matter to unite these nations. It will require someone who has some form of supernatural charisma and authority. The Bible prophesies this very thing. This is why we read, "The dragon gave him his power, his throne, and great authority" (Rev. 13:2).

Continue to watch the events in Egypt, Libya, and Ethiopia. I *do not believe* the Antichrist is presently waiting in the wings to seize power. Bible prophecy indicates that first there will be three kings or leaders over these three nations and that they will be overthrown in the middle of the Tribulation. However, we are beginning to see the shaking and upheaval that will create the void for the arrival of the Antichrist.

THE OSAMA FACTOR
AND AMERICA

MORE THAN 120 YEARS AGO AN ISLAMIC LEADER, Muhammad Ahmed, united the tribes in Sudan to defeat Egypt, using sticks and swords. Over a century later, another Muslim who lived in Sudan was expelled in 1996. He was familiar with the history of the Sudanese leader Ahmed and his exploits. Thus, Osama bin Laden was following in the pattern of an Islamic hero. Both Ahmed and bin Laden lived in a cave. Both were recognized as warriors—Ahmed fighting the Egyptian army, and bin Laden fighting the Russians in Afghanistan. Ahmed promised to take Egypt, Mecca, and Jerusalem captive, just as bin Laden promised. According to both Ahmed and bin Laden, all infidels who would not submit to Islam should be killed by beheading. And both stood against the Western culture.

Muhammad bin Laden (Osama's father) was a contractor, billionaire, and founder and head of the Bin Laden Corporation. For forty years he spoke of the coming Mahdi. He established a fund of twelve million dollars to help the Mahdi restore the grandeur of Islam in the world. Little did he realize that his son, who would be forced to leave Saudi Arabia, would one day lay claim to this title.

There is circumstantial evidence that Osama bin Laden attempted to get the Islamic world to perceive him as the anticipated Islamic Mahdi. Consider the following: Apocalyptic tradition predicts that a war will take place between the West and the East and believes the East will overpower the West, which includes Spain, Britain, and America. Osama masterminded an attack against the United States—the strongest nation of the West, causing economic turmoil, fear, panic, and distress in America and the world. After 9/11 Osama used his full name more frequently—Osama bin Muhammad bin Awad bin Laden, perhaps to mirror the tradition of the coming Mahdi, whose name is said to be Muhammad, after the Islamic prophet Muhammad. A series of videos have been captured by US troops showing bin Laden writing in Arabic the words "the awaited one" on a dry-erase board. Even some of the detainees at Guantanamo Bay (Gitmo) have said that bin Laden thought he was the "awaited enlightened one."

AL-MAHDI—HIDING IN A CAVE

One of the interesting Islamic traditions related to the future Islamic savior is where it is believed he is hiding. A Turkish sheikh stated:

> The Great War will break out between East and West. These will be very difficult days for mankind. There will be very strong fighting. Very many people will be killed. Then the Lord will command al-Mahdi Alaihi as-Salam to appear. Now he is in a cave, in a big, deep cave. No one can approach it. *Jinns* [genies] are protecting and guarding him.[1]

Many Muslims, especially from the Shi'ite branch, believe the Mahdi is being protected and supernaturally preserved in a empty desert area in Arabia. The very thought of someone hiding in a desert area reminds me of the warning Jesus gave concerning false prophets and false Christs, when He said:

> Therefore if they say to you, "Look, He is in the desert!" do not go out; or "Look, He is in the inner rooms!" do not believe it.
>
> —MATTHEW 24:26

Intelligence sources believed that for some time Osama was hiding in a series of caves and caverns in the mountains of Afghanistan or Pakistan. What was unknown was that he had found secret refuge in a large compound where he was eventually slain.

In Luke 21:11 Jesus predicted there would be great and fearful signs from heaven prior to His return. These would include strange signs in the sun, moon, and stars (v. 25). For centuries Christian students of Bible prophecy have followed times of unusual cosmic activity, beginning with the eyewitness account of the Jewish historian Josephus, who gives numerous cosmic signs that occurred four years prior to the destruction of the temple in Jerusalem in A.D. 70. These signs included a large comet that was seen over the city for about one year and a strange phenomenon where a sword appeared in the sky over the city. Wise men believed these were warnings of the impending destruction of the Holy City.

Among those who anticipate the arrival of Islam's Mahdi are those who point out several predictions concerning signs in the heavens that are to occur in the last days. One such hadith teaches that the moon will eclipse twice during Ramadan, the holy month in Islam when Muslims believe Muhammad received the revelation written in the Quran. Another cosmic sign said to be a portent of the arrival of the last days is when "a star with a luminous tail will rise from the East before the Mahdi emerges."[2]

During the late 1990s, two events occurred that brought a sensation to many Muslims in the Middle East. One was the appearance of a comet that had been hidden and was revealed in 1993, called the "comet Hale-Bopp." It was much brighter than Halley's Comet.[3] This comet was visible to the naked eye and was considered a sign to Jews, Christians, and Muslims who study the signs of the last days according to their religious traditions. Jews and Christians noted that the comet was last seen in Noah's day, about the time Noah was building the famous ark. As the large comet appeared, many Muslims remembered the tradition of the star with the long tail. This comet exited the galaxy far from the human eye in 1998. In 1999, in the month of August, a total solar eclipse occurred over the Middle East.

Ramadan fell in the months of October and November in 2004. It was interesting that Osama bin Laden made a videotape prior to the American presidential election. Why did this terrorist mastermind choose five days before the election to show his face to the world when he had been silent for so long? The answer may lie in the fact that during Ramadan in 2004, two eclipses occurred. The Islamic tradition that two eclipses will occur during Ramadan prior to the appearance of the Mahdi may have given bin Laden an opportunity to cryptically make a self proclamation.

It is unlikely that many Muslims around the world saw Osama bin Laden as their long-awaited messiah. To many Muslims, the influence of his al Qaeda network has had as much negative influence on the radical Islamic agenda as its positive effects. For those who did believe he was the Mahdi, their hopes died with one bullet and the proclamation of Osama bin Laden's death on May 1, 2011.

THE LOYALTY OF OSAMA CLONES

Those who thought that the death of Osama bin Laden was the grand finale of the war on terror don't understand the passionate allegiance of the *clones of bin Laden*. Statistics are widely varied on the number of radical Islamists in the world today, but some researchers have suggested that as many as 37 percent of the Islamic world are part of the radical element of the religion. With about 1.2 billion estimated Muslims, 37 percent would be about 439 million radicalized Muslims in the world.[4]

Most Americans are now familiar with the attacks on 9/11 at the World Trade Center and the Pentagon, but many are unaware that numerous attacks by bin Laden *wannabes* have been thwarted through the efforts of the Department of Homeland Security, the FBI, and CIA operatives posing undercover as potential jihadists. The United States federal government has been successful with the war on terror on two fronts: preventing further major attacks within the United States, and keeping the information concerning the plots from the general public. The reason for an information blackout is threefold. First is to prevent a fear or panic from spreading through the general population by revealing the location of the planned assault. Second, so as not to give away the people, agencies, or undercover operatives who are infiltrating the Islamic terror cells. And third is to prevent the news media from digging into how the planned attacks were prevented, which could give the adversaries needed information to avoid detection.

These clones of bin Laden have engaged in a nonstop effort to initiate another 9/11 type of assault that would have even greater effect on the nation than the attack on September 11, 2001. Having traveled throughout the United States meeting thousands of individuals, I have been told by informed persons of several of the plots that have been disrupted. To keep their identities secure, I have chosen not to give the names of the sources or the locations of the plots.

Several years ago a group of Middle Eastern men from Florida purchased several school buses from a man who sells older used buses to churches and organizations that need a bus to transport children and youth. Shortly thereafter, a martial arts specialist was meeting with hundreds of public school teachers, explaining how to defend themselves if someone came on their bus to do harm to them or the children. Following the seminar, a man came up to the speaker and informed him that he had sold five buses for cash to a group of Middle Eastern men and was suspicious as to their intentions. When the proper authorities were informed, it was discovered that these men were Muslims who intended to fill the five older buses with explosives, then hijack five normal buses packed with school children and transfer the children to the buses with explosives driven by their own jihadist drivers. They intended to blow up these buses—with the children—in front of the school! Thankfully the plan was exposed.[5]

I have a Pakistani friend (whom I will leave nameless) who in 2004 related to me a stunning event that occurred in California. Because of his last name and his family, my friend's name was on an FBI watch list. He is a Christian, the only one in his Muslim family. Months after 9/11 he was visited in his office by five men, all Muslims from different countries. They asked if he wished to invest in a new business—a bakery that the men wished to start in the community. After my friend said he would listen to more from them concerning the offer, the leading man also asked if he wished to help them purchase several small crop duster planes. The association of the bakery with crop dusters didn't "go together" for my friend. The spokesmen for the group said he would contact him later and left a cell phone number for my friend to call.

When the men left, another group of men from the FBI showed up, wanting information about the conversation, as several other such conversations had been monitored recently. My friend agreed to stay in contact with the five Muslim men from different countries. In a matter of time, the plot was exposed. There had been a very large evangelistic meeting that was planned to be held in a stadium in the area. These men wanted to purchase crop dusters, arrange for them to be filled with fuel, and then fly over the stadium and spray the open-air stadium filled with thousands of Christians with gasoline from these planes. Then they planned to crash another plane in the stadium. Once again, this strategy failed.[6]

While ministering on the eastern shore of Maryland, the host of my trip passed a restaurant and a hotel in one of the smaller communities. One of his close friends worked for the police force in the city. He related to me that the hotel and restaurant were formerly owned by a group of Middle Eastern men, all who were Muslim. Right after 9/11, the men left the area, and the buildings and property were sold to a new owner. As the new owners were remodeling the interior of the facility, they discovered cash and weapons behind the walls. Based on collected evidence, it appeared they were placed there when the former owners had worked in the facility.

These are only three of about ten examples I could give showing where plots were stopped in the early stages. What is troubling is the large number of foreign and even homegrown radicals who are scattered like weeds in a garden, waiting to grow strong and choke out the lives of surrounding Americans.

Current estimates show that there are more than 8 million Muslims in the United States, due to immigration, a high birth rate, and an astounding conversion rate. According to one report, more than 200,000 individuals convert to Islam in America each year. According to projections, the Shi'ite demographic, the more radical group of Muslims, comprises approximately 1.8 million of the 8 million large US community of Muslims.[7]

Why It Took Ten Years to Catch Bin Laden

With advanced technology, including satellites that can see a dime lying on a parking lot from their position in space, cell phones calls that can be intercepted, and e-mails that can be captured and read on government computers, why couldn't one of the greatest intelligence communities in the world, in cooperation with British, French, German, and Israeli sources, find the world's most wanted terrorist? Allow me to make a series of personal observations in attempting to answer this question.

The first fact is that the best information concerning the location of a wanted person often comes from firsthand, eyewitness sources on the ground. When the United States placed a twenty-five-million-dollar bounty on bin Laden's head, we assumed some Muslim in Afghanistan or Pakistan would immediately seize the opportunity to turn over the terrorist kingpin to the United States to gain such a massive prize of instant wealth. This offer meant nothing to those who knew bin Laden personally, a fact explained when you recognize our lack of understanding of *Arab honor* and *Islamic tradition*.

The nations of Afghanistan and Pakistan are all tribal regions. In Afghanistan there are four chief tribes—the Pashtuns, Tajiks, Uzbeks, and Hazaras. Each tribe has its own customs, traditions, ethics, and moral code, often unwritten but passed down for generations.[8] Among all Arab and tribal communities, there is an inbred and generational teaching calling for *family honor,* which is the highest-regarded characteristic to be demonstrated in the community. A family member never, and I mean never, dishonors a leader in the tribe, and children never dishonor their father. In strict Islamic countries, a father will kill his own son or daughter who dishonors the family. On the news we have seen *honor killings* in which a family stoned a daughter for fornication or a wife for adultery.

Osama bin Laden became a world-recognized jihadist leader and, although a terrorist, was admired and respected among most

Muslims, especially in numerous Pakistan and Afghanistan tribal regions. Turning him over to the United States military, even for twenty-five million dollars, would be considered the highest form of dishonor in the community and would bring the wrath of the entire community on the whistle-blower who revealed his whereabouts. In fact, someone would eventually kill the whistle-blower and also mark every member of his family for death!

A second fact is the manner in which Muslims will defend other Muslims when they are being *targeted*—by Israel, the United States, or the West in general. In the mind of the more fanatical Muslims, the Jews and Christians are considered infidels, especially since the Christian faith believes that Jesus is the Son of God and the Islamic faith denies that God has a son. With Jerusalem being the third holiest site in the Islamic religion and the Temple Mount being surrounded by Jews and Christians, the Islamic world sees Jerusalem as an occupied territory belonging to them and believes in the need for Islam to liberate Jerusalem from the hands of their spiritual-political enemies, the Jews and the Christians. When bin Laden was hiding from cave to cave, mountain to mountain, and village to village, he was successful in keeping himself out of the public eye. However, there were a small number of people who knew his whereabouts, but because he was a fellow Muslim and had world recognition, his followers would protect him to the death and never turn him over to Western powers.

Another important reason it took so long to locate him is that it is difficult to maneuver military vehicles through the huge mountain regions of Afghanistan and Pakistan into the mountains and crevasses of these two nations. Only three modes of transportation are accessible to travel from small village to small village nestled in these mountain regions—mule, horseback, and foot travel. During their war in Afghanistan, the Russians discovered how successful bin Laden and his mujahideen were in preventing the Russian military from taking over Afghanistan. The Russians used tanks, jeeps, and planes, while the Islamic warriors on ground rode on horses, shooting surface-to-air missiles from the back of a horse! The rugged and rough terrain in that part of the world, the numerous caves, remote villages, and Islamic loyalty made the search for the world's most wanted terrorist last ten years.

THE RISE OF BIN LADEN CLONES

I have heard individuals, some in the military, suggest the United States may have known the whereabouts of bin Laden for some time, but they kept the terrorist mastermind alive so as not to make him a hero among other radicals who would have made proclaimed him to be a martyr for the cause of Islam if he was killed. When the Navy Seals shot bin Laden in his compound about one hour's travel north of Islamabad, Pakistan, there was a concern that if the operation was mishandled, it could make him a hero and only produce more clones of bin Laden. A *clone* is a person who takes on the same mental, emotional, political, and spiritual thinking of another. Osama bin Laden clones pattern their lifestyles, religious beliefs, and hatred after their departed warrior.

The unnamed Navy Seal who placed a bullet just above the left eye of bin Laden made a deadly shot to the head that instantly killed Osama, leaving a corpse with his eyes still open (according to photos). The body was loaded aboard the Seals' helicopter to a US ship, the USS *Carl Vinson*, where it was prepared for burial in the North Arabian Sea.[9] The Arabian Sea is a large body of water between two other bodies of water—the Red Sea and the Persian Gulf. Both empty into the Arabian Sea and the larger part of the Indian Ocean. This Arabian Sea is surrounded by the countries of Pakistan, Iran, Yemen, Oman, and Somalia. When the information of his death and sea burial swept the world, radical Muslims began renaming the sea where the body sank the "Martyr's Sea," according to one of Britain's leading Islamic scholars.[10]

There is an odd parallel between two passages of the Book of Revelation juxtaposed against the facts of Osama being shot in the head and his corpse lowered into the sea. The beast, or the future Antichrist, is seen "rising up out of the sea" (Rev. 13:1). We also read that he will have a deadly wound to one of his heads that has been healed (v. 3). Bin Laden, the world-renowned terrorist, was shot to death in the head and dumped into a sea that connects with the coastlines of some of the very nations of End Time prophecy! Let me make this clear. Bin Laden is dead, he is not the Antichrist, and he is not coming out of his fiery chamber of eternal damnation to rule the world. Here is the point, however. His death made him the ultimate hero among radicals throughout the world, and his demise and burial at sea will only form a new group of men and women who will seek to avenge the death of their hero.

POSSIBLE TERRORIST ASSAULTS AND AMERICA'S RESPONSE

It is not a matter of *if* but a matter of *when* the United States will be struck again with a major terrorist attack at the hands of Islamic jihadists. We witnessed a shooting on November 5, 2009, at Foot Hood, Texas, that killed thirteen people and injured twenty others. The single shooter was a Muslim of Palestinian descent and a US Army major named Nidal Malik Hasan. Despite the fact that the major had been in contact with radical Yemen-based cleric Anwar al-Awlaki for a long time prior to the shootings and yelled a statement made by all suicide bombers, "Allahu Akbar," before he fired his gun, the administration still had difficulty identifying Nidal as an Islamic terrorist![11]

I was quite amazed at the discipline and patience expressed by the families and friends of the slain. Instead of mass numbers of Americans threatening local Muslims and promising retaliation, they prayed at the site of the murders and spoke of their hope in a resurrection for their believing loved ones. It revealed to me the marked difference when a family member of a Christian is slain versus the family member of a Muslim in the Middle East. The grieving Christian knows there is a hope of a resurrection, and there is no talk of retaliation. However, throughout the world, if a Muslim is slain, there is instant talk of retaliation and death to the enemies of Islam. But this one thing is certain: those seeking future jihad on US soil should never interpret our Christian faith and love for people as some type of weakness that disables us from defending our families should jihadists plan and succeed in multiple attacks again on US soil.

One of the strengths of America is the second amendment to the US Constitution, which gives each citizen the right to bear *arms*, or to possess guns for his or her own defense and protection. When a potential attacker realizes the targeted victim is armed with a weapon, there are second thoughts before initiating the assault that could end with the death of the assailant. America is not the aggressive nation often painted by liberals in Europe and radicals in the Middle East. The average US citizen is a peace-loving individual who will put up with a lot—until it affects his or her family and children. Then, when the line of love for family is crossed or defiled by an intruder, the nature of the average American father will be to defend his family himself.

If, in the future, the clones of Ben Laden rise up like wild beasts and begin assaulting the freedoms and lives of the children of peace-loving Americans, I have no doubt that the eagle of America will become a lion of authority, and with or without government assistance, we will defend our families, our faith, our pride, and our honor. The Arab world is not the only group that believes in defending its honor. Honor is inbred in every honest American. The war on terror did not end with the death of Osama—it only transferred into the hands of new leaders, copycats who will continue to plan their attacks, hoping to find a crack in the hedge that protects America.

AMERICA—ISRAEL IS YOUR BLESSING OR YOUR CURSE

> I will bless those who bless you,
> And I will curse him who curses you;
> And in you all the families of the earth shall be
>   blessed.
> —GENESIS 12:3

In the Old Testament era, two words are commonly used to describe favor or disfavor. God spoke of *blessing* His people for following His revealed instructions in the Torah (the five books of Moses), but He also spoke of a *curse* if they rebelled and refused to walk in God's covenant. The entire Bible is a book based upon the foundation of the covenant. In English we speak of contracts and agreements, but God used the word *covenant* 272 times in just the Old Testament alone. The Hebrew word for *covenant* is *berith* and is the frequent object of the verb *karath*, meaning, "to divide or to cut in two." This cutting refers to the fact that covenants were sealed with the blood sacrifice of a selected animal. In later references, the Hebrew male child was circumcised in the flesh of his foreskin at eight days of age as a sign of the covenant (Gen. 17:10–12).

THE LAND, CITY, AND COVENANT PEOPLE

The most important fact to remember about Israel is that this nation was birthed through a covenant with God. The Almighty chose a man called Abraham from the land of Ur of Chaldea and brought him to the Promised Land where He said He would make him a "great nation" (Gen. 12:2), a "great and mighty nation" (Gen. 18:18), a "righteous nation" (Gen. 20:4), and a "nation and a company of nations" (Gen. 35:11). Abraham's descendants would become a "kingdom of priests and a holy nation" (Exod. 19:6). Israel grew from one man, Abraham, to six hundred thousand men (Exod. 12:37) within about four hundred years! From this nation came the tribe of Levi, which served in the tabernacle (later in the temple) as full-time ministers and priests (Num. 1:50). We read:

> For what great nation is there that has God so near to it, as the LORD our God is to us, for whatever reason we may call upon Him? And what great nation is there that has such statutes and righteous judgments as are in all this law which I set before you this day?
> —DEUTERONOMY 4:7–8

God delivered the Hebrews out of Egyptian bondage because He "remembered His covenant with Abraham, with Isaac, and with Jacob" (Exod. 2:24). God's covenant for Abraham and the Hebrew nation included special blessings on their crops, lands, and animals and promised the defeat of their enemies (Deut. 28). God made a promise that the land Abraham possessed—called Israel today— would be given to the seed of Isaac and Jacob forever (Gen. 22:17–18; 28:4; 35:12).

THE JERUSALEM COVENANT

Many years later a covenant was established for the city of Jerusalem. In the time of Abraham the city was called Salem, and two major events occurred there. First, Abraham paid tithe to the first king-priest, Melchizedek, in Jerusalem (Gen. 14). Later Abraham led his son, Isaac, to the hill of Moriah to offer him before God (Gen. 22). Abraham called the name of the place "Jehovah Jireh" (v. 14). Rabbis teach that when combining the two words *Jireh* and *Salem*, you have the foundation for the name Jerusalem.

From that moment Jerusalem was marked for the Hebrew people. It would be the site of the future redemptive covenant through Christ. When David was made king over Israel, he moved the headquarters of Israel from Hebron to Jerusalem after conquering the ruling tribe called the Jebusites (1 Chron. 11:3–7). David was the first Israelite king to rule from Jerusalem, and he ruled from there for thirty-three years (2 Sam. 5:5). Read the promise David received concerning the Israelites dwelling in Jerusalem:

> For David said, "The LORD God of Israel has given rest
> to His people, that they may dwell in Jerusalem forever."
> —1 CHRONICLES 23:25

Jerusalem was chosen by the Lord years before the Israelites ever conquered the mountain and marked it as Israel's capital in the time of David. Moses wrote:

> But you shall seek the place where the LORD your God
> chooses, out of all your tribes, to put His name for His
> dwelling place; and there you shall go.
> —DEUTERONOMY 12:5

God selected a specific place to put His name (v. 11) and to make His name "abide" (Deut. 14:23). The feasts were to be observed in this place (Deut. 16:2), and the city was to be a place for families and servants to rejoice (v. 11). This place was Jerusalem, the site of Solomon's temple (2 Chron. 3) and the "second" temple, the temple from Christ's time (Matt. 21:12). God ensured that His covenants with Abraham and David were as certain as the laws of creation:

Thus says the LORD: "If My covenant is not with day and night, and if I have not appointed the ordinances of heaven and earth, then I will cast away the descendants of Jacob and David My servant, so that I will not take any of his descendants to be rulers over the descendants of Abraham, Isaac, and Jacob. For I will cause their captives to return, and will have mercy on them."
—JEREMIAH 33:25–26

Jerusalem is a city marked by God Himself and promised to the seed of Abraham—the Jewish people—through David.

THE COVENANT FOR THE HEBREW PEOPLE

The natural seed of Abraham are called *Hebrews* (Gen. 40:15; 43:32). Later, at the time of the Babylonian captivity and afterward, they were called *Jews*, as the ten tribes had been dispersed and the tribe of Judah was the leading group in the land. God called the Hebrew people, "My people" (Exod. 3:7, 10; 5:1; 7:4; 8:1). By identifying them as *His people*, God was marking them as His covenant people whom He had raised up in the earth through the man Abraham.

Herein lies the key point. Israel is the only nation on Earth, Jerusalem the only city on Earth, and the Jews the only people on Earth who were birthed and formed through a direct covenant of God! Every other nation or Christian group could dedicate their nation to God and make promises to Him to raise up a Christian nation. This appears to have been the intent of many of America's Founding Fathers. However, these covenants were established by the founders who approached God; Israel was founded by God approaching a man! This Hebrew covenant was based upon God placing His name upon Jerusalem and upon His chosen people.

> Yet I have chosen Jerusalem, that My name may be
> there; and I have chosen David to be over My people
> Israel.
>
> —2 CHRONICLES 6:6

When the priest would pray a prayer of blessing, it included God's name, as it is written:

> So they shall put My name on the children of Israel,
> and I will bless them.
>
> —NUMBERS 6:27

Knowing that Israel, Jerusalem, and the Hebrew people were God's covenant nation, city, and people, then how does God react when world leaders, including an American president, demand that Israel give up land, promised by God Himself, for the sake of peace with individuals whose agenda is the destruction of the Jewish state?

THE PRE-1967 BORDERS

In biblical prophecy, when the Antichrist arises on the scene, he will make a seven-year agreement with Israel and break this "covenant" in the middle of the seven years (Dan. 9:27). He will then divide the land for gain (Dan. 11:39). The greatest division during the Tribulation will be when the Antichrist divides the city of Jerusalem into two halves, causing the Jewish people to go into captivity in their own city:

> For I will gather all the nations to battle against
>   Jerusalem;
> The city shall be taken,
> The houses rifled,
> And the women ravished.
> Half of the city shall go into captivity,

> But the remnant of the people shall not be cut off from
> the city.
>
> —Zechariah 14:2

The important nugget to note here is that half of the city goes into captivity. Before the 1967 Six-Day War, Jerusalem was divided between East Jerusalem and West Jerusalem, with the west being Jewish and the east being Jordan. After the Six-Day War, Jordan lost control of Jerusalem and the entire West Bank of the Jordan River, and the land was annexed into Israel. Since 1967 the Palestinians have desired not only the West Bank back (ancient Judea and Samaria), but they have determined that East Jerusalem will be the capital of a new Palestinian state. There are even those in Washington DC who know little or nothing about Bible prophecy and God's covenants who are demanding that Israel withdraw to the pre-1967 borders.

This would require the Jews to give up the Western Wall, where thousands of devout Jews and millions of tourists pray yearly. Today, if a Jew or Christian is caught praying on the Temple Mount, that person is removed by Muslim police. Imagine the Western Wall becoming a complete Islamic prayer wall where Jews or Christians are not allowed to pray at this holy site! The Jews would also be giving up the Eastern Gate, the Garden of Gethsemane, the Mount of Olives, and the Kidron Valley, which are the main tourist sites for millions of Christians who visit the Holy Land. In the Tribulation, all of the above-mentioned territories will be seized by the Antichrist and his armies, forcing the city to be divided again and causing Jews who are living on the western side of the city to be brought into captivity! If Israel returns to the pre-1967 borders, it will be impossible to defend the nation, as the enemies would have the high mountains on the Golan Heights, the West Bank, and even areas overlooking Jerusalem from which to send in missiles. In addition, there would be untold danger to tens of thousands of apartments and Jewish settlements.

GOD'S WARNING TO LEADERS

There is vast difference between dividing the land of Israel when the Jews were out of the land as opposed to when they returned back to the land from their captivity. From A.D. 70 to 1948, Israel did not exist as a nation, and the Jews had no homeland. For nineteen hundred years Jerusalem and Palestine exchanged hands in heated battles, often between Christian empires or nations and Islamic empires or nations. There was no warning given to any nation concerning how God would judge them if the Jews were not in the land. However, once God restored Israel from her captivity the second time (Isa. 11:11) and brought them to the land, He would judge severely anyone attempting to divide the land again:

> I will also gather all nations,
> And bring them down to the Valley of Jehoshaphat;
> And I will enter into judgment with them there
> On account of My people, My heritage Israel,
> Whom they have scattered among the nations;
> They have also divided up My land.
> —JOEL 3:2

Ezekiel describes the enemies of Israel who plan on dividing the land into two nations. Read God's rebuke:

> "Because you have said, 'These two nations and these two countries shall be mine, and we will possess them,' although the LORD was there, therefore, as I live," says the Lord GOD, "I will do according to your anger and according to the envy which you showed in your hatred against them; and I will make Myself known among them when I judge you. Then you shall know that I am the LORD. I have heard all your blasphemies which you

have spoken against the mountains of Israel, saying,
'They are desolate; they are given to us to consume.'
Thus with your mouth you have boasted against Me and
multiplied your words against Me; I have heard them."
Thus says the Lord GOD: "The whole earth will rejoice
when I make you desolate. As you rejoiced because the
inheritance of the house of Israel was desolate, so I will
do to you; you shall be desolate."

—EZEKIEL 35:10–15

When the Jews re-formed Israel in 1948, reunited Jerusalem as the
capital in 1967, and annexed their original Promised Land with the
1948 Israeli boundaries, God restored His promise to Abraham and
David. When a world leader demands a division of the land, he or
she is actually coming against the covenant that God sealed with His
own name!

Our generation is different from those of the past nineteen hundred years when Israel was expelled from the land, when numerous
nations were permitted to live in what was called *Palestine*. However, when the people were brought back from the Holocaust and
God raised them up as an army in a land of unwalled villages (Ezek.
38), the game changed! Anyone who publicly demands a new division of the land into two separate nations is saying he or she does
not believe in the Abrahamic covenant of the Bible, and that person
holds no regard for the promises God gave to Abraham, David, and
the Jews concerning the future of Jerusalem. By his or her unbiblical
demands, that person is also calling God a liar, because God swore
by Himself to Abraham when He established this covenant (Heb.
6:13–14).

Thus the only way the Almighty can seize the attention of anti-
covenant leaders is to allow their own nations to become impacted
economically in some manner. Over the years, often when a US president or leader placed public demands for Israel to give up land or

withdraw from its promised territory, usually within seventy-two hours the nation experienced a severe weather pattern that caused much damage and cost money to repair.

America has always been a safe haven nation for the Jews. America and her allies helped defeat Hitler and the Nazis in World War II, helping to liberate Holocaust survivors and leading the way for the reestablishment of Israel. Since 1948 Israel has trusted and received the support of every US administration.

However, let present and future leaders be warned—demanding the division of a covenant land means you are mocking the words and promises given to Israel, Jerusalem, and the Jews that were sealed in the blood of animal sacrifices and by the blood of circumcision of male Hebrew sons.

When God remembers His covenant with Israel, He will either release mercy or judgment. For Egyptian slave owners God released judgment, but for His people in captivity He gave them mercy and freedom to leave Egypt and return to the land of promise. God is now extending covenant mercy for His people in the land of Israel, and He will eventually visit the Gentile nations in judgment for their treatment of His covenant people. The Antichrist will confirm the covenant then break the covenant in the middle of the seven years (Dan. 9:27). But destruction will eventually come because God will stand up and fight for Jerusalem! God's name is at stake—and He remembers His covenant!

9

THE BIBLE AND THE QURAN— ISLAMIC AND CHRISTIAN PROPHECIES

And I looked, and behold, a white horse. He who
sat on it had a bow; and a crown was given to him,
and he went out conquering and to conquer.
—REVELATION 6:2

BIBLE-BELIEVING CHRISTIANS QUOTE SPECIFIC SCRIPTURES
when pointing to End Time prophecies, and Muslims refer to
the Quran and the hadith when referring to their beliefs on the time
of the end. At times, Christians and Muslims use the same scriptures to identify the final Antichrist of Christian prophecy or the
Muslim's final awaited one. This apparent contradiction of interpretation can be rather confusing to Christians and Muslims who are
aware of each other's interpretation.

As we have already discussed in this book, Scripture gives many
predictions concerning the Antichrist, his kingdom, his peace treaty,
his sudden invasion of Jerusalem, and his assault on Israel and the

Jewish people. The Islamic hadith reveal the rise and rule of the Mahdi. An example of Scripture used in both the hadith and in biblical prophecy is found in the Book of Revelation.

THE FOUR HORSEMEN

According to the Book of Revelation, the beginning of the seven-year Tribulation period is initiated when a mysterious white horse and its rider come galloping on the world scene:

> And I looked, and behold, a white horse. He who sat on it had a bow; and a crown was given to him, and he went out conquering and to conquer.
>
> —REVELATION 6:2

Many biblical scholars identify this rider as the Antichrist. In John's day, Roman emperors and military conquerors were pulled in chariots by white horses. A white horse was also reserved for use by a major leader or military person. The Greek word *toxon* is used for "bow," which is the bow of a warrior or a fighter. There are two Greek words for crown in Revelation. The Greek word for "crown" in the verse above is *stephanos,* which is a word used for a wreath placed on the head of the winner of the prize at the games or contests. This crown is given for the person's conquest.

In 1993, I was surprised to learn that Muslims believe the Mahdi will appear on the world scene riding upon a white horse.

> It is clear that this man is the Mahdi who will ride the white horse and judge by the Qur'an (with justice) and with whom will be men with marks of prostration on their foreheads [marks on their foreheads from bowing in prayer with their head to the ground five times daily].[1]

> I find the Mahdi recorded in the books of the Prophets—
> For instance, the Book of Revelation says: "And I saw
> and behold a white horse. He that sat on him—went
> forth conquering and to conquer."[2]

In John's vision there are two different riders on white horses: the rider introduced as one of the four horsemen (Rev. 6:2), and a rider in Revelation 19, identified as the "King of kings and Lord of lords" (Rev. 19:11, 16). The first horseman (Rev. 6:2) is linked to the Antichrist, and the rider in chapter 19 is Christ Himself. The Antichrist arrives on the world scene on a white horse seven years before Christ appears on His.

It is interesting to note that most Islamic leaders own white stallions. Saddam Hussein was often seen in large military parades riding on a white stallion. I was told that Moammar Kadafi in Libya owns one, and even the son of Osama bin Laden has personal white stallions and has said he desires to be a peace negotiator in the future. Islamic tradition teaches that the Mahdi will appear on a white horse, and some Islamic scholars believe the white horse rider in Revelation 6 is a prediction of the coming Mahdi.

Christian scholars note that the rider has a bow but no arrows. Some conclude this could be a hidden clue that this white horse rider will come in "peace" instead of war. Some refer back to Daniel 9:27, where the Antichrist makes a treaty, or a "covenant," for seven years. This treaty will involve a false peace with Israel and surrounding nations. The Bible indicates: "By peace [he] shall destroy many" (Dan. 8:25, KJV), and "When they shall say, Peace and safety; then sudden destruction cometh upon them" (1 Thess. 5:3, KJV).

This covenant for *peace* is more of an agreement for Israel's security than a standard peace treaty. The word *peace* in Daniel 8:25 is not *shalom*, the common Hebrew word used for "peace, blessing, and prosperity." It is *shalvah*, meaning "security" (false or genuine), or "making things quiet." This final world dictator will initiate his own laws to create a false sense of security in order to destroy those opposing him. The word *destroy* in the Hebrew means to "decay, ruin, lay them in waste." If the Antichrist has a Muslim link, then this prediction alludes to Islamic-style peace, not the type of peace we think of in the West. If individuals follow strict Islamic law (called *Sharia*), then you will have security. If these laws are broken, then the trespasser will be punished—at times with death.

Islam has an apocalyptic belief that there will be peace treaties signed before the arrival of the Mahdi.

> There will be four peace agreements between you and the Romans. The fourth agreement will be mediated through a person who will be from the progeny of Hadhrat Haroon (A.S.) and will be upheld for seven years.[3]
>
> —MUFTI A. H. ELIAS

> The Prophet said…"He will divide the property and will govern the people by the Sunnah of their Prophet …and establish Islam on Earth. He will remain seven years, then die, and the Muslims will pray over him."[4]
>
> —NARRATED BY JABIR IBN SAMURAH

> [The Prophet said,] "The Mahdi…will fill the earth will equity and justice as it was filled with oppression and tyranny, and he will rule for seven years."[5]
>
> —NARRATED BY ABU SA'ID AL-KHUDRI

Biblical scholars believe the coming Tribulation is seven years in length (Dan. 9:27), and contemporary Islamic scholars are stating that there will be a rule of the Mahdi lasting seven years!

BEHEADING OF PEOPLE

For centuries, liberal scholars have criticized one prophecy found in the Book of Revelation. In fact, these doubt peddlers would relegate the Book of Revelation to some mysterious, strange book whose application applied to the first century only. The criticized prophecy says:

> And I saw thrones, and they sat on them, and judgment was committed to them. Then I saw the souls of those who had been beheaded for their witness to Jesus and for the word of God, who had not worshiped the beast or his image, and had not received his mark on their foreheads or on their hands. And they lived and reigned with Christ for a thousand years.
>
> —REVELATION 20:4

This scripture indicates that during the final seven years of the Tribulation, people who turn their faith toward Jesus Christ will face execution by beheading. In the Greek text, the phrase "I saw souls beheaded" literally reads, "I saw souls who were beheaded with the ax." For years, twentieth-century commentators pointed out that *civilized* nations today no longer behead people; thus this reference alluded to the Roman Empire slaying believers during the Roman persecution in John's day. Paul himself was beheaded in Rome. Today, however, men are slain by guns and bombs and not beheaded by an ax or a sword.

Since the war on terror, the entire world has been shocked to see groups of masked Islamic fanatics reading a decree against innocent men or women and then literally beheading them. This radical form of execution is promoted among the sayings of Muhammad in the Quran:

Therefore strike off their heads and strike off every fingertip of them…because they acted adversely to Allah and His Messenger.[6]
—Surah 8:12–13, Shakir

Seize them and slay them wherever you find them.
—Surah 4:89

When you meet the unbelievers in the battlefield strike off their heads and, when you have laid them low, bind your captives firmly.
—Surah 47:4, N. J. Dawood translation

When a few United States troops were photographed humiliating men in the Abu Ghraib prison in Iraq, practically every Islamic leader in the region went into a rage as Arabic-speaking papers and journalists united to condemn and demand the punishment of the American soldiers who would humiliate these possible terrorists.

However, the same Islamic world was strangely silent when violent and bloody pictures of fanatics beheading Western businessmen in Iraq hit the newspapers and Internet. Why were these same leaders who went into a rage because of events at the Abu Ghraib prison incident suddenly silent when viewing an innocent headless victim of Islamic fanaticism? Because Islam not only believes in beheading, but also several of the large Muslim nations practice it!

The only religion in the world whose religious book and traditions believe *and practice* the act of beheading is the religion of Islam. This is one of many reasons why I believe that the final world dictator identified in the Bible as the Antichrist will not have a Jewish link but an Islamic one.

CHANGING LAWS AND THE CALENDAR

If and when an Islamic leader unites the Islamic world and seizes the surrounding Gentile nations, what would be some of the first changes under Islamic rule? The first changes an Islamic *messiah* would initiate are the laws governing religion and worship. These changes are alluded to in Daniel 7:25 (KJV):

> And he shall speak great words against the most High,
> and shall wear out the saints of the most High, and think
> to change times and laws: and they shall be given into
> his hand until a time and times and the dividing of time.

Muslims call God *Allah*. They do not use the Hebrew name of *Yahweh*, the God of Abraham, Isaac, and Jacob. The future Islamic dictator will speak great words against the Hebrew God (Dan. 7:25; Rev. 13:6). Muslims consider Allah the same God of Abraham, Isaac, and Ishmael, but the Arabic name *Allah* was not a name revealed to Muhammad. It was a name already in existence in pre-Islamic times.

The Antichrist will change times. The word *times* can allude to changing the *year* or the *calendar*. Any global Islamic leader would set out to change the "times" in three ways:

1. *By changing the Gentile and Jewish calendar to the Islamic calendar.* Islam uses a different calendar than Western nations. Most Gentile nations, especially those familiar with Western culture, use a solar calendar, which dates time before and after Christ's birth. For the West, the year 1979 was 1,979 years from Christ's birth. The Islamic calendar began in the year A.D. 622; thus all time for Muslims is counted from 622 forward. The Islamic calendar reached the 1,400th year in 1979 during the

Iranian revolution. In a final conquest of the world by an Islamic leader, all nations would be forced to follow the Islamic calendar and not the Christian or Jewish calendars.

2. *By changing the year from 365.25 days to 354 or 355 days a year.* The West (and most modern nations) uses a solar calendar that consists of 365.25 days to complete one solar year. The Islamic calendar is a lunar calendar, with 354 or 355 days completed to make a complete Islamic year.

3. *By changing the day of worship to Friday—the Islamic day of worship.* Hindus worship on Thursday, Muslims on Friday, Jews on Saturday, and traditional Gentile Christians on Sunday. Under Islamic rule, only one day, Friday, would be chosen to worship Allah.

This power to change *times* and *laws* is for a "time (one year), times (two years), and dividing of times (one half a year)," which totals forty-two months (Dan. 7:25, KJV; 12:7; Rev. 12:14).

Note that Daniel 7:25 states the Antichrist will change times *and laws*. While this could allude to the Law of Moses in the Torah, the Aramaic word is *dath*, and in the context could allude to changing the religious laws. This interpretation agrees with the religious agenda of a global Islamic leader. According to Muslim tradition, the time will come when the entire world will be converted to the Islamic religion, and no other religion will be practiced.

Under Islamic rule there would be four main assignments that any new Islamic kingdom would initiate.

1. *The first assignment would be forced conversion or death.* In such nations as the Sudan and parts of Nigeria today, armed Muslim warriors enter villages demanding the entire village to meet together. Those who convert to Islam are spared. Those who do not are killed to create fear. Often, the men are killed while the wives and daughters are raped and the children taken and raised as Muslims. In Indonesia, more than eight thousand Christians were forced to convert to Islam or face death. The magazine *Voice of the Martyrs* often documents the persecution of Christians from around the world.

2. *The second assignment would be to destroy churches and synagogues.* Indonesia is the largest Islamic nation in the world, with 1.7 million people. Although the president is a moderate Muslim leader, radical Muslims—jihad warriors— have killed more then ten thousand Christians in two years. At least six hundred church buildings have been set on fire, bombed, or destroyed since 1995. While many moderate Muslims have gotten along with Christians for years, the rise of the fanatics is a serious threat to the stability of many Asian nations, including Indonesia.[7]

3. *The third assignment would be to capture and retrain the youth.* When Christian youth are taken as captives, they are forced to convert or become slaves. If they convert, they are sent to Islamic schools where they are taught the Quran and Muslim doctrine. While the Bible, the

principal foundational book of America's documents, is banned from public schools in America, in Islamic countries the Quran is taught in the school systems the moment a child can read. Muslims are aware that in order to win the next generation, it begins with the youth.

4. *The fourth assignment would be to spread the message to new areas.* Islam is taking new converts and having them travel into other nations in order to bring the Islamic message. This missionary effort is supported with millions of dollars from Islamic nations, especially Saudi Arabia. Saudi Arabia has provided more than $50 million to organizations to help "evangelize" America for Islam. Overall, the Saudis have spent approximately $95 billion since the mid-1970s to export Wahhabism (the sectarian form of Islam that is both the Saudi state religion and a chief theological component of Islamism, the totalitarian ideology guiding global jihadism and terrorism) on a global scale, and there is no evidence of decreased activity in its missionary effort.[8]

Any religion has the right to proclaim its message to people and then allow the people to choose what they wish to believe. This is the universal method by which the Christian message is to be presented. Ministers preach a gospel message and conclude with an altar invitation. True Christianity never forces anyone to convert. However, among the fanatical Muslims, no opportunity is given to reject the Quran or teachings of their prophet—because rejection is the path to death. The following explanation of apostasy is given, including the consequences for the apostate:

Apostasy (*irtidad*) is the act of turning away from Islam having accepted it. This involves the rejection of *tawhid* and *nubuwwa* and the essentials of Islam (e.g. that the Qur'an is a book of God). There are 2 types of *murtad—fitri* and *milli*. A *fitri murtad* is one who was born of Muslim parents (or at least one parent) and then rejects Islam. If he rejects Islam, then, according to the fatwa of our *maraji* (including Ayatullahs al-Khu'i and Khumayni) he is to be killed. A *milli murtad* is one who converts and then rejects Islam—he is to be given 3 days to repent and accept Islam again. If he does not accept by the fourth day he is to be killed.[9]

Hatred toward Israel, the West, Jews, and Christians is a common thread among the fanatical communities. Among moderate Islamic countries, such as Jordan, Christians experience limited freedoms. Secular Muslims are often repulsed at the twisted thinking of many Muslims. However, among the Shi'ite branch of Islam, many Muslims blame America for the rebirth of Israel and despise our support of the Jewish state. In their minds, if they can't defeat Israel, they'll defeat America from within for supporting Israel.

THE KINGDOM OF PERSECUTION

The beast's kingdom will be marked as the greatest season of persecution against Jews and those who convert to Christianity that has ever been experienced. This will produce the greatest number of religious martyrs in history (Rev. 6:9–11). Numerous prophecies speak of this time:

> But tidings out of the east and out of the north shall trouble him: therefore he shall go forth with great fury to destroy, and utterly to make away many.
>
> —DANIEL 11:44, KJV

The phrase "make away many" means to utterly slay and destroy. According to the Hebrew dictionary, it can mean to seclude and ban for religious reasons. The rage of the beast is visible in his treatment toward the Jews.

> And his power shall be mighty, but not by his own power: and he shall destroy wonderfully, and shall prosper, and practise, and shall destroy the mighty and the holy people.
>
> —DANIEL 8:24, KJV

The phrase "holy people" alludes to the Jewish people living in Israel. Notice the prophecy says "not by his own power," because the power and authority the Antichrist receives will initiate from Satan.

> Now the beast which I saw was like a leopard, his feet were like the feet of a bear, and his mouth like the mouth of a lion. The dragon gave him his power, his throne, and great authority.
>
> —REVELATION 13:2

During the final forty-two months of the beast's kingdom, Daniel informs us:

> And at that time shall Michael stand up, the great prince which standeth for the children of thy people: and there shall be a time of trouble, such as never was since there was a nation even to that same time.
>
> —DANIEL 12:1, KJV

Jesus described this same upheaval of humanity in Matthew 24:21 as the "great tribulation." The wars and destruction and loss of life will be so great that without divine interruption (the return of Christ), the entire human race would be in danger of extinction:

> For then there will be great tribulation, such as has not been since the beginning of the world until this time, no, nor ever shall be. And unless those days were shortened, no flesh would be saved; but for the elect's sake those days will be shortened.
>
> —MATTHEW 24:21–22

The apostle Paul also spoke of this time of trouble and predicted:

> For when they say, "Peace and safety!" then sudden destruction comes upon them, as labor pains upon a pregnant woman. And they shall not escape.
>
> —1 THESSALONIANS 5:3

The seven-year peace treaty initiates a false sense of security, as the Gentile nations and Israel will declare, "Finally, peace and security!" Suddenly, the armies of the beast invade northern Africa, controlling the Suez Canal sea-lanes. His soldiers of jihad sweep into the oil-rich nations of the Persian Gulf, seizing the black gold of the Arabian deserts. Israel will have been forced to disarm after the war of Gog and Magog (Ezek. 38 and 39), thus left unprotected from the Antichrist's forces. The Antichrist will use the Palestinian cause to create a massive uprising on the streets inside of Israel, thus retaking East Jerusalem. He will station his command center in Jerusalem as indicated in Daniel 11:45:

> And he shall plant the tents of his palace between the seas and the glorious holy mountain; yet he shall come to his end, and no one will help him.

Scholars indicate the "glorious holy mountain" is actually Jerusalem or Mount Moriah, the original location of the two ancient Jewish temples. The word *seas* (plural) alludes to the Dead Sea and the Mediterranean Sea. (Jerusalem is positioned between these two seas.) The following passage in Daniel says: "There shall be a time of trouble [referring to the Great Tribulation—Matthew 24:21]" (Dan. 12:1). At that time, the words of Daniel 11:39 will be fulfilled: "He shall… divide the land for gain." The Palestinians will be given the land they are demanding. Then, the predictions from the Quran and the hadith will be reality. The Muslims will be permitted to "kill the swine [Jews] and destroy the cross [anything representing Christianity]."

This one man will turn against the Jews with a vengeance. Anyone who receives Christ during this season will be added to the Antichrist's hit list. Thankfully, this time of trouble will only last for forty-two months. It will be interrupted by the return of the Messiah, Jesus Christ.

The peace treaty will be signed with Israel for one prophetic week, which is seven years (Dan. 9:27). The Antichrist and his armies invade Jerusalem in the middle of the seven years, known as mid-Tribulation. (See Revelation chapters 11 and 13.) During the final half of the seven years, the Antichrist reigns from Jerusalem and will eventually be defeated by Christ, who returns at the conclusion of the seven years (Rev. 19:11–16). If the beast lives in Jerusalem for the last forty-two months, where will his throne of rule be the first forty-two months? We will find out where in the next chapter.

IRAQ—THE FUTURE
HEADQUARTERS OF THE
COMING ANTICHRIST

"For I will rise up against them," says the LORD of hosts, "and cut off from Babylon the name and remnant, and offspring and posterity," says the LORD.
—ISAIAH 14:22

NAMED BY THE WEST THE BUTCHER OF BAGHDAD, SADDAM Hussein took control of Iraq in July 1979. A Baathist, Saddam's vision for Iraq was one of power and grandeur. Fully aware of the historic significance of his nation, Saddam set in motion plans to rebuild the ancient city of Babylon, erect the world's largest mosque with the Euphrates River running though it, and eventually become the leader of a new Islamic crescent that would include Israel as its prize possession. A lengthy war with Iran canceled many of his plans, but not before Saddam began spending millions of dollars rebuilding buildings in the region of ancient Babylon.[1]

The Mystique of Ancient Babylon

After Noah's flood, men began to rebuild cities in the plains and valleys. One of the first cities among many was Babel, built by Nimrod, the grandson of Noah through his son Ham (Gen. 10:1–10). According to Josephus, Babel was built in the plains of Shinar as an act of rebellion against God for sending the flood and destroying the world. Nimrod began erecting a tall tower, intending it to be so high that any future floodwaters would never reach the top. Josephus indicates that God destroyed the tower by sending a strong wind.[2] The tower was called the *Tower of Babel*, which can translate as "confusion," alluding to the incident where God scattered the people by confusing their languages.

The modern area of Iraq became known in early history as Mesopotamia. The next reference to the plains of Shinar is during the time of Abraham, when a war was raging between five kings in Canaan and four kings from Mesopotamia who were being led by Amraphel, the king of Shinar (Gen. 14:1). The three other kings listed in Genesis 14 as allies of Amraphel are:

- ◆ Chedorlaomer, the king of Elam—this is modern Persia or Iraq.

- ◆ Tidal, the king of the nations—this was a king over Gentile tribes.

- ◆ Arioch, the king of Ellasar—this was a city near Ur, or Mesopotamia.

These four kings ruled from the area of modern Syria and Iraq. Abraham, the father of the Hebrews, engaged in war against these four kings and reclaimed the possessions seized during the battle. Following his war victory, Abraham went to Jerusalem where he met with Melchizedek, the first priest of God (Gen. 14).

Abraham's first battle was with kings from the same area where Israel's worst enemies still live. Since 1979, the countries of Syria and Iran have been the leading opposition against the Jews, the rebirth of Israel, the reunification of Jerusalem, and the return of the Jews to their historic land. Just as the kings surrounding ancient Babylonia initiated the first conflict with the father of the Hebrew nation, the future Islamic kings of a new Babylon will instigate the final mother of battles that will climax in the valley of Megiddo in central Israel (Rev. 16:16).

After Abraham, the next mention of the Babylonian area is penned in the prophetic Book of Daniel. By this time, Babylon was not just a city built on the Euphrates River, but it had grown into a mighty kingdom, powering over Mesopotamia and extending its dominion by conquering Israel and Jerusalem. Thousands of Jews were taken captive in Babylon for seventy years, including the prophet Daniel. It was the Babylonian armies who destroyed Solomon's temple, seizing the priceless vessels of gold and silver and storing them in the treasure houses of Babylonian gods (Jer. 52).

Ancient Babylon (the area of Iraq today) was eventually seized by the armies of the Medes and Persians in approximately 546 B.C. Many years later, the Greek Empire under Alexander the Great conquered the Persians and took possession of Babylon, extending their global dominion into more countries. Following the Greeks, the Roman Empire began to form and eventually became the fourth kingdom in Daniel's prophecies (Dan. 2:40; 7:23).

Hundreds of years later, in the seventh century, the Arabs would possess the land of Shinar and set up the headquarters of various branches of Islam near the banks of the Euphrates River. In A.D. 637, the Arabs defeated the Persian Army and established the first Arab empire in Mesopotamia. The first Arab government was called the *Umayyad Caliphate*, with several caliphates following. Then, in 750, a dynasty called the *Abbasid Empire* came into power.

THE ARABIANS TAKE BABYLON

Throughout history, the Babylonian area was occupied by the Sumerians, Assyrians, Chaldeans, Persians, and Greeks—but never by the Arabians. A prophecy in Isaiah implies the Arabians would be there, but after the Babylonian destruction they would no longer live there:

> And Babylon, the glory of kingdoms,
> The beauty of the Chaldeans' pride,
> Will be as when God overthrew Sodom and Gomorrah.
> It will never be inhabited,
> Nor will it be settled from generation to generation;
> Nor will the Arabian pitch tents there,
> Nor will the shepherds make their sheepfolds there.
> —Isaiah 13:19–20

This prophecy of destruction must allude to the present, since the Arabians did not pitch their tent there until A.D. 637. Between 661 and 750, the Arabs conquered Babylonia and the town of al-Kufa, which was situated near the ruins of ancient Babylon. This town became the capital of Iraq and the headquarters for the Umayyad dynasty. Between 744 and 750, the Islamic caliph Marwan II ibn Muhammad transferred his residence to Harran, Iraq. Beginning in 717, fanatical caliphs began to persecute the Jews living in and around Babylon. Throughout Islamic history, the fate of the Jews often depended upon who the regional Islamic governors were at the time.

In 850 the Islamic caliph al-Mutawakkil, a religious fanatic, demanded Jews to wear a yellow head covering. The poor and those who worked as servants of the Arabs had a yellow patch attached to their clothes either on their chest or back. During the early centuries of Islam, Jews and Christians were often forced to wear yellow clothes with patches on them to identify them as Jews. In most instances, Jews and Christians were levied with heavy taxes.

Clearly, the plains of Shinar, the Tower of Babel, the city of Babylon, and the kingdom of the Babylonians have played major roles in biblical history and prophecy. Iraq and the city of Baghdad have served as headquarters for caliphs in Islam since the infancy of the religion.

THE NEW BABYLON—RISING FROM THE ASHES

The final battle of battles involving Israel and her enemies will be with a future king of Iraq. Prophetically, he will be the king of neo-Babylon. On October 11, 1990, the *New York Times International* said:

> Under Saddam Hussein, one of the ancient world's most legendary cities has begun to rise again. More than an archaeological venture, the new Babylon is self-consciously dedicated to the idea that Nebuchadnezzar has a successor in Mr. Hussein, whose military prowess and vision will restore to Iraqis the glory their ancestors knew when all of what is now Iraq, Syria, Lebanon, Jordan, Kuwait, and Israel was under Babylonian control.[3]

The ancient king Nebuchadnezzar left instructions for the future of Babylon on cuneiform script tablets. On these clay tablets, twenty-five hundred years ago the scribes instructed those who found the tablets to rebuild the temples and palaces. This message was so clear to Saddam Hussein that during this building project he had bricks impressed with his image and that of old king Nebuchadnezzar!

One Iraqi archeologist, Shafqa Muhammad Jaafar, said: "Because Babylon was built in ancient times and was a great city, it must be a great city again in the time of our great leader Saddam Hussein."[4] According to Paul Lewis of the *New York Times*, the motivation for Saddam rebuilding Babylon was to strengthen Iraqi nationalism by appealing to history. It also portrayed Saddam in the eyes of his people as the new Nebuchadnezzar, a leader who eventually conquered the world in his day.[5]

After Saddam spent $100 million, thousands of workers laid sixty million bricks along new walls in the new Babylon. Every six feet along the wall there is a brick with an inscription in Arabic saying, "The Babylon of Nebuchadnezzar was reconstructed in the era of Saddam Hussein."[6] After the laying of sixty million bricks and the rebuilding of gates, walls, and palaces, the last Babylonian festival was in 1988. The war with Iran had taken its toll on Iraq, and the building program ceased. Instead, Saddam began placing hundreds of millions of dollars into his lavish palaces, scattered throughout the country.

Saddam's invasion into Kuwait was not for its oil deposits. Iraq has huge amounts of the world's reserves of oil. The *spiritual* motive was to begin annexing the land that once belonged to ancient Babylon. It would have also given Iraq a much-needed coastline. Even the name *Babylon* comes into play constantly in the minds of Iraqis. In the early nineties, Saddam built a supergun with a 16-inch barrel that was 172 feet long. The gun was tested and set a world record by shooting a projectile 112 miles straight up. The supergun was code-named *Baby Babylon* by the Iraqis.

A second gun was being built when the parts were intercepted by special agents. The gun had a 39-inch barrel and was 512 feet long, with the potential rage of hundreds of miles. This larger gun was being named *Big Babylon!*[7]

The Demise of Saddam

Saddam Hussein, the *Butcher of Baghdad*, met his doom on the gallows in the very land he ruled. Just like Hitler and evil dictators before him, Saddam's rule has come to an abrupt finish. He will never become the leader of a new Islamic crescent or the new king of a new Babylon. Yet, in the future, under a new and different leadership, the ancient land of Shinar (Iraq) could once again expand with wealth from the oil wells and be rebuilt into a strong nation.

After all, the Bible teaches a season of false peace. This peace must involve Israel and her Arab-Muslim neighbors. Yet, out of this region of the world will arise the leader of the new Islamic republic, a Muslim who will at first be received by the Islamic world but in the end will be the most violent, bloodthirsty human to have ever walked on Earth.

According to Paul, this man's appearance is now being restrained, but one day he will be revealed in his full identity (2 Thess. 2:1–10).

IRAQ WILL BECOME THE HEADQUARTERS OF THE BEAST

Modern Iraq was once the center of the ancient Babylonian empire. Baghdad served as the headquarters and center of operation for several Islamic dynasties. Today, the Shi'ite branch of Islam needs a headquarters, and I believe Iraq, in the future, will become the center for Shi'ite Muslims who will claim this prophetic territory. Prior to the 2002 invasion of Iraq, I wrote that the new government would be a Shi'ite government. Iraq is important since the Antichrist does not invade Israel until the middle of the seven-year period. He will be living and ruling from another nation prior to making his move against Israel. The prophet Daniel was told: "He [the Antichrist] shall come up and become strong with a small number of people" (Dan. 11:23). His authority is identified through the symbol of a *little horn* (Dan. 7:8). Not well known during his first forty-two months in power, the Antichrist will not be a powerful leader (such as an elected official over the EU), but he will control a small number of people. He will gain his power through deception and demonic power (Rev. 13:1–5).

Another indicator that Iraq will be heavily involved in this End

Time prophetic conflict is found in the Book of Revelation. John speaks of activity linked with the Euphrates River and a massive two-hundred-million-man army that will cross the Euphrates, passing through the nation of Iraq.

THE EUPHRATES CONNECTION

The Euphrates and Tigris rivers divide Iran from Iraq. The Euphrates begins in Turkey not far from Mount Ararat. It travels through Turkey, Syria, and Iraq, emptying into the Persian Gulf (1,700 miles long). The Euphrates was the eastern boundary of the Roman Empire. This river is the only river mentioned by name in apocalyptic prophecies related to the final days of the rule of the beast kingdom.

Biblically, there are several powerful ancient spirits that have been confined under the great river Euphrates, which will be released during the Great Tribulation:

> ...saying to the sixth angel who had the trumpet, "Release the four angels who are bound at the great river Euphrates." So the four angels, who had been prepared for the hour and day and month and year, were released to kill a third of mankind.
>
> —REVELATION 9:14–15

These wicked angels will rise up and motivate a massive army of two hundred million soldiers to slay one-third of mankind during a thirteen-month period (Rev. 9:13–19). I personally believe these angels are the same ancient prince spirits (called "principalities" in Ephesians 6:12) that once ruled from the past empires of prophecy. These include the spirit of Babylon, the spirit of the Medes and Persians (Dan. 10:13), along with the prince spirit of Greece (v. 20). The above-mentioned empires all ruled from ancient Babylon, and, according to Daniel, each kingdom had a strong demonic spirit dominating the atmosphere over the kingdoms (Dan. 10).

Later, toward the conclusion of the Tribulation, the Euphrates River will dry up to make a way for a massive army, headed by the kings of the east:

> Then the sixth angel poured out his bowl on the great river Euphrates, and its water was dried up, so that the way of the kings from the east might be prepared.
>
> —REVELATION 16:12

John, in Revelation, indicates severe drought and famine will precede this event (Rev. 6:8; 11:6). Presently, during the dry season, the water level of the Euphrates may drop as low as twenty-four inches. The country of Turkey has constructed several massive dams that can shut off the flow of the Euphrates like a knob on a faucet. Why is the emphasis on the Euphrates so important? Because ancient Babylon was built along the Euphrates, and Baghdad, the capital of Iraq, sits near the Tigris River, not far from the Euphrates.

When the Euphrates dries up and a massive army marches across, they will march from the East, which includes Iran, Afghanistan, and Pakistan. These nations are located on the east of the Euphrates. These three nations are home to millions of Islamic radicals, all promoting their fanatical form of Islam and strict radical agenda. The Antichrist will be "great...toward the east" (Dan. 8:9), which includes these Islamic-controlled areas mentioned above.

Armies marching from the East would also need to pass through Iraq as they proceed into Israel and the valley of Megiddo, the site of the future battle of Armageddon (Rev. 16:16). We cannot underestimate the historical, spiritual, and political importance of the Iraqi nation. The land of Iraq was ancient Shinar, the land of the first battle Abraham fought, and it will be the land where the last king will rise and battle the Jews in their homeland. Important historical facts about Iraq include:

- It is the site of the Tower of Babel.

- It has the same territory as ancient Babylon.

- Its territory has been ruled by three prophetic empires.

- It is the heart of the 10/40 window.

- It is the headquarters for Shi'ite Muslims.

- Ali, Muhammad's son-in-law, was murdered here.

- Some believe the twelfth imam disappeared in Iraq.

- Many Shi'ites believe the Mahdi will appear here.

- It is the country where the Euphrates River flows.

- It is located toward the east from Israel—where the Antichrist will be strong.

- Iraq, Syria, Kuwait, and Lebanon united will form the old Babylon.

The importance of Iraq can be summarized in this way: Iraq was the cradle of civilization and the area where Abraham lived (in Ur) before migrating to the Promised Land (Gen. 11:31). It was home to the four kings whom Abraham and his servants fought (Gen. 14:1–8). It is the place of the Tower of Babel, the site of the first global religion and first world government (Gen. 11). It was the area where three major empires of Bible prophecy set up their kingdoms. It was the headquarters of the Shi'ite branch of Islam and the site where many Muslims believe the twelfth imam disappeared and where the

Mahdi will reemerge to take possession of the world, forming an Islamic empire.

It is not necessary for a future Iraqi ruler to continue rebuilding the ancient ruins of Babylon. The *spirit of Babylon* will be released during the Tribulation and will work in the heart of the beast and his ten kings. This new Babylon will eventually consist of Iraq, Syria, and Lebanon, and, from a religious perspective, it will also include Iran.

THE MAIN ARGUMENT OPPOSING THE NEO-BABYLON

Scholars may argue that ancient Babylon has been destroyed, and the Bible says it will not be rebuilt. Pastor Mike Coleman, a friend of mine, once said that he was told by a Hebrew professor this is one of the reasons Saddam desired to rebuild Babylon—to prove the Bible was wrong! Throughout the Old Testament, the prophets gave grave warnings about the utter destruction of Babylon. Many references are found in Jeremiah, chapters 50 and 51:

> Therefore the wild beasts of the desert with the wild beasts of the islands shall dwell there, and the owls shall dwell therein: and it shall be no more inhabited for ever; neither shall it be dwelt in from generation to generation.
> —JEREMIAH 50:39, KJV

> And thou shalt say, Thus shall Babylon sink, and shall not rise from the evil that I will bring upon her: and they shall be weary. Thus far are the words of Jeremiah.
> —JEREMIAH 51:64, KJV

In Jeremiah's time, Babylon had invaded Israel, destroyed Jerusalem, burned the temple, and led the Jews into captivity. Jeremiah was predicting the utter destruction of Babylon. Yet, Jeremiah's prophecy is very parallel to the prophecy in Revelation 17 and 18 concerning "Mystery Babylon." Jeremiah's Babylon is a political city, and John's Babylon is a religious and economic system.

During the Gulf War, I flew on a plane with a rabbi from Hungary. We discussed the Gulf War. He believed Jeremiah alluded to a future war in the area of ancient Babylon, today Iraq. He noted America's involvement in the Gulf War appeared to parallel the warnings of Babylon's destruction:

1. Jeremiah said a nation from the north would rise against Babylon (Jer. 50:41). The Medes and Persians who overthrew Babylon were from the east. America is called *North America.*

2. Jeremiah said many kings would be raised up from the ends of the earth (Jer. 50:41). The largest coalition in history was raised up during the Gulf War.

The rabbi then showed me in Scripture where the Babylon of Jeremiah 51 was a future Babylon, or the area of modern Iraq. He noted that the original Babylon was never destroyed in the manner that we read in Jeremiah's prophecy. Ancient Babylon slowly deteriorated into ruins and rubble. Jeremiah said the Babylon he saw would be destroyed by a "destroying wind" (Jer. 51:1). He noted that "bright arrows" would be used (v. 11) and the reeds would be "burned with fire" (v. 32). The rabbi said, "During the Gulf War or a future conflict, America or Israel may be forced to use nuclear or other modern weapons [the destroying wind] or missiles [arrows] tipped with powerful weapons that will burn the area with fire." He continued, "If this prophecy does not happen in this war, it will in the future, and old Babylon will be destroyed."

If the headquarters of the Antichrist will be Iraq—the area of ancient Babylon, then at what point in time could this area be destroyed? It could be devastated during a war with Israel or the

West and rebuilt for the Antichrist. After all, the nations of the earth would never allow Iraq to be destroyed without demanding that the West rebuild it, the same as we did in Japan after World War II.

Others suggest that in the middle of the Tribulation the Antichrist's headquarters will be destroyed, and he will move his armies into Israel. Since John, in Revelation, sees "Mystery Babylon" burned with fire in one hour, and this prophecy is fulfilled during the final forty-two months of the Great Tribulation, Iraq could become the command center for the beast's kingdom during the first forty-two months. Following a major conflict with the king of the North (Turkey, Dan. 11:40–44), the area of Iraq could be destroyed, and the Antichrist would then make his move into Israel.

Without doubt, Iraq will become the center of attention in the last days. Just as Jerusalem is the gate of heaven and the place where God placed His name, ancient Babel was the gate of wickedness and the place where deceit and spiritual corruption were birthed (Zech. 5:5–11).

A final reason I believe that Iraq will be the headquarters of the future Antichrist is the destruction coming to surrounding nations prior to the seven-year Tribulation. Isaiah 17:1 predicts the utter destruction of Damascus and Syria. Damascus is the world's oldest continuing city and has never been completely destroyed in a war. It will, however, become nonexistent in the future. We also read where the Persians (Iranians) will participate as a leading nation in the upcoming war against Israel, called the battle of Gog and Magog. In the future, with Damascus (Syria) and the Iranians destroyed, the one nation that will continue to exist will be the nation sitting between Syria and Iran—Iraq.

THE MARK OF THE BEAST
AND THE ISLAMIC LINK

He causes all, both small and great, rich and poor,
free and slave, to receive a mark on their right hand
or on their foreheads.... Here is wisdom. Let him who
has understanding calculate the number of the beast,
for it is the number of a man: His number is 666.
—REVELATION 13:16, 18

Assuming the future Antichrist of Bible prophecy is a Muslim or represents one branch of the Islamic religion, then how does the Bible's most recognized prophecy, dealing with the infamous mark of the beast, fit into an Islamic scenario? The Bible teaches that the Antichrist kingdom will head up an economic system of buying and selling by using a mark, which will be his name or the number of his name.

> He causes all, both small and great, rich and poor, free and slave, to receive a mark on their right hand or on their foreheads, and that no one may buy or sell except

one who has the mark or the name of the beast, or the number of his name. Here is wisdom. Let him who has understanding calculate the number of the beast, for it is the number of a man: His number is 666.

—REVELATION 13:16–18

Verse 18 from the Amplified Bible reads:

Here is [room for] discernment [a call for the wisdom of interpretation]. Let anyone who has intelligence (penetration and insight enough) calculate the number of the beast, for it is a human number [the number of a certain man]; his number is 666.

For this kingdom to control all purchasing and selling is important for several reasons. First, the famines and judgments created during the first forty-two months of the coming Tribulation will bring about a massive shortage of both water and food. John indicated that there will be no rain for forty-two months during the first part of the Tribulation (Rev. 11:2–6). This drought impacts the food supply, causing a famine on one-third of the earth, and a water crisis, also identified in Revelation as the time when the entire Euphrates River (1,700 miles long) dries up. The Middle Eastern nations already have encountered shortages of fresh drinking water, and other regions struggle with wheat and rice food supplies, especially during drought or seasons when locusts emerge.

The one Middle Eastern nation with the technology and ability to feed its people and ship out more than 400 percent of its produce is Israel. There are numerous underground reservoirs of water, hidden since the time of Creation, which are now being tapped for irrigation purposes for hundreds of farms stretching from Galilee in the north to the Arabah desert lands in the south.

Governments or individual leaders who can control or manipulate the buying and selling—especially of food reserves—will have the masses literally *eating out of their hands* and submitting to their wishes. People do bizarre things when they are starving. In the Bible, during one severe famine women ate their own children to survive (Lam. 2:20). Others ate dove's dung and donkey heads to delay starvation and death (2 Kings 6:25–29).

According to Josephus, in the time prior to the destruction of the temple in A.D. 70, a severe famine struck Judea, resulting in people boiling their leather shoes and attempting to eat them. Most starving people would follow any religion that provides food.

WHAT IS THE MARK?

Since the second century, early Christian fathers, Bible scholars, and students of prophecy have debated the "mark" prophecy, dissecting each word, exploring history, and comparing verses to unlock the mystery of the mark of the beast. The lack of understanding is evident when reading the older commentaries by Christian theologians:

> Despite numerous attempts to identify the mark of the beast with names, computers, monetary systems, and the like, its precise nature is unknown, remaining to be disclosed as the end draws near.
>
> —MERRILL UNGER

> I confess my ignorance as to the number six hundred and sixty-six. I cannot present you with anything satisfactory to myself. We find, answering to the number six hundred sixty-six, the words *apostasy* and *tradition*: but I cannot say anything positive at this point.[1]
>
> —JOHN DARBY

Irenaeus has only uncertain guesses to offer, and he thinks the Apocalypist intended the name remain hidden till Antichrist should come. The language, however, implies that it is discoverable by those who have the requisite wisdom; and the command, "let him that hath understanding calculate the number," shows that the author expects some to solve the enigma.[2]

—Isbon Beckwith

It seems to me to be one of those seasons which God has reserved in His own power; only this we know, God has written *Mene Tekel* upon all his enemies; he has numbered their days, and they shall be finished, but his own kingdom shall endure for ever.[3]

—Matthew Henry's Commentary

While older scholars during the past two hundred years have been unable to decipher this enigma, Scripture teaches we should count, or calculate, the number of the beast. What does it mean to "count the number of a person's name"?

Hebrew Gematria

There are two main languages in which the letters of the alphabet can be interchanged with numbers: Greek and Hebrew. The Greek language contains twenty-four basic letters, and the Hebrew language has twenty-two main letters. Hebrew uses only consonants and no vowels. The dots and marks underneath or above certain letters determine the vowel pronunciation. The Greeks would learn to interchange the letters for numbers by the influence of a mathematician named Pythagoras.

The Hebrew mystics believe that the alphabet conceals certain secrets that can be discovered through the method of *gematria*.

Hebrew gematria is rule twenty-nine of the thirty-two rules of rabbinical hermeneutics.

Using this system, each individual Hebrew letter has a numerical value. After exchanging a letter for a number, the numbers can be summed up, producing the total number value of the word. Occasionally an entire sentence will be added up to give a sum total of the meaning of the letters. Below is a Hebrew chart showing the twenty-two Hebrew letters along with the number value of each letter. When John alluded to counting the name of the beast, he was referring to this system, which was well known among leading rabbis and students.

The basic translation code for the standard gematria for the Hebrew alphabet is as follows:[4]

Decimal	Hebrew	Glyph
1	*Aleph*	א
2	*Bet*	ב
3	*Gimel*	ג
4	*Daled*	ד
5	*He*	ה
6	*Vav*	ו
7	*Zayin*	ז
8	*Heth*	ח
9	*Teth*	ט
10	*Yodh*	י
20	*Kaph*	כ ך
30	*Lamed*	ל
40	*Mem*	מ ם
50	*Nun*	נ ן
60	*Samekh*	ס

Decimal	Hebrew	Glyph
70	*Ayin*	ע
80	*Pe*	ף פ
90	*Tsadi*	צ ץ
100	*Qoph*	ק
200	*Resh*	ר
300	*Shin*	ש
400	*Tav*	ת

EARLY FATHERS USED THIS SYSTEM

The early fathers were familiar with this system of interchanging the letters with numbers. Revelation 13:18 states, "Count the number of the beast: for it is the number of a man" (KJV). The Greek word for *man* is *anthropos*, which is a singular word for man and also a word used for mankind. Some say the phrase could read, "It is the number of mankind." Several church fathers attempted to calculate certain names or phrases and identify the Antichrist or the system from which he would arise.

The apostle John had a student named Polycarp, who taught Irenaeus (A.D. 140–203). One rather famous example of gematria is when Irenaeus took the letters forming the word *LATEINOS* and showed the sum was 666.

L	A	T	E	I	N	O	S	Total
30	1	300	5	10	50	70	200	666

Irenaeus said, "It seems to me very probable: for this is a name of the last of Daniel's four kingdoms; they being the Latins that now reign." Since the fourth empire of Bible prophecy was Rome, and

Rome ruled in the first four centuries, it was commonly accepted by many early fathers that the final empire prior to Christ's return would be some form of the Roman Empire.

Eventually, the political Roman Empire faded into history and was replaced by the Roman Church, whose influence in Europe and part of the Middle East controlled the rise and fall of kings who controlled much of the old Roman territory. The Latin language was accepted and used in the Roman Church, thus the interpretation of the phrase *LATEINOS*, numerically interpreted to be 666, maintained a strong following.

Objections later formed when it was pointed out that the correct spelling by Greek authors of the word in Latin would be *LATINOS* and not *LATEINOS*. The correct spelling (dropping the English letter *e*) changes the numerical value to 661 and not 666. (The reason *ei* was used in the original spelling was because *ei* is used for the long letter *i* in Latin.)

Another opposing theory developed when a parchment of an old scroll was discovered in Egypt and found to be a small scroll fragment from Revelation 13—the same section dealing with the number of the beast. This fragment totaled to the number 616 and not 666. Most scholars, however, believed that this was a later version and have dismissed this theory.

Because of severe persecutions in the first-century church, initiated with the wicked emperor Nero, many Christians in the first-century church felt Nero would become the beast of the Apocalypse. Nero ruled Rome for fourteen years but was sentenced to death for setting fire to Rome. He escaped, but he later committed suicide on a dirty cot at age thirty-one. In A.D. 69, the historian Tacitus wrote about a rumor that Nero faked his death and was hiding, to emerge in the future.

After John penned the Apocalypse (around A.D. 95), he mentioned that the Antichrist would have "...one of his heads as if it had been mortally wounded, and his deadly wound was healed" (Rev. 13:3). Centuries later, some early fathers (in the second, third, and as late as the fourth century) interpreted this to mean that Nero would rise again and his "death wound" would be healed. Thus this wicked, ungodly emperor would become the Antichrist. Below are three quotes:

> Nero will be raised from the dead, appear again at Rome, persecute the church once more, and finally be destroyed by the Messiah, coming in his glory, and being accompanied by the prophet Elijah.
>
> —Victorinus (a.d. 304)

> Nero will become the precursor and forerunner of the Devil, coming to lay waste the earth.
>
> —Lactantius (a.d. 250–325)

> Nero, the basest of men and even of monsters, was well worthy of being the first persecutor; I know not whether he may be the last, since it is the current opinion of many that he is the Antichrist to come.
>
> —Sulpicius Severus (a.d. 400)

The theory that Nero would return from the "pit" and rise again as the future Antichrist was reinforced according to some; then his name was transliterated from Latin into Hebrew. The letter *n* is added in the transliteration to conform to the Hebrew spelling of Nero's name. Thus the Latin name "Nero Caesar" becomes *Nrwn qsr*. These individual letters are given their Hebrew equivalent, and with each letter given its respective numerical value, they total 666. (See LATEINOS chart on page 130.)

Why would intelligent and biblically knowledgeable scholars accept a theory that an emperor who had passed away more than three hundred years earlier could return from the grave to become the Antichrist? It appears to have been a misunderstanding in the interpretation of passages from the Book of Revelation. As stated earlier, John saw this beast with a wound to one of its heads, and the deadly wound was suddenly healed. Since Nero was the first perse-cutor, it was *assumed* he would return and be the last.

A second reference also added fuel to this speculation of Nero returning:

> The beast that you saw was, and is not, and will ascend out of the bottomless pit and go to perdition. And those who dwell on the earth will marvel, whose names are not written in the Book of Life from the foundation of the world, when they see the beast that was, and is not, and yet is.
>
> —REVELATION 17:8

An interesting observation is gleaned from this prophecy. First, the beast (Antichrist and his kingdom) *was* (meaning previously existed), and *is not* (did not exist in A.D. 95 when John penned the Apocalypse), and *is* (or now confined into the abyss—a location under the earth). Because Nero was, and at the time of John's writing (A.D. 95) was not, and in the future will come forth from the abyss, the assumption was that Nero would one day come back from out of hell and be permitted to rule again, bringing destruction to the earth.

MARKING EVERY PERSON

For centuries, trying to understand how every person could receive a mark on his or her hand or forehead confounded ministers and scholars. The world was so large and the population so spread out that it would take many years to brand the entire world. Yet the Bible says, "He causes all to receive a mark."

With the invention of modern computers, many scholars and students of prophecy began to teach that the "mark" was linked to some form of a computer, since information was linked globally through computer systems. In the 1980s a story was widely circulated that stated that the European Union, with its headquarters in Brussels, Belgium, had constructed a new supercomputer capable of placing information about everyone on Earth into its large database systems. The report continued that this supercomputer was so large that it was nicknamed *The Beast*. Suddenly, prophetic interest in Revelation 13 surfaced again. The main contradiction to making this or any other computer the *beast* of Revelation is that the beast is identified using the personal pronoun *he*, and a computer is an *it*, not a *he* (personal pronoun). Secondly, the "beast is given to the burning flames" at the return of Christ, which alludes to hell. There is no purpose for Christ to send a computer and its hardware into hell.

Eventually, another system connected to purchasing and storing information on products emerged. It was the barcode system printed on product labels and boxes that could, allegedly, in the future be printed on the skin with invisible ink.

The most recent theory involves a new type of computer chip, smaller than a grain of rice, which could be imbedded with millions of bits of information and implanted just under the skin. These devices are presently implanted in pets to help track them if they are lost from their owners. In the early 1990s, I was ministering in Brooksville, Florida, and was invited to meet a man who was welding parts for Russian satellites. He could communicate with the space shuttle from his home, using advanced computers and special equipment. He related to me that they were testing a small chip that would one day be implanted just under the hairline of a person's forehead and under the outer skin of the right hand. The chip operates with a special battery that is charged continually by the heat of the human body. The gentleman believed that this chip would one day replace all identity cards.

Since the development of these special chips, it has been reported that on a predetermined date, everyone in the United States will be required to have one of these implanted in either their right hand or forehead. Each chip will hold personal information that can be scanned. Another type of scanner already exists that is used in major theme parks, such as Disney World in Orlando, Florida. When checking into your hotel in a Disney Park, you receive a special card. However, cards can be lost. When entering the main park, you insert your card and place your finger in a scanner. This amazing scanner actually reads the lines in your finger and gives each line a number. Each human being has a fingerprint pattern that distinguishes that person from all others on Earth. Thus if the card is lost, the scanner can accurately identify any person who has access to the park.

There are also new scanners that can read the retina design in the human eye. These have been used successfully in prisons and will possibly be used in the future in airports to identify passengers boarding planes. Just like the fingerprint, the retina of the human eye has a distinct design.

With the large computers, computer chips, hand scanners, and eye scanners, there is now nowhere to hide. These scanners can record and store information. However, looking back at the text in Revelation, there are three ways given by which a person can buy or sell:

◆ The *mark* of the beast

◆ The *name* of the beast

◆ The *number* of his name

THE OLDEST MANUSCRIPTS

Another interesting insight about the mark of the beast emerges when examining one of the oldest Greek manuscripts. In most of today's translations of the Holy Scriptures, the number 666 is spelled out using "six hundred, threescore and six." However, in some of the oldest manuscripts of the New Testament, the 666 is actually identified by three Greek letters.

αυτων της δεξιας, η επι των μετωπων" αυτων, 17 "και" ινα
'their   'right, or on   'foreheads 'their ;   and that

μὴ.τις δύνηται ἀγορᾶσαι ἢ πωλῆσαι, εἰ.μὴ ὁ ἔχων τὸ
no one should be able   to buy   or   to sell,   except he who has the

χάραγμα "ἢ' °τὸ ὄνομα" τοῦ θηρίου, ἢ τον ἀριθμὸν τοῦ
mark   or   the   name' of the   beast,   or   the   number

ὀνόματος αὐτοῦ. 18 ᵀ Ὧδε ἡ σοφια ἐστιν. ὁ ἔχων ᴾτὸν"
'name   ²of ²its.   Here   ²wisdom   ¹is.   He who has

νοῦν,   ψηφισάτω τον ἀριθμὸν τοῦ θηρίου· ἀριθμὸς.γὰρ
understanding let him count the   number of the beast :   for °number

ἀνθρώπου ἐστιν, καὶ ὁ.ἀριθμὸς.αὐτοῦ ꟼ ᵀχξς'."
'a 'man's   it is ; and   its number   [is]   666.

14 Καὶ ˢεἶδον," καὶ ἰδού, ᵗ ἀρνιον ᵛἐστηκὸς" ἐπὶ τὸ ὄρος
   And   I saw,   and behold, [the] Lamb   standing   upon   mount

Σιών, καὶ μετ' αὐτοῦ ἑκατὸν ᵂτεσσαράκοντα τέσσαρες"
Sion   and with him   a hundred f   ...

say of sell, save he
that had the mark, or
the name of the beast,
or the number of his
name. 18 Here is wis-
dom. Let him that
hath understanding
count the number of
the beast : for it is the
number of a man ;
and his number *is* six
hundred threescore
and six.

XIV. And I looked,
and lo a Lamb stood

Erasmus (1516) relied on twelfth- and thirteenth-century manuscripts, which represented the *Byzantine text*, the *Koine text*, or
the *Majority text*. All Greek New Testaments translated before the
middle of the fifteenth century were copied by hand, using one of
these three manuscripts.

After the middle of the fifteenth century, modern versions of the
Greek New Testament were based on the *Byzantine* manuscript,
also known as the *Textus Receptus*, compiled by Erasmus in 1516,
or on the *Novum Testamentum Graece*, edited by Eberhardt Nestle
in 1898.

For three hundred years—until the 1900s, the *Textus Receptus*
remained the main text. It is the text used by the 1611 King James
translators of the Bible, who translated the first English Bible that
was approved by the king. When the early fathers quoted from the
Greek New Testament, we know they used the manuscript identified as the Byzantine text, also known by the name *Textus Receptus*.

In an old Greek manuscript, the mark of the beast is identified by
three Greek letters, known as *chi*, *xi*, and *stigma*. These three letters
are found in the third-century Egyptian text and in the Majority
text. Modern Greek spells out these letters. It was in the later 1800s
that Nestle, instead of using these three letters, added up the numerical value of these letters to total 666.

The reason for the number 600, 60, and 6 (666) is the gematria of the three Greek letters. The letter *chi* has the Greek numerical value of 600. The letter *xi* has a value of 60, and the letter *stigma* has a value of 6. Thus the three Greek letters penned in the oldest manuscript of Revelation 13:18 totals to 666. The Greek letter *chi* has a form similar to the Hebrew letter *tav*, the twenty-second and final letter of the Hebrew alphabet. The latter *chi* appears as an *X*, and the ancient form of *tav* is a + or an *X*. The Greek title *Christ* begins with the letter *chi* (*X*). In the early Roman church, the letter *chi-rho* was the mark or monogram of Christian Rome.

The second Greek letter found in the Revelation manuscript is the letter *xi*. This letter is transliterated as the *x*. Our English letter *x* is the same form as the letter *tav* in Hebrew and *chi* in Greek. The numerical value of *xi* is 60.

The final letter is unique. According to commentaries on the Greek New Testament, there are twenty-four letters in the Greek alphabet plus three archaic letters, one of which is the *digamma*, also known as the *stigma*. The letter *stigma* is not used in modern Greek; today it is the letter *sigma*. In ancient times, it was used as the sixth letter of the Greek alphabet. It was used as a letter to represent the number 6. The *stigma* was also a mark that was placed on slaves in the Roman period. The *stigma* is transliterated as the letter *s*, and its number equivalent is 6.

The standard gematria for the Greek alphabet is as follows:[5]

Greek Letter	Greek Name	Numeric Value
A, α	*Alpha*	1
B, β	*Beta*	2
Γ, γ	*Gamma*	3
Δ, δ	*Delta*	4
E, ε	*Epsilon*	5
		6 is *sigma*, ς final form

Greek Letter	Greek Name	Numeric Value
Z, ζ	Zeta	7
H, η	Eta	8
Θ, θ	Theta	9
I, ι	Iota	10
K, κ	Kappa	20
Λ, λ	Lamda	30
M, μ	Mu	40
N, ν	Nu	50
Ξ, ξ	Xi	60
O, o	Omikron	70
Π, π	Pi	80
		90 is ϙ
P, ρ	Rho	100
Σ, σ, ς	Sigma	6, 200
T, τ	Tau	300
Y, υ	Upsilon	400
Φ, φ	Phi	500
X, χ	Chi	600
Ψ, ψ	Psi	700
Ω, ω	Omega	800
		900 = sampsi ϡ

What is the reason for using these three Greek letters and not just the number 666? Barnes comments:

> There can be no doubt that the number 666 is the correct reading, though it would seem that this was sometimes expressed in letters, and sometimes written in full. Wetstein supposes that both methods were used by John; that in the first copy of his book he used the letters, and in a subsequent copy wrote it in full.[6]
>
> —BARNES' NOTES ON REVELATION 13:18

The fact is that no one has been able to give a clear, solid understanding as to the actual prophetic meaning of these three Greek letters and how they will fit into the name, number, or mark of the beast. However, there may be a rather bizarre "link" between the form or shape of these three letters and possible symbols that are connected to the Islamic religion.

COULD THE LETTERS BE SYMBOLS?

All twenty-two letters of the Hebrew alphabet are not only used to form words, but each individual letter also has a particular symbol it represents. The first letter, *aleph*, represents an ox. The second letter, *beit*, represents a house, and the third letter, *gimel*, represents a camel. The symbols predate the time when the alphabet took on the form of letters. Before letters, it was first represented in the form of symbols in the same manner that the Egyptians used hieroglyphics, or word pictures, which when *read* revealed a message.

Is it possible that these three Greek letters—*chi*, *xi*, and *stigma*—are actually hidden clues that reveal certain symbols that give us more insight on the future beast and his religion?

Greek Letters Representing "666" (Revelation 13:18–Byzantine Text)		
Χ	ξ	ς
CHI	XI	STIGMA
600	60	6

Chi

The first of the three Greek letters is the letter *chi*. This letter takes on the form of a symbol that looks like the English letter *x*. In Greek, this letter has a *ch* sound and is the first two letters in the Greek word *Christos*, a Greek word meaning *Christ*. If this letter is intended to be a *mark* or a *symbol*, is there a link in some nation or religion that would use an emblem or mark similar to the letter *chi*?

It is interesting to note that the Saudi Arabian civil ensign is in the form of two swords that cross one another, laid out over a green background. Saudi Arabia is the most important nation on Earth in relation to the Islamic religion. It is where Islam's prophet, Muhammad, received his revelations that formed the Islamic religion at Mecca, located in Arabia and presently the world headquarters for all Muslims. Mecca houses the famous Ka'ba, where millions of Muslims each year perform the *hajj* (pilgrimage). Saudi Arabia is also the home to Medina, where Muhammad is buried. Saudi Arabia is such a strict Islamic nation that all other religions are suppressed, and any other form of religious worship other than Islam is forbidden and even punishable by prison and in some cases by death. Certain punishments have been met by beheading, which is permissible under certain circumstances according to the Quran.

Xi

It is quite interesting to observe the form of the second Greek letter used in Revelation 13:18, the Greek letter *xi*.

Former Muslims have noted that the Greek letter *xi* was very similar in appearance to the Arabic letter that forms the name *Allah*, the name for God used worldwide among all Muslims. The name *Allah* is the Arabic name for God and is the name all Muslims use when speaking of God. Christians will use the term "the Lord" or simply say "God." Jews use the name *Adonai*, which is a common name for the God of Abraham. The Muslims, however, use the name *Allah*.

All Muslims will tell you that this name Allah is the name of the same God worshiped by both Jews and Christians. However, scholars note that the name Allah was actually not a name formed by Muhammad but was the name of a pre-Islamic moon deity that was worshiped in pre-Islamic times among the Arabs throughout the Arabian Peninsula. Some scholars go as far as to allege that

Muhammad may have used the name Allah to help win many of the tribal people who had been involved in the worship of the moon prior to the time of Muhammad's revelations.

Stigma

The third Greek letter, *stigma*, has a form that is also a symbol of something or someone connected to the Islamic religion. As stated earlier, the *stigma* is not a letter in modern Greek, but it is a letter that was a brand placed on slaves. E. W. Bullinger states, "Now the word στίγμα (*stigma*) means *a mark*, but especially a mark made by *a brand* as burnt upon slaves, cattle, or soldiers, by their owners or masters; or on devotees who thus branded themselves as belonging to their gods."[7]

Several years ago a lamb was born in Durmen Village, Uzbekistan, just three days before a major Islamic holiday. This lamb caused quite a stir, because on the black fleece of the lamb was a white pattern that formed the Arabic word for Allah on one side and Muhammad on the other side. When the third Greek letter, *stigma*, is turned sideways, which is the way it appeared on the fleece of the lamb in Uzbekistan, then it is similar to a letter that the villagers believed represented the name *Muhammad*.

This concept, that these letters could represent symbols, may be a new idea to contemporary Christians; however, keep in mind that throughout nineteen hundred years of church history, no one has successfully broken the code of the mark during this entire period. There has been speculation that it is linked to computers, special chips, or invisible tattoos, but this mark of buying and selling is initiated by the false prophet of Revelation 13:11–18. Thus, the economic control is linked to the religion of the beast and benefits those following his orders. The mark, name, and number are three different methods employed to control the limited resources available, especially food, during the Tribulation.

It is clear that the beast empire rules in and around the

Mediterranean Sea, which is a stronghold for the Islamic faith. If these three letters are symbols, as some former Muslims suggest, then:

1. The letter *chi* could allude to a symbol of two swords used in Saudi Arabia, the headquarters of the Islamic religion.

2. The letter *xi* could refer to the name of the god that will be worshiped during the time of the Tribulation.

3. The mysterious letter *stigma* could refer to the mark that will be used on the right hand and forehead enslaving the followers of the Antichrist during the Tribulation.

Remember, the *chi, xi, stigma* together represent the number of a man.

THE NUMBER SIX

Throughout the Bible, numbers have had special meanings. For example, the number three refers to unity:

◆ Faith, hope, and love

◆ Body, soul, and spirit

◆ Outer court, inner court, and holy of holies

The number seven is found 463 times in the Bible. Seven always alludes to fullness and completion and is often found alluding to some form of perfection. It has been called God's perfect number. Other numbers, such as twelve, allude to government and divine order. There were twelve tribes of Israel, twelve disciples, and twenty-four elders (twelve times two). The number six is recognized as the number of man. God formed man on the sixth day of Creation (Gen. 1:27–31). Man was given six days to work and was to rest on the seventh (Exod. 20:9–10). Goliath, the giant from Gath, was six cubits and a span, with a description of six weapons, including the head of his spear, which weighed six hundred shekels of iron (1 Sam. 17:4–7).

The image set up by Nebuchadnezzar in Babylon (a picture of the future image of the beast) was sixty cubits high and the breadth was six cubits (Dan. 3:1).

It is unique how the number six is linked to the Islamic religion.

- Muhammad was forced to flee from Mecca to Medina in the year 622 (the *Hijra*).

- Muslims worship on the sixth day of the week (Friday).

- Muhammad's name can total to 666.

It may seem a coincidence that the number six has a link to the Islamic faith, but consider how the number seven is connected to the Jewish people. The religious Jews worship on the seventh day, have a jubilee every seventh year, and were commanded to honor a national jubilee every seven times seven years (Lev. 25). When considering the significance of a mark that would seal the followers of a future world dictator, I realize many people will simply "blow off" this particular theory. While I am not personally dogmatic on this concept, I am offering it to you as a topic to consider and investigate on your own; I believe there is merit for its consideration.

A Name, a Number, and a Mark

The forehead and the right hand

When Muslims pray, they bow facing toward Mecca in Saudi Arabia. The more pious Muslims will press their forehead against the floor, eventually creating a light red spot on the center of the forehead. Devout Muslims also carry prayer beads with them and move the beads with their fingers as they pray.

Sanctions against nations

In the past, the United Nations Security Council has voted to place sanctions upon certain nations involved with building weapons of mass destruction or the slaying of multitudes of innocent victims under the command of a ruthless dictator. At other times, the United States has placed economic sanctions or blocks upon other nations, such as Iran, Libya, and Iraq, for supporting terrorism or selling dangerous weapons.

Often these imposed sanctions have little impact upon the dictator or leadership of the nation, but they have a terrible impact upon the average families living in the nation. Necessary items such as medicine, baby formula, diapers, and basic food staples are in short supply and high demand. The average citizen suffers, but the leader uses his connections in the black market to smuggle into the country everything his heart desires through poorly monitored borders.

Part of the anger against the West, especially against the United States, is caused by the sanctions placed for many years on Islamic countries. Much of the Arab and Islamic world see these as political tools to kill the nation's poor and those dependent upon Western powers to survive. Because of the propaganda they are given, they are unaware that the sanctions are placed to pressure the dictator/ruler to act in a civilized manner. The propaganda machine emphasizes the evils of the West and reveals the negative impact upon the children and their parents.

This future mark of the beast will be a *reverse sanction*. No man can buy or sell without the mark, name, or the number of the beast. The ultimate option of not receiving the mark is death by beheading (Rev. 20:4). Thus, if the Antichrist is supported by or descended from an Islamic background, Islam will have its own form of retaliation by controlling ten nations and the economic power.

THE TWO MOST VALUABLE ASSETS

I am not an economist, a specialist in the stock market, or an investor. For more than thirty-four years of ministry, I have placed all income from offerings or book and tape resource sales back into my ministry. I have numerous friends and associates who are quite informed in the areas of investments. Presently, there are several areas where investors have placed strong emphasis.

For several years the stock market has been on a roller-coaster ride, climbing, then suddenly dipping, leaving investors with a strange feeling in the pit of their stomach as they try to catch their breath when the market graph begins sliding toward the low end. Unseen variables such as terror attacks, corporate scandals, and sudden loss of jobs can cause loss of thousands of dollars to common investors.

Others say that investing in land is the best future investment. My grandfather owned several pieces of rental property, which were a source of income for him and my grandmother, especially in their latter years. Single dwellers and families will always need apartments, duplexes, and houses to rent and to own. However, any major recession, depression, and job market slash can impact this area. On many occasions my grandfather had men staying in his apartments who had lost their mining jobs and were unable to pay the rent for several months.

There are some who insist that a percentage of a person's portfolio should be in precious metals, including silver and gold bullion or coins. History does note that in times of economic crisis, precious metals seem to do well as investments. Of course, a person must know someone who is willing to purchase what he has. During the Great Depression, the American government established a food rationing system. Families received food ration stamps each month. The stamps limited the amount of bread, sugar, wheat, and lard a family could purchase.

In examining the future according to the prophecies, there are two items that every human being must have, and I know of few if any people who are making investments in these two items—*food and water.*

As mentioned earlier, during the time of the coming Tribulation, there will be extended famines and disasters that will impact the sea, land, grass, trees, and water, resulting in global hunger. A national famine always produces civil unrest and eventual hunger and possible starvation to the masses.

The Euphrates River, a life source for those living along the Fertile Crescent, which runs the length of Iraq, will dry up. Thousands of farmers and farming communities that thrive along the banks of this famous river will cease to exist during this severe drought.

In the future, it will be food and water that will become the valuable assets. We can live without stocks, mutual funds, property investments, and gold coins. However, the human body must have water and food. Whoever can own and control the future supply of food and water will be able to gain the respect of people.

This is clearly demonstrated in third-world countries. We know of missionaries who personally travel to remote regions on the earth and feed the hungry in nations where the poor and unloved are allowed to starve in the streets. One missionary feeds lepers, and another, a pastor of a twelve-thousand-member youth group, left the multitudes of believers to whom he had been ministering to feed two thousand Muslims a day. The love demonstrated by these Christians has touched the hearts of those they feed, until many have turned their hearts to Christ!

It is clear that controlling the food and water supplies will be the key to the beast's kingdom controlling the masses, as he rations food through his own economical system.

Let's wrap up with a summary of the evidence in Scripture:

1. The beast will arise out of the Great Sea region, which is the Mediterranean (Dan. 7:1–2).

2. The beast will arise out of the territory of the former empires of biblical prophecy (Dan. 8:1–9).

3. The beast will turn against the Jews and attempt to destroy them (Dan. 12:7).

4. The beast will behead those who resist his system of rule and refuse to worship him (Rev. 20:4).

5. The beast is great toward the east, the south, and in Israel (Dan. 8:9).

6. The beast will split control of Jerusalem into two parts (Zech. 14:2).

7. The beast will demand worship and issue his own economic system (Rev. 13:17–18).

As we observe the times in which we live and the alignment of nations along with the expectations of Muslims around the world, anticipating the reforming of an Islamic empire and the arrival of the Mahdi, there is little doubt of the role of a future Islamic dictator and that somehow the mark of the beast will come into play during the final forty-two months of his rule.

FANATICAL ISLAM'S PLAN
TO CONTROL THE WORLD

"Who is like the beast? Who is able to make war with him?"
And he was given a mouth speaking great things and blas-
phemies, and he was given authority to continue for forty-
two months. Then he opened his mouth in blasphemy
against God, to blaspheme His name, His tabernacle, and
those who dwell in heaven. It was granted to him to make
war with the saints and to overcome them. And authority
was given him over every tribe, tongue, and nation.
                                          —REVELATION 13:4–7

F IFTY YEARS AGO, THE VERY THOUGHT THAT A MILITANT
    Islamic leader could unite a radical Islamic coalition into a
feared global threat would have been considered a severe stretch
of fiction. Twenty-five years ago, the possibility of a violent Middle
Eastern dictator gaining access to weapons of mass destruction was
discussed among military brass behind closed doors. Today, the
threat is not *if* this possibility exists but *when* a frightening assault
with weapons of mass destruction will come.

All religions have a commission to teach others about their beliefs, and this includes the Islamic religion. Their agenda is both practical and prophetic. The practical plan is to expand the Islamic crescent from its Middle East stronghold into Europe and Asia, eventually dominating the large cities in North America. The prophetic agenda is to ensure that the predictions and traditions of its founder, Muhammad, are fulfilled. In Muhammad's day the Islamic religion grew by the use of the sword and forced conversion. Today it grows through large Muslim families, conversion, and, in some countries, forced conversion. Despite the smooth tongues of educated Muslims who tell the West not to worry, the sword of fanatical Islam is once again slashing its way through nations, slaying the *infidels* who would resist conversion to the religion of Allah. As the Quran says:

> The punishment of those who wage war against Allah and His Messenger, and strive with might and main for mischief through the land is: execution, or crucifixion, or the cutting off of the hands and feet from opposite sides, or exile from the land.
>
> —Surah 5:33

It was once thought impossible that small, third-world nations would ever become a threat to modern democratic nations. After all, America and the Soviet Union were the two superpowers possessing weapons that created mushroom clouds with devastating impact. After the fall of communism, the Soviet Union became a black marketer's dream. Weapons were exchanged for drugs and much needed money.

In the early nineties one source informed me that the Iraqi government had hired more than five hundred former Soviet Union scientists who were working on Iraq's weapons program. These included several men knowledgeable in the development of nuclear weapons. Today, numerous Islamic nations are on the road to nuclear weapons development, including rogue nations such as Iran.

HOSTAGE TO THE WEAPONS

Imagine this scenario. A Middle Eastern diplomat working at the United Nations has secretly arranged to have certain packages delivered into the United States via a foreign cargo ship. The individual packages are as small as a briefcase. Upon arrival, a contact intercepts the packages, delivering them to the *proper* sources. Within a few months, a small nuclear bomb has been built and hidden in Brooklyn, New York.

On the West Coast, another *cell agent* has arranged for a series of packages to arrive via ship to a specific location. This package holds five sealed vials of a deadly biological plague. The vials are secured at an undisclosed location until a coded signal is given.

A third *cell leader* effectively crosses the Mexican border into Texas with the assistance of the M-13 Mexican gang. He too is carrying a special chemical, called *X-1*. It is a nerve agent that can be released in the air without being detected. The deadly chemical is placed in a secure room in an apartment building, shared by two men who are part of the numerous *sleeper cells* Americans have been warned about for months.

On a predetermined signal, the head of an Islamic coalition from the Middle East contacts the United States president, demanding that he pressure the Israelis to once and for all pull out of Palestinian territories and get out of East Jerusalem. He demands that within seven days Israel release to the international community all information and location of their nuclear weapons. If the American government and Israel fail to respond within seven days, the nuclear bomb will be released in the largest Jewish community in the world—Brooklyn, New York. The biological agents will be spread across Los Angeles and in Houston, Texas. Because the sleeper agents were careful to conceal their arsenal, no one in our federal or state governments knows where the dangerous bomb and the deadly biological substances are hidden. Suddenly America is held hostage by an invisible threat. The fear factor strikes at the hearts of Americans as, on the evening news, the media leak the possibilities of millions of deaths resulting from this possible attack.

What does the president do? If he says no, then he will be blamed for millions of Americans' deaths. What do you think the average American would do? I believe American citizens would force Israel to do what the terrorists have demanded. After all, they reason, why should Americans suffer for what a group of Jews are doing ten thousand miles away in another country?

The above scenario taking place is not impossible. In fact, it is quite probable. All Muslims desire the *liberation* of Jerusalem and want Israel replaced by the Palestinian state—including the physical removal or death of the Jewish population. This may be why the biblical prophet Zechariah said Jerusalem would become "a cup of trembling unto all the people round about" (Zech. 12:2, KJV). The prophet also predicted that Jerusalem would become a "burdensome stone for all people" (v. 3, KJV). This verse infers that dealing with Jerusalem will be like carrying a huge, very heavy stone on one's shoulders.

All methods of expulsion of Jews from Jerusalem have, and will, fail—until the intrusion of the Antichrist. He and his people will successfully *liberate* Jerusalem from the *infidels*. His success will be his ability to merge a coalition and successfully hold nations hostage with his spectacular arsenal of weapons.

THE ANTICHRIST AND HIS WEAPONS

In Revelation 13, John announced the appearance of the beast and his kingdom. John poses the questions, "Who is like the beast? Who is able to make war with him?" (Rev. 13:4). Later in the same prophetic book, we read where the beast and his ten kings destroy a large city in one hour (Rev. 18:10, 17, 19). This powerful blast produces a "smoke" that creates fear in the hearts of those who are standing "afar off" observing the destruction (vv. 9–10, 18, KJV). Within one hour these ten kings will give their kingdoms (nations) over to the beast (Rev. 17:12). After carefully researching the chapters alluding to these passages, I believe the reason nations submit to the beast is the fear that he will destroy both the leaders and their people who resist him. This is how Saddam was successful in retaining power in Iraq. He murdered thousands of his own people, including anyone who disagreed with his mode of operation.

The biblical prophets visualized many wars prior to the return of the Messiah. During these battles, men would die in a manner unknown to the prophet. Imagine when Zechariah saw the vision of the final battle for Jerusalem and how men would die:

> And this shall be the plague with which the LORD will strike all the people who fought against Jerusalem:
>
> Their flesh shall dissolve while they stand on their feet,
> Their eyes shall dissolve in their sockets,
> And their tongues shall dissolve in their mouths.
> —ZECHARIAH 14:12

This prophecy alludes to the time when the armies of the Antichrist are surrounding Jerusalem. Some say the flesh of men melting alludes to the moment that Christ returns, when, by the brightness of His coming, He destroys the global armies, thus eliminating those who would attempt to exterminate the Jews (2 Thess. 1:1–10). Others believe it reveals a weapon of unbelievable power that literally melts human flesh while people are still standing on their feet. This verse may be alluding to a neutron bomb, whose explosion literally melts the flesh from a human body. Such weapons, nonexistent in Zechariah's day, are now locked in silos on military bases!

China, North Korea, and Russia are actively selling ballistic missiles to Middle Eastern nations, including Iran. The real danger is not a traditional ballistic missile but a missile warhead tipped with biological, chemical, or nuclear weapons.

After the Gulf War, United Nations inspectors entered Iraq and were shocked to discover 50 chemical-filled ballistic warheads, 12,694 mustard gas–filled artillery shells, and over 10,000 sarin-filled artillery shells and rocket warheads. They also discovered 300 tons of bulk agents ready for use.[1]

All of this with Saddam claiming he had no "weapons of mass destruction"!

The future beast will use his own stash of weapons to institute his own forms of justice on surrounding nations. No one will be successful in conquering him or stopping his progress of taking possession of nations. This is why Daniel identified this beast as "exceedingly dreadful" (Dan. 7:19). Daniel said this man would use peace to destroy many.

> Through his cunning
> He shall cause deceit to prosper under his rule;
> And he shall exalt himself in his heart.
> He shall destroy many in their prosperity.
> He shall even rise against the Prince of princes;
> But he shall be broken without human means.
> —DANIEL 8:25

Daniel is saying that through the Antichrist's knowledge, he will be successful with deceiving many. This deceit will be linked to his so-called peace agreements, which will eventually be broken. Daniel 11:27 paints a picture of deception through negotiating:

> Both these kings' hearts shall be bent on evil, and they shall speak lies at the same table; but it shall not prosper, for the end will still be at the appointed time.

The Antichrist will initiate a covenant (a firm agreement) for one "week" (Dan. 9:27). The Hebrew word *week* is *shabuwa´* and alludes to a week of years—or seven years. The Antichrist will lie and break the agreement in the middle of the seven years, invading Jerusalem and setting up an image of himself to be worshiped by his followers (Rev. 13:14–15). Daniel saw the process:

> Then he shall confirm a covenant with many for one
>   week;
> But in the middle of the week
> He shall bring an end to sacrifice and offering.
> And on the wing of abominations shall be one who
>   makes desolate,
> Even until the consummation, which is determined,
> Is poured out on the desolate.
>
> —DANIEL 9:27

> And through his policy also he shall cause craft to prosper in his hand; and he shall magnify himself in his heart, and by peace shall destroy many: he shall also stand up against the Prince of princes; but he shall be broken without hand.
>
> —DANIEL 8:25, KJV

The Antichrist will promise peace, yet "by peace shall destroy many." The word for *peace* in this passage literally means *security*. He will tell people they will have security if they follow him. How ironic that this is the same theme the Palestinians use when negotiating with the Israelis. Israel demands security, and the Palestinians promise "land for peace." Just as the Oslo peace accords collapsed, the future promises of peace signed by Islamic nations with Israel will be a covenant of deceit. The word for *destroy* in this passage means *ruin* or *decay*. This passage could read, "And promising security he will ruin many."

It may seem strange, but some Muslims are expecting peace treaties to be signed, after which the Mahdi will rule for seven years.

The Prophet Muhammad reportedly said:

> Al Mahdi will be from my progeny. His forehead will be broad and his nose will be high. He will fill the world with justice and fairness at a time when the world will be filled with oppression. He will rule for seven years...large number of people from Iraq will come to him and pledge their allegiance to him.... This person (Imam Mahdi) will distribute the spoils of war after the battle. He will lead the people according to the Sunnat and during his reign Islam will spread throughout the world. He will remain till seven years (since his emergence). He will pass away.[2]

Another interesting observation is made in the following statement:

> There will be four peace agreements between you and the Romans. The fourth agreement will be mediated through a person who will be from the progeny of Hadhrat Haroon (A.S.) and will be upheld for seven years.[3]

Three observations can be made from these Islamic traditions:

1. They believe a peace agreement will be signed and upheld for seven years.

2. The agreements will come after a major war.

3. The Mahdi will rule for seven years (some teach longer); then he will die.

Now, compare these traditions with the various revelations given in Scripture concerning the last days and the kingdom of the Antichrist.

1. The coming dictator signs a peace treaty for seven years (Dan. 9:27).

2. The treaty will be signed after major wars in the Middle East (Ezek. 39:9).

3. The man who signs the treaty will be destroyed at the end of the seven years (Rev. 19:20).

Muslims have not taken their traditions from the Bible, but their expectations of the Mahdi are very similar to the predictions found in the prophetic books of the Scriptures. The common question is, How will surrounding Arab-Muslim nations make peace with Israel when there is such hatred between these two ancient relatives?

THE TIMING OF A FALSE PEACE

At the present time, many Islamic nations are uninterested in a true peace with Israel. The majority is supporting the Intifada, an internal uprising between the Palestinians and Israelis. Others are calling for an all-out holy war (jihad) against Jews living in Palestine. (Many refer to the entire country of Israel as *Palestine*.) If Israel were to defeat surrounding nations in a major war, which they will in events prophesied in Ezekiel 38 and 39, the international community would demand a peace settlement.

During the battle of Gog and Magog, all but one-sixth of the enemy armies will be killed. This will be the greatest war victory in Israel's history. Some scholars speculate this could also be the time when Damascus, Syria, will be utterly destroyed, as predicted in Isaiah 17:1. Since 1948, Israel has fought five wars with its Arab neighbors. Syria has been involved in four of the past five conflicts.

If Syria sent a chemical or biological weapon to be released upon the Israeli population, Israel would not restrain itself from utterly destroying its enemy.

After the Gog and Magog war, many believe the seven-year agreement of Daniel 9:27 will be signed. It may be that at that time individuals connected with Hamas, Hezbollah, and other radical groups will realize that Israel, as a nation, is here to stay. They may acknowledge that future wars could mean a total annihilation of all human beings in the Middle East. Most Islamic nations will only agree to peace with Israel after a huge war, resulting in countless deaths in Muslim countries, has ended. This is one reason why I suggest that the aftermath of the war of Gog and Magog could initiate the seven-year agreement between Israel and her surrounding enemies.

I am certain that organizations like the United Nations will lead the way for a major peace treaty at the beginning of the seven-year Tribulation. This may be alluded to in Revelation 6:2, when John saw the rider on a white horse. This verse indicates this white horse rider receives a crown and power to conquer. Each time I read this I am reminded that all United Nations (UN) vehicles throughout the world are white in color. The United Nations is offering Israel and the Palestinians the opportunity to use UN security forces to guard the roads and checkpoints in Israel. The United Nations peacekeeping forces are scattered throughout the world, and the UN has power to place economic and military sanctions on entire nations, thus limiting their banking, selling, and purchasing activities.

The white horse rider goes forth to conquer. The Greek word for *conquer* in Revelation 6:2 means "to subdue." This rider introduces the seventh kingdom of prophecy, which will continue for a brief time (Rev. 17:10–11). He will ride his way across the globe, subduing nations and eventually forming his final eighth kingdom with a ten-nation coalition.

How to Destroy Using Peace

Destruction under the guise of peace was visible in Afghanistan. As long as the Afghans observed the strict laws of the Taliban, they were unharmed. If any person resisted or disagreed with even one small point of Taliban rule, they were met with swift Islamic justice. Crowds gathered in stadiums to watch people shot, hung, or beheaded for such *evils* as having a television, owning a VCR, or stealing to feed their hungry children. Even a woman who exposed her face in public faced severe punishment.

During his forty-two-month rule, the beast and his kings will control all global economics and influence world political decisions. Those who differ or oppose these policies will be beheaded (Rev. 20:4). I am certain the Antichrist will take this passage from the Quran as his inspired reason for beheading the *infidels*.

> "I will instill terror into the hearts of the Unbelievers: you smite above their necks and smite all their finger-tips off them."…It is not you who slew them; it was Allah.
> —Surah 8:12, 17

Those who will submit to his plans, purposes, and policies will be permitted to buy and sell using the "mark of the beast" (Rev. 13:17). Those rejecting the mark will be killed. The peace initiated by the Antichrist will bring survival to his followers and death to his enemies (Rev. 20:4).

According to Islamic tradition, the Mahdi will institute Islamic justice through peace. But his justice will be exacted by the sword of Islam. Anyone who rejects the Quran or Muhammad as the prophet and refuses to follow their strict, twisted concepts will be killed. Again, this accurately fits the description given by biblical prophets about the coming beast and his kingdom!

THE (ISLAMIC) SUN
WILL RISE IN THE WEST

I saw still another mighty angel coming down from heaven,
clothed with a cloud. And a rainbow was on his head,
his face was like the sun, and his feet like pillars of fire.
—REVELATION 10:1

H AVING TRAVELED TO THE MIDDLE EAST AND SPECIFICALLY
to Israel on more than thirty-two occasions, I have had
opportunity to make acquaintances with Messianic believers, Arab
Christians, secular and religious Jews, and Muslims. My Muslim
friends are some of the most considerate and friendly persons I have
encountered in the country. Some are bus drivers, others are businessmen, and all are trying to make a living for their families. They
have little or no interest in the politics occurring and get along well
with people of other religions, including Jews and Christians. In fact,
while some say they are Muslims, they seldom if ever take time to
pray five times a day, and they miss services in the mosque. Of course,
the more devout Muslims remind them they are not being a "true
Muslim."

In the West and the Middle East, Muslims can be divided into basically three categories. There are secular Muslims who are "Muslim in name only" and have been influenced by Western thought at liberal universities. Devout Muslims who keep the five main pillars of Islam—daily prayer, charity, fasting, faithfully attending the mosque, and the *hajj* (pilgrimage to Mecca, if able)—comprise the second and largest segment. The third group are Islamic fanatics, those who consider Jews and Christians infidels and believe that in the last days they must participate in jihad to kill the infidel, force conversion to Islam, and spread the Islamic religion to non-Islamic nations through terrorism, war, or any method required to eventually turn the world to Islam. A friend who served as secretary in an important federal agency once told me that they suspected up to 200 million Muslims could be classified as leaning, or possibly leaning, toward engaging in jihad.

Muslims from all three groups believe that the Islamic religion will eventually become the accepted single religion of the entire world. According to Islamic history, by 711 A.D., much of what was the old Roman Empire had come under the control of Islam. Islamic influence ran from Morocco to Persia and into Europe. At the height of the Ottoman Turkish Empire (the sixteenth and seventeenth centuries), Islam stretched over three continents, including North Africa, southeastern Europe, and the Middle East. The Turks also controlled Palestine and Jerusalem from 1517 to 1917. After World War I, the empire declined, and in 1923 it was succeeded by the Republic of Turkey. Muslims have since dreamed of restoring not just a single Islamic empire under one leader, but they want to avenge themselves of their military defeats that eventually came through France and Spain. Moderate Muslims believe Allah will make this happen in his time and by his will. Fanatical Muslims, however, believe they are given authority by Allah to kill the unbeliever and force Islam upon those who survive this jihad.

In the time of Muhammad, the "West" was considered the regions now known as Great Britain, France, Spain, and Portugal. With the rise of the United States as the leading economic and military nation on Earth, the West has taken a new direction. When Muslims in the Middle East speak of the "West," the term has become more than one nation or region of the word. It encompasses Great Britain, Spain, France, and, of course, America (and Canada). If these Western nations formed a body, then the United States would be the heart. Islam does not distinguish a separation between "religion and state," as America does with "separation of church and state." In devout Islamic countries, the state rides on the back of the religion. The nation's leaders must be Muslims, the laws are Islamic, and the Islamic religion embraces the government as the government is the mirror of Islamic law and tradition. When Muslims speak about America, most perceive the United States as a "Christian nation" whose government is dominated with and controlled by wealthy Jews or Zionists. Since the goal of Islam is to make Islam the only true religion in the world, then the West must eventually be defeated and crushed by jihad (terrorism) or converted to Islam. Knowing these concepts and Islamic ideas, I was curious to learn of an Islamic prediction relating to the last days, that the sun would one day rise in the west.

Islam has about seventy signs that indicate the "last days." Some are major, and others are considered minor in nature. Some predictions are ominous and disastrous, including many cosmic signs and signs of nature similar to signs mentioned by Christ. Muslims, Christians, and Jews consider earthquakes, plagues, and wars as "signs" of the time of the end, or the last days.

Listed among the major signs is a rather strange, curious prediction stating the sun would rise from the west:

> Allah's Apostle said, "The Hour will not be established...till the sun rises from the West. So when the

sun will rise and the people will see it (rising from the West) they will all believe (embrace Islam) but that will be the time when: (As Allah said,) 'No good will it do to a soul to believe then, if it believed not before, nor earned good (by deeds of righteousness) through its Faith.'"[1]

—SAHIH BUKHARI

After researching the possible interpretations to this prediction, I discovered there are basically three main schools of thought as to the meaning of this hadith.

The first and very common interpretation is that the literal sun will one morning rise in the west instead of the east. As evidence that this could happen, some Muslims state that the planet Mars has shifted, and consequently the sun is not rising on Mars' western side. However, the hadith prediction says nothing about Mars. Obviously it would be impossible for the sun to rise in the west as the earth's rotation causes the sun to appear on the horizon from the east.

The second interpretation is that before the world ends, Islam will spread and be received in the nations of the West. Traditionally, Islam has been strong in the eastern part of the world, especially when traveling from northern Africa eastward toward Iraq, Iran, Pakistan, and Afghanistan, and throughout the southern Russian states that were once a part of the ancient Roman Empire. The sun rising indicates the spread of Islam from the east to the west, which includes Spain, Great Britain, France, and eventually the United States. France's population is about 65 million, approximately 6 million of which are Muslims. Islam is the second largest religion in the United Kingdom, with over 1.5 million Muslims. Islam is growing in America. However, there are no reliable definitive statistics for the number of Muslims living in America. A 2001 article by Daniel Pipes in the *New York Post* made this observation:

Uncertainty has generated some wildly divergent numbers. A large 1990 demographic survey counted 1.3 million Muslims. In 1998, a Pakistani newspaper put the number at 12 million. Even the usually authoritative Yearbook of American and Canadian Churches found 527,000 American Muslims in 1996 and six times as many (3.3 million) in 1998. Needing some kind of consensus figure, Muslim organizations came up with a self-acknowledged "guestimation" of 6 million, which this year they decided to raise to 7 million.[2]

Thus, to some moderate Muslims the sun, or "light of Islam," is rising in the areas of the West with the spread of the message of Islam and the acceptance of the religion among the Western nations.

The third interpretation is perhaps the most intriguing. Several years ago while ministering in Pensacola, Florida, I watched the head of the Nation of Islam, Minister Louis Farrakhan, teaching about the spread of Islam. The Nation of Islam's national headquarters is located in Chicago, Illinois, and provides thousands of votes to any politician running for office in the Chicago area or in the state of Illinois. When a handsome and bright young man, Barack Obama, was running for state senator in 1996 to serve the Thirteenth District, the area included Chicago's South Side neighborhoods, "including areas in which Farrakhan was considered to be highly influential."[3]

At the conclusion of Farrakhan's televised message he quoted the prediction that the sun would rise in the west. As I understand his interpretation, he suggested that a special messenger would arise in the West (America) and help spread the light of Islam into the darkened minds of the American (the Western) population. As I listened carefully, I sensed that Minister Farrakhan was suggesting that he might be the "sun" that would impact the West.

The Emblem of the Rising Sun

When Senator Barack Obama began campaigning in the primaries, several interesting facts were brought to the surface by those wanting to learn more about this "dynamic and charismatic" African American candidate. It was known that he was born in Honolulu, Hawaii, on August 4, 1961, to Ann Dunham, a white American from Wichita, Kansas, and Barack Obama Sr., who was from Kenya. When Obama was two years old, his parents separated and later divorced. His biological father returned to Kenya and was killed in an automobile accident in 1982. Barack's mother eventually married Lolo Soetoro, an Indonesian student, and eventually the family moved to Indonesia where Obama attended school until age ten. Returning to Hawaii, he lived with his maternal grandparents from 1971 to 1979, graduating from high school.

Obama eventually graduated with a BA from Columbia University in 1983. After four years in New York, he moved to Chicago to work with church-based community organizations. He eventually entered law school at Harvard in 1988, and graduated *magna cum laude* in 1991 with a doctor of laws degree (JD). The list of accomplishments continues, until he reached the pinnacle of his career and became an instant American legend by becoming America's first African American president.

During the primaries, opponents of Obama were quick to call attention to several points of "interest" that were made public. The first was that the senator's nickname was Barry, but Obama later demanded he be called by his formal name, Barack. It was pointed out that Barack is a deviation of Barak and is an Islamic name and was the name of Muhammad's horse. The Islam name means "lightning." I pointed out that Barack was also a biblical name (spelled Barak), found in the Book of Judges, chapters 4 and 5. During the campaign it was claimed by some that Senator Obama's father and stepfather were Muslims (although "others" claimed they were nonpracticing Muslims). The third point was Barack's middle name was Hussein, the same exact name of the former president of Iraq, Saddam *Hussein*. Soon the secular media made it clear that anyone calling the senator Barack *Hussein* Obama was attempting to scare the American people and attempting to link the senator to the Islamic religion.

The senator's campaign made it clear that his present faith was Christianity and that he had been a member of one church, Trinity United Church of Christ, for twenty years. The interest in Obama's religion led to investigating the messages and background of the pastor, Rev. Jeremiah Wright. According to an article written in March 2007 by Ryan Lizza, senior editor at *The New Republic*, "...Wright was a former Muslim and black nationalist who had studied at Howard and Chicago..."[4] Other journalists dug into the church's website, bulletins, magazines, and recorded sermons and alleged that the church had posted a Hamas manifesto in the church's bulletin. It was also noted that Wright was a very close friend with Louis Farrakhan, the radical leader of the Nation of Islam, who once called Jews "blue-eyed devils" and white people "white devils"—the same Louis Farrakhan who had spoken on television after 9/11 about the sun rising in the west.

During the primaries and even after Senator Obama became the Democratic nominee for president, there was much behind-the-scenes concern in his campaign that just the perception of an "alleged Islamic link," or at least the perception that Obama may have strong secret links to Muslims, could hurt the possibilities of Obama becoming president. Contacts inside of Israel reported there were questions among key Israeli military personal and Knesset members as to whether or not Obama would continue his support for Israel and how would he react if another possible war were to erupt in Islamic nations, such as Iran. The concern among some Israelis grew as occasionally leaders in Muslim nations in and around the region began to make speeches to their audiences and address the possible future president as, "Our brother Muslim Obama." To these individuals, a man who has a Muslim father is automatically a Muslim himself by birth, unless the birth son confesses publicly to another religion. An article in *USA Today* summed up the feeling of American Muslims:

> After months of balancing their support for the presidential candidate with concerns that their allegiance could do more harm than good, millions of relieved Muslims cheered the election of the son of a Muslim immigrant whose middle name is Hussein.[5]

During the presidential campaign, the apprehensions among some Obama opponents reached a peak when something interesting was noted about a seal that had been created in Chicago for the Obama campaign.

The Symbols in the Seal

The Obama campaign eventually introduced a special seal that became the campaign logo. While the imagery of the seal can be interpreted one way to all living in the West, to a Muslim with a "prophetic imagination," some suggested the seal could have sent a "cryptic" or hidden message. The seal was the letter *O* (representing the *O* in *Obama*) with a rising sun within the circle. The explanation given was that it represented the sun rising on a new day in America, representing hope. When exploring the Internet during the campaign, I found where the Associated Press said this about the new seal (emphasis is mine):

> A new seal debuted on Obama's podium Friday, sporting iconography used in the U.S. presidential seal, the blue background, the eagle clutching arrows on

*left and olive branch on right, but with symbolic dif-
ferences. Instead of the Latin "E pluribus unum" (Out
of many, one), Obama's says, "Vero possumus," rough
Latin for "Yes, we can." Instead of "Seal of the President of the United States," Obama's website address is
listed. And instead of a shield, Obama's eagle wears
his "O" campaign logo with a rising sun representing
hope ahead.*[6]

The newly designed large eagle emblem, similar to the presidential
seal, was massively criticized during the primaries and was immediately dropped by the campaign. However, the large "O" with the
rising sun remained as the main logo throughout the primaries until
the election of President Obama. I doubt that few if any people in
America would have questioned if there was a "cryptic message"
being sent to Muslims throughout the world that the anticipated and
predicted "sun was now rising in the west." I knew of the Islamic
hadith and also noticed the unique seal with the rising sun. However, the "conspiracy" that this seal was a secret message seemed to
fail in the fact that no single Muslim, Islamic leader, or news agency
from any Islamic nation noted the rising sun or made a comment
concerning it. However, the leader of the Nation of Islam made a
very controversial statement.

Prior to the election, Rush Limbaugh reported that Louis Farrakhan used a controversial term when describing Senator Obama. In
a transcript posted on Limbaugh's website, Farrakhan, addressing
an audience, said, "You are the instruments that God is going to use
to bring about universal change. And this is why that Barack has
captured the youth. And he has involved young people in a political
process that they didn't care anything about. That's a sign. When
the Messiah speaks, the youth will hear. And the Messiah is absolutely speaking."[7] In the Christian faith, the word *Messiah* comes
from a Hebrew word that means "anointed one." There is only one

true Messiah, and that is Jesus Christ. However, Scripture warns that false prophets and false christs would appear (Matt. 24:24). The individuals would be religious leaders who would lead people astray from the truth.

Why would the leader of the largest black Islamic movement in America call at that time a presidential candidate the Messiah? It was reported on Worldnetdaily.com that senior staffers with the Obama campaign were members of the Nation of Islam.[8] When combining the Islamic link in Obama's family, his name, his former pastor's past, the friendship of Farrakhan, and the seal, it added fuel to the controversy and suggestions that Obama was a "secret Muslim" who would eventually compromise with our enemies. The statement that "the Messiah is absolutely speaking" could lead one to believe that Farrakhan has accepted Obama as the "sun rising in the west."

Let me personally state that I believe Obama has accepted the Christian faith and is not a "secret Muslim," as some suggest. He has numerous minister friends, especially in the African American community. It is evident that President Obama is completely familiar with black Christian churches and their pastors, having worked in Chicago. He was sworn in using Abraham Lincoln's Bible (not the Quran) and allowed Rick Warren to use the name of Jesus in the inaugural prayer. I do, however, see how his family background could assist him in being easily accepted and warmly received in moderate Islamic nations.

POLITICALLY AND RELIGIOUSLY CORRECT

Christians who acknowledge a born-again experience also believe that Jesus Christ is the way, the truth, and the life, and that He is the only mediator between God and man (John 14:6; 1 Tim. 2:5). We believe that if any other religion that preceded Christianity or followed Christianity was sufficient to bring mankind into an eternal relationship with God, then the death and resurrection of Christ would not be needed. It is clear that all other religions, while they may contain elements of truth, fell completely short in their teachings and among their followers, thus the need for the Messiah and the Redeemer.

America is now in the season of not just being politically correct but also of becoming "spiritually correct." It is taboo to teach that Christ is the only Savior and that the Christian faith has the premium on truth. Today we are informed that all religions are a path in the same direction that ends at the gates of heaven. According to this watered-down theology, no one is a "sinner," and a good moral person has the same right to enter the pearly gates as a dedicated Christian. The prevailing attitude is that God would never send a person to hell (although Hitler is there). It is this type of liberal theology that will eventually deny that Christ is the Son of God and introduce the spirit of antichrist to the world (1 John 2:18, 22; 4:3). In the Book of Revelation, a future religious leader identified as the lamb with two horns will merge two major religions together under his control (Rev. 13:11–18). I believe those two religions will be apostate Christianity and Islam. For Muslims to receive an alleged Christian leader, the leader must deny that Christ is the Son of God, since 1.4 billion Muslims deny that Jesus is God's Son and teach that "Allah is not begotten neither does he beget."

It stands to reason that at some point a noted world leader must arise on the global scene who promotes peace and unity among all faiths. I am certainly able to get along with anyone who chooses to get along with me, despite our political or religious differences. However, when the divinity of Christ is rejected and the Savior becomes just a good man or just another prophet, then I will stand for Christ! Since the future "lamb with two horns" rules from Jerusalem, and the two religions with the largest followers in Middle East and Europe are traditional Christianity and Islam, then any leader with both religions in his background would be an excellent forerunner to prepare for the future fulfillment of the prophetic scriptures.

From a biblical and prophetic perspective, there will be several wars that will transpire in the future, including wars involving Israel and her internal and external enemies. Eventually, however, there will be major peace treaties signed with Israel and her surrounding enemy nations. It is yet to be seen how long President Obama will serve, what wars he will encounter during his administration, and what treaties will be signed under his leadership. We must remember that there is a false peace that will prevail prior to the final End Time events. It may be that it will take a leader with the sort of dual religious background (Islamic and Christian) of our president to help create the climate needed to bring the Muslims and the Jews together at the same table. The election of the forty-fourth president may be much more prophetic than anyone realizes. It is also important for all believers to remember this passage:

> Blessed be the name of God forever and ever, for wisdom and might are His. And He changes the times and the seasons; He removes kings and raises up kings; He gives wisdom to the wise and knowledge to those who have understanding.
>
> —DANIEL 2:20–21

ISLAM SPREADING IN THE WEST

America is a melting pot and a mixed multitude of nations. Prior to 1963, any children immigrating to America from foreign nations attended a public school where each morning they heard a Bible story read and heard a prayer offered to God, often concluding in the name of Christ. Through the influence and political pressure of an outspoken and radical atheist named Madalyn Murray O'Hair, both prayer and Bible reading were removed from our public schools by a decision of the US Supreme Court. Prior to this time, anyone coming to America understood this nation to be a *Christian nation*, with moral and spiritual values based upon the Bible. Many early immigrants arriving from Europe were Catholic, Protestant, or Orthodox Christian in their faith. During the past fifty years, millions of immigrants from the Middle East, Asia, and India have begun pouring into America, bringing with them Islamic, Hindu, and other religious faiths to the United States.

After 1963–1964, as people from other faiths began pouring into the nation, they no longer heard a story from Scripture or a prayer prayed to our God. Thus they continued to follow their own religious indoctrination, continually growing families in many of the major cities in America. Our nation is based upon religious freedom, and true Christians would never force conversion upon anyone. Conversion is a matter of personal faith and a personal decision.

Many Muslims settle in America and build their homes, families, and businesses. There are, however, various individuals and groups whose motives for being here have nothing to do with becoming a prosperous American citizen, and they refuse to blend in to any type of American tradition or culture or assimilation.

Once such person is Abdul Alim Musa, a Washington DC imam who has stated that he is working to replace the US government with an Islamic state by 2050. He has stated he will establish a complete way of Islamic life in the United States.[9] The Council on American Islamic Relations (CAIR) chairman has stated, "Islam isn't in America to be equal to any other faith, but to become dominant."[10] He is also reported to have said, "I hope to see an Islamic government over the U.S. one day."

The plans that many Muslims have for America include (but are not limited to):

- ◆ Establish mosques in every city
- ◆ Call on society to embrace and accept Islam
- ◆ Establish full-time Islamic schools to raise leaders

- ◆ Establish businesses and finance Islam through the businesses

- ◆ Encourage Muslims to build a community near the mosques

- ◆ Establish social welfare institutions

There is also a lesser-known agenda that is subtler and could have an impact not only upon Christianity but also upon the freedom of Christian ministers to speak the truth when comparing Christian teaching to Islam or when exposing the contradictions found in Islamic teaching. This sly agenda includes (and, again, is not limited to):

- ◆ Make speaking against Islam a hate crime (to silence all critics)

- ◆ Make inroads into the black community, which is often more accepting of Islam

- ◆ Engage in debates to show that Islam is equal to Christianity and Judaism

- ◆ Begin appointing Islamic leaders—regionally, statewide, and nationally

- ◆ Begin buying out media outlets, papers, and companies

- ◆ Hold America hostage with high oil prices

As an example, in 1991, Siraj Wahaj prayed at the House of Representatives and quoted from the Quran. One year later he spoke to a Muslim group in New Jersey, stating that if only Muslims were more clever politically, they could take over the United States and replace its constitutional government with a caliphate.[11] He also stated:

> If we were united and strong, we would elect our own
> emir [leader] and give allegiance to him.... [I]f 6–8 mil-
> lion Muslims unite in America, the country will come
> to us.[12]

And according to CAIR founding chairman Omar M. Ahmad,
"Islam isn't in America to be equal to any other faith, but to become
dominant.... The Koran, the Muslim book of scripture, should be
the highest authority in America and Islam the only accepted religion on Earth."[13]

The question arises, Why would certain Islamic leaders and organizations be interested in eventually establishing Islamic dominion
over the United States? I have never heard any Christian minister
or organization declare that the goal of Christianity is to eventually
take over Saudi Arabia and make the sacred Islamic site of the Ka'ba
an evangelistic headquarters! Christians witness of our faith to all
people, but we have never made plans to overthrow a government of
any Islamic nation and force the Muslims to convert or else.

Back to the question, Why is there an agenda to make the government of America Islamic under Islamic law? There are three
basic reasons:

1. To control the economic and educational centers
   of the world, which in this case is the United States

2. To rise above the rival religion of Christianity and
   the liberalism found in the Western civilizations

3. Most importantly, to establish a visible and active
   Islamic kingdom on Earth

Recent events in Britain and France prove the possibility that Muslims can increase their numbers and influence in Western nations.
In the fall of 2005, Muslim riots in France continued for days as

mobs torched over four hundred cars, set on fire warehouses, and threw stones and sticks at police. In all Islamic cultures, the families have numerous children, often as many as ten to fifteen per family, whereas in the West, the average number of children per household is two.[14] Thus Islam grows by birth rate and not just through conversion. When asking the question, "Will Britain convert to Islam?" a reader commenting on an article called "The Islamic States of America" wrote:

> The Christian churches have all but disappeared from the lives of the British people. The chapels of Wales are gaunt ruins, the great Roman Catholic churches of the industrial North West are often empty and derelict, the Anglicans scuttle about in their hallowed, lovely buildings like mice amid ancient ruins, rarely even beginning to fill spaces designed for multitudes.
>
> The choirs and the bells gradually fall silent, the hymns are no longer sung and one by one the doors are locked and places which in some cases have seen worship for centuries become bare museums of a dead faith.
>
> Few listen to what these churches say. They have become exclusive clubs, whose members celebrate bizarre rituals which are baffling to outsiders.[15]

I once read on an Islamic blog that has since been removed from the Internet a statement from a Muslim immigrant to America who was boasting about how easy it is to operate the Muslim beliefs and system in America. It was written that:

- ◆ American laws will protect us.

- ◆ Democrats and leftists will support us.

- ◆ The UN will legitimize us.

- CAIR and MAB (Muslim Association of Britain) will incubate us.

- The ACLU will support us.

- Western universities will educate us.

- Mosques in the West will shelter us.

- OPEC will finance us.

- Moderate Muslims will fertilize us.

- We will use your (West) welfare system.

Let me again emphasize that there are Muslims who are happy to be here and simply want to make a good living and raise a family. However, when digging deeper into Islamic books and blogs on the Internet and listening to Muslims discuss their future, I see that America is a part of their agenda of evangelism and eventual influence in the government.

THE INFLUENCE OF BLACK ISLAM

The largest American Islamic organization among African Americans is the Nation of Islam. Over the years I have heard certain statements made by the ministers of the Nation of Islam, including Louis Farrakhan. Such statements include racist ideas that Christianity is a "white man's religion" and Islam is for the "black man." In fact, this black supremacy theology is central to the early teachings of the Nation of Islam.

> According to the Nation of Islam, Allah (God), created man, and the man he created was black. They believe that Allah himself is the original and supreme black man. He is the Supreme Being among a mighty and powerful race

of black men. In this The Nation of Islam differs strongly with the monotheism of traditional Islam.

It is the teaching of Elijah Muhammad that all black men today are a part of this God-race. The black race is thus divine and superior to all other races. Modern day blacks came into existence some 66 trillion years ago when a great explosion ripped the moon from the earth. These people were black and called the tribe of Shabazz. They explored the earth and settled the better places to live, two of which are the Nile Valley and Mecca. Again, neither the Qur'an nor the Bible support such a concept.[16]

The thought is that a black man should never be a Christian or support the Christian faith, which is based upon and followed by white men. Black men should follow Islam. The religion of Islam is often connected to Africa, thus the link mandating that black men with an African heritage should reject American Christianity and join the ranks of their fellow Muslims from around the world.

Is Islam a black man's religion? Was the founder of Islam, Muhammad, black in color? There are no known drawings or pictures of Muhammad, but there are people who personally met him who have revealed his skin color. According to Islamic hadith:

> While we were sitting with the Prophet in the mosque, a man came riding on a camel. He made his camel kneel down in the mosque, tied its foreleg and then said: "Who amongst you is Muhammad?"...We replied, "This white man reclining on his arm."[17]

Muhammad is described as a "white man."

I said to Abu-Juhaifa, "Describe him for me." He said, "He was white and his beard was black with some white hair. He promised to give us 13 young she-camels, but he expired before we could get them."[18]

Anas reported: I saw the Messenger of Allah (may peace be upon him) raising his hands (high enough) in supplication (for rain) that the whiteness of his armpits became visible.[19]

Let me be clear that religion should never be about skin color. However, to imply that Islam is for black men and ignore that Muhammad was white would be deceptive to say the least. It was a black man from Africa, Simon from Cyrene, who helped carry the cross for Christ when he fell under the load (Mark 15:21). One of the first biblical churches was started by a black Ethiopian who was baptized by Phillip the evangelist (Acts 8). An early biblical teacher, Simon from Niger, came from a western African nation (Acts 8:26, 40). The African people were heavily involved in the formation of the Christian faith!

According to the Nation of Islam, white people are responsible for slavery. However, there again the Muslims allow a willful historical omission by not revealing that Muhammad himself had black slaves. The following information is from the translation of *Sahih Bukhari* and other hadith.

- Muhammad had a black slave named Anjasha.[20]

- He displayed black slaves in the mosque.[21]

- Muhammad had slave girls, and at times they were whipped.[22]

- Muhammad referred to blacks as "raisin heads."[23]

Arabs invaded northern Africa in the seventh century, sending black African slaves to Asia and Arab countries. In the Islamic Republic of Mauritania, which is Arab, Berber Muslims hold possibly more than one hundred thousand black slaves.[24] In Saudi Arabia, a common word for black is *abd*, meaning "slave."

In Sudan, black Muslims are kidnapping black Christians and making them slaves. Therefore, for Minister Farrakhan to suggest that Islam is favorable to black Africans is ignoring early Islamic history and defiantly ignoring the conflicts in the Sudan, Nigeria, and other African nations where black Muslims are killing, raping, and attacking their own people—all in the name of the spread of radical Islam.

The unique aspect of the Christian faith is that love is the center of the religion. Christians are taught: "You shall love your neighbor as yourself" (Matt. 19:19). The Bible teaches Christians to: "Pray for those who spitefully use you and persecute you" (Matt. 5:44) and "…not to resist an evil person. But whoever slaps you on your right cheek, turn the other to him also" (v. 39). The Bible even teaches us to: "Love your enemies, bless those who curse you, do good to those who hate you" (v. 44). This is far different from the response promoted by fanatical Muslims against others, which instruct followers of Islam to attack their enemies and cut off their fingers and heads.

Only time will reveal how the prediction of the "sun rising in the west" will be fulfilled in the minds of Muslims. Time will also reveal if Muslims will perceive a present or future American leader to be the "sun" of Islam, shining the light of the religion among the Western unbelievers. Whatever their perception will be, the message of Islam, the increase of immigration and births in Muslim families, and the desire to convert the West will certainly continue.

The Arab world, which is predominantly Muslim, has learned that one of the greatest inroads into the West is to control the governments and the economies through oil.

THE OIL BEAST
RISING OUT OF THE SEA

He shall enter peaceably, even into the richest places of
the province; and he shall do what his fathers have not
done, nor his forefathers: he shall disperse among them
the plunder, spoil, and riches; and he shall devise his
plans against the strongholds, but only for a time.
—DANIEL 11:24

THERE IS NO SHORTAGE OF OIL. THERE ARE OIL TANKERS sitting in our waters off the coast, and they are not allowed to unload." The man speaking was working for the CIA and related this information to my father during the famous 1972 oil embargo. The OPEC nations, led by Saudi Arabia, felt that the United States had intervened in the Yom Kippur War, thus saving the nation of Israel from calamity. As punishment, the Arab oil barons united in an embargo to teach America a lesson.

At the time, our family lived in Northern Virginia, fifteen miles from the nation's capital. A person's license tag number determined the days that car owner could purchase gas—odd numbers only on one day, and even numbers the next. As Americans complained, they also demanded that our government become independent from Arabian oil. Eventually, the crisis ended, the prices dropped, and the issue faded like a morning fog in the rising sun. The only good legislation passed was the decision to open an area called the *strategic reserves*, where oil would be stored in the event of a national catastrophe or an emergency.

In 2008, the price of fuel at the pump again rose to record levels. The reasons varied. The OPEC nations cut production to drive up the price during the highest driving season in America. Other nations were demanding more fuel globally due to the fact that more people were purchasing vehicles. During the summer months in America, a specific blend of gas was mandated, which could only be mixed by specific refineries. It was also pointed out that Americans were driving larger vehicles that demanded more fuel but got less miles per gallon. A combination of these factors, along with two major hurricanes, shot the price of fuel over four dollars a gallon in some states.

Again, the politicians and people screamed, "We need options…we need to be less dependent…we need to build more refineries…" However, when the price went from $4 a gallon to $3.25 a gallon, the cost looked cheap by comparison! As I write this book, the price has continued to decline. As usual, members of Congress did nothing about this oil crisis but blamed the opposing party in order to get voting points with their constituents back home.

OIL IN PROPHECY

It may come as a surprise to learn that a prophecy in Daniel may be a cryptic allusion to the power of oil and how the coming dictator called the Antichrist will control the nations with oil.

> He shall enter peaceably even upon the fattest places
> of the province; and he shall do that which his fathers
> have not done, nor his fathers' fathers; he shall scatter
> among them the prey, and spoil, and riches: yea, and he
> shall forecast his devices against the strong holds, even
> for a time.
>
> —DANIEL 11:24, KJV

Some would say, "How could this refer to our time? Oil wells did not exist in Daniel's day." This is correct, but this is the amazing supernatural evidence of biblical prophecy. The prophetic visionaries saw things centuries before they occurred, yet wrote about them with pinpoint accuracy.

The setting of this prophecy deals with a leader whom many identify as the Antichrist of Bible prophecy. The passage deals with the Antichrist taking possession of important land areas and promising to take the wealth of the region and divide it among his followers. In this prophecy, the word *fattest* is often translated as "richest" or "wealthiest." However, the root word is *shaman* and can mean "oil" or "to shine." With modern understanding, we could say the fattest places (bringing huge amounts of wealth) would be the oil states in the Persian Gulf region.

A second interesting clue is the word *province*, which is the word *mediynah* or, as we spell it in English, *Medina*. There is a desert region situated between Egypt and Israel named the Median Desert. However, there is also a famous city in the nation of Saudi Arabia called Medina. This city is where the founder of the Islamic religion, Muhammad, is buried, and this city is the site of one of the largest Islamic mosques in the world.[1]

I believe this verse could allude to a future dictator who will control the *places of oil in the area of Medina*. The largest oil producer in the Gulf is Saudi Arabia, which is also the heart of the world's oil supply and the world headquarters of the Islamic religion. If an

Islamic radical with a substantial following overthrew the royal house of the Saudi king, he could seize the oil wells, and within a few days the global oil markets would panic, sending the world's stock markets into the abyss. All nations that depend upon oil, including America, would feel the immediate economic squeeze. Islamic fanatics would gladly grasp the opportunity to watch America's economy plummet and American citizens spending their incomes to fill the coffers of this new Arabian king.

The passage in Daniel indicates the *reason* the future dictator will enter the "fattest [*oily*] places of the province." His goal will be to redistribute the wealth from the wealthy to the common man.

> He will take the property of the rich and scatter it out among the people.
>
> —Daniel 11:24, TLB

> He will divide among his followers the goods and property he has captured in war.
>
> —Daniel 11:24, GNT

One of the primary complaints about the Saudi royal family is that they hoard the oil wealth for themselves and their families while many of the Arabs living in the huge desert nation remain in poverty. This was why Osama bin Laden had appeal among many common and simpleminded Muslims. Osama was from a wealthy family and inherited millions before being expelled from Saudi Arabia. However, according to a Christian from Pakistan, Osama used part of his fortune to establish schools for students in Pakistan and Afghanistan.[2]

I have several friends who have worked for oil companies in the Gulf of Arabia. They are very familiar with the Arabian mind-set. They have told me that large majorities of people actually despise the Saudi royal family. It is only a matter of time until there is a major uprising in the Gulf, and one man will emerge as the new leader of the region. Oddly, the Islamic tradition states that the Mahdi will appear in the area of Saudi Arabia.

PLAYING GAMES WITH OIL

It seems everyone in the world is seeing the need to drill and look for new sources of oil—except the legislative branch of government in America. Why are so many politicians afraid of opening up offshore drilling or even drilling in Alaska? The simple answer is that environmentalist groups from the West Coast have a strong influence over the media and have given large sums of money to political coffers to prevent the drilling process by blocking legislation through lobbyists or lawsuits.

However, China is reputed to be drilling off the coast of Florida, and Russia has already claimed the polar icecap. China is working to build numerous refineries and realizes that with their growth they will be the top oil consumer in a short time. In America, we have such brilliant ideas as taking much-needed farmland that should be used to plant food and using it instead to plant corn that will be used for ethanol fuel. In the meantime, costs for food are skyrocketing!

WHAT AMERICA DID NOT REALIZE

Was invading Iraq the right thing to do? Absolutely! Saddam Hussein had used poison gas upon the Kurdish population, killing thousands. He not only invaded Kuwait, setting more than five hundred oil wells on fire, but he also had murdered millions of Muslims. He and his two sons tortured countless others for their own twisted pleasure. Evidence is mounting that Saddam had close links to al Qaeda and was planning to develop deadly weapons of mass destruction that, within a few years, would be given to terrorists to attack key targets in Europe and America.

Saddam's two sons were demons clothed in human flesh. One on

221

occasion, according to a bishop from Iraq, Saddam's son Uday drove up to a public restaurant, spotted a young Christian girl, entered the facility, raped the girl in front of her parents, and then shot her and her family in cold blood.[3] For those who say the war wasn't worth it, was the war with Germany and the removal of Hitler worth the effort? Ask the Jews! Was the removal of Saddam worth the effort? Ask the persecuted Iraqis!

American military leaders were told by former Iraqi defectors that when Iraq had been liberated, the Americans would be considered as heroes and liberators. The impression was that democracy was desired, and after the removal of Saddam, peace would follow. This is not what occurred. The main reason is that Iraq is a nation consisting of three different groups of Muslims—the Kurds to the north, the Shi'ites to the south, and the Sunni Muslims in the center of the country. The Sunnis and Shi'ites have fought one another during fourteen centuries, and throughout Islamic history, Iraq was one of the centers of the conflict.

THE NEXT STRIKE ON AMERICAN SOIL

During the years following 9/11, there has been a strange lull in America from terrorist attacks. Special agents from government organizations have pulled financial and intelligence resources together, creating a large barrier to the possible initiation of the plans of terrorists. However, the lack of activity seems to be lulling Americans to apathetic, lethargic sleep.

We must remember, however, that there was a more-than-eight-year gap of time between the first attack on the World Trade Center in February 1993 and the 9/11 assault in 2001. Individuals who are part of the radical Islamic *sleeper cells* known to exist in America have extreme patience, and they will wait for years before initiating another big attack. All the individuals with whom I have spoken who are directly involved in counterterrorism or with Israeli or American military organizations say it is only a matter of time before we experience another strike on America soil.

There are various opinions as to what an attack from a terrorist group could actually do. Counterterrorism organizations who have intercepted "chatter" indicate that a plan to engage in the next attack will be much more dramatic and cost more lives than even 9/11.

Some experts are suggesting that a dirty bomb will be used. This possibility stems from several sources. According to an inside source, several components for such a bomb were confiscated in a shipping terminal in the Chicago area. Shortly thereafter an arrest was made, and the accused allegedly was plotting to construct a dirty bomb.

In 1998, Sultan Bashiruddin Mahmood, a Western-educated nuclear physicist and chairman of the Pakistan Atomic Energy Commission, was hailed by many Pakistanis as a hero for his work in developing Pakistan's first nuclear bomb. However, in the year 2002 he was placed under house arrest. Sultan Bashiruddin Mahmood had become an Islamic fanatic.[4]

One month after the September 11 attacks, the US Army and CIA intelligence intercepted communications with Sultan Mahmood speaking with Taliban leader Mullah Omar. Eventually, Sultan Mahmood's residence in Kabul, Afghanistan, was invaded. In the building were discovered drawings of a helium hot air balloon designed to release large quantities of anthrax spores. What was more frightening was that according to Sultan Mahmood, he had been in contact with Osama bin Laden in August of 2001, and the terrorist mastermind had revealed that he had in his possession radioactive material and was interested in making a "dirty nuke."[5]

THE BLACK WIND OF DEATH

I believe it is quite possible that the second wave against the United States will come in the form of a chemical or a biological attack. I base this on intelligence information and upon a statement made by an al Qaeda leader that is part of an Islamic prophecy, predicted to occur at the end of days.

> Then you watch for the Day that the sky will bring forth a kind of smoke (or mist) plainly visible, enveloping the people: this will be a grievous Penalty.
>
> —SURAH 44:10–11

An Islamic commentary elaborates more by saying:

> Smoke will appear all over the earth, which will cause believers to catch something similar to a slight cold, whereas the unbelievers will be hit harder by it.[6]

I can recall hearing discussions among journalists and news commentators as to the meaning of the phrase "black wind of death." Some suggested it was a hidden code or a cryptic term for the name of a future attack. Others believed it was a suggestion of a chemical or biological attack.

Actually, the sign of "smoke" is mentioned in Islamic predictions as one of the signs of the last days.

Islamic writers have a variety of opinions as to what this "smoke" actually alludes to. Some take it as a supernatural sign sent by Allah against the unbelievers. Others indicate it will be something Muslims will initiate; however, they will be protected from this chastisement by Allah. This portent is one of the many signs that, according to Islamic teachers, will precede the arrival of the Mahdi. One is a black wind that some believe will kill up to one-third of the population.[7]

I believe this prediction could actually become self-fulfilling. That is, a group of Islamic fanatics will develop a chemical or biological agent that will manifest as a visible form of smoke or a type of bomb that will cause death to those with whom it comes in contact.

100,000 IN THE NEXT ATTACK

A person named Abu Salma al-Hijazi, said to be a close commander to Osama bin Laden, was interviewed in Iraq months after the liberation by the United States and its coalition forces. This al Qaeda commander was asked about a large-scale future strike against the United States of America. Al-Hijazi was quoted as saying: "A huge and very courageous strike will take place and that the number of infidels expected to be killed in this attack, according to primary estimates, exceeds 100,000." He added that he "...anticipates, but will not swear, that the attack will happen during Ramadan." The attack will be carried out in a way that will "amaze the world and turn al Qaeda into [an organization that] horrifies the world until the law of Allah is implemented, actually implemented, and not just in words, on His land.... You wait and see that the balance of power between al Qaeda and its rivals will change, all of sudden, Allah willing."[8]

Apocalyptic Muslims are as certain that their predictions will come to pass as religious Jews who believe in a coming Messiah and Christians who believe in the biblical signs of Christ's return. By initiating such an attack, it will be a global "sign" to all Muslims that the last days are here and their long-awaited leader who will soon bring the world under Islamic dominion is about to arise.

PLANS TO HARM THE AMERICAN ECONOMY

The crackdown on illegal immigration, new laws governing entering and exiting America, and the institution of the new Patriot Act have made it more difficult for Islamic fanatics to hide within America without being detected or observed. However, the propaganda war is very difficult for America to win, especially when the Islamic government owns the television and satellite stations in the Middle East and in parts of Europe. This propaganda battle takes on some strange forms at times.

The Coca-Cola Scare

Some time back, one of my staff workers spoke to a woman from South Carolina who was warned outside of a grocery store by a man who appeared to be Middle Eastern to avoid all Coca-Cola products. I later learned that the same "warning" was given out in Florida, Tennessee, and Alabama by individuals who appeared to be Middle Eastern but "out of concern" were informing people about a warning they had received.

A short time later I contacted a friend in the Justice Department in Washington and told them about these series of warnings that were coming to my attention. They called the man on my staff personally to get more information. After detailed investigation, the following information was discovered.

A Muslim businessman in France had developed a new soft drink named *Mecca Cola*. It was supposed to be very similar to the traditional Coca-Cola. However, whenever someone purchased Mecca Cola, a portion of the proceeds went to support the Muslim religion. There are six million Muslims in France, and the businessman saw an opportunity to sell a product that was not from America, and, in return, the Islamic religion would gain a commission.[9]

It is believed that someone linked to supporting the new Mecca Cola attempted to plant the false idea that somehow the Coke in America was being tainted and could be dangerous to consumers. If the rumor would spread to enough people and the national media picked up on the warning, then the Coke products in America could suffer, and this would work well for the new Mecca Cola in France.

The entire scare was a hoax that failed.

MUSLIM IMPACT ON AMERICA'S ECONOMY

There are, however, other areas in which some Muslims may be attempting to hurt the economy of the United States. These three areas include:

- The changing of the use of the dollar for the euro
- The future oil crisis
- The hoarding of gold

Exchanging the dollar for the euro

The European Union (EU) introduced the euro currency several years ago. It is now common for the euro to maintain an equal or higher value than the dollar. The British use the pound; the Japanese, the yen; and the Americans, the dollar. For years the nations of the world desired to have hard currency in hand, and the dollar was the premium currency.

I recall visiting Bulgaria and Romania after the fall of communism. In Romania, one American dollar was equivalent to six hundred Romanian dollars. A beautiful man's suit could be purchased for twenty dollars. A full mink coat, which would be priced in the United States for as much as six thousand dollars, could be bought for four hundred American dollars.

The same is true with many third-world countries. Since World War II, the dollar has sustained the buying power in nations of the world. However, the euro has now changed the equation.

From time to time, the euro has been a desired investment and currency in much of Europe. It appears that Muslims who are angry at America for entering Afghanistan and Iraq are now spreading word that the Muslim nations should avoid using dollars and begin to use euros as their international currency. While the change is difficult for many because some Arab leaders have huge amounts of cash (American dollars) stored away in vaults in secret places, the rising tide of voices against the American dollar is increasing in volume.

The hoarding of gold

Gold is very important to Islamic apocalyptic traditions. *The Musnad* of Imam Ahmad ibn Hanbal states:

> Abu Bakr ibn Abi Maryam reported that he heard the Messenger of Allah, may Allah bless him and grant him peace, say: "A time is certainly coming over mankind in which there will be nothing [left] which will be of use save a dinar and a dirham."[10]

In early Islamic history, a gold coin was minted, which was called the *dinar*. After the collapse of the Ottoman Turkish Empire in 1924, there was a lapse in the Islamic currency, as most Muslim countries accepted the currency of the Western nations, including the British pound and the American dollar. Several years ago, an Islamic group in West Malaysia began minting the gold dinar again. Meetings have been conducted in Egypt and in Arabia discussing the need for Muslims to accept the new coinage as the official coin of the Islamic nations. In brief, many apocalyptic Muslims who hold traditions concerning the last days believe there will be a worldwide economic crisis in which all paper money will be useless. The only money of value will be money consisting of gold and silver.[11]

Many speculate that this is one reason why gold and silver prices have, from time to time, risen by 40–50 percent in a short time. In early 2003, the price of gold and silver was rising, but after the invasion of Iraq, the price increased by about 30 percent! There was no explanation for this, since the stock market was rising, the jobless rate decreasing, and the economy was again on the move. The explanation may be found when exploring who is hoarding the gold and silver.

Intelligence research indicates that Muslims are now telling fellow Muslim businessmen to purchase as much gold as possible and get an edge on the market. Huge amounts of gold would provide enough material to produce large numbers of the thin gold dinars, which, through an Islamic banking system, could then be sold to fellow Muslims.

Before you think this sound too farfetched, remember that in the 1980s silver went to $50 an ounce and gold spiked at over $800 an ounce.[12]

History confirms that when a major economic crisis blankets the world, precious metals such as gold and silver are sought after by investors, businessmen, and private individuals. Biblical prophecy seems to indicate that it is oil that will become the most sought-after commodity as End Time events begin to take place. This is only one of many reasons why America must become oil independent by using our natural resources.

THE CONTROVERSIAL
DOME OF THE ROCK

Therefore when you see the "abomination of desola-
tion," spoken of by Daniel the prophet, standing in the
holy place (whoever reads, let him understand), then
let those who are in Judea flee to the mountains.
—MATTHEW 24:15–16

T HE MOST VOLATILE REAL ESTATE ON PLANET EARTH IS A
small mountain that sits in the heart of the old city of Jerusalem. Called the Temple Mount by Jews and Christians, this site
is sacred to the three leading monotheistic religions of the word—
Judaism, Christianity, and Islam. The Temple Mount is holy to the
Christians because Christ was crucified nearby on Mount Moriah.

It is holy to Muslims because of the two Islamic mosques: the
Dome of the Rock (the *Qubbat Al-Sakhra*) and the Al-Aqsa, which
is a second mosque on the southern end of the Temple Mount, originally commissioned by 'Abdul Malik ibn Marwan and built between
A.D. 709–715 by his son Caliph al-Waleed.[1] At this present time,
the Muslim Supreme Awqaf Council controls access to the entire

mountain. Christians and Jews are not permitted (at this point of time) to read the Scriptures or to offer prayer on the mountain where the Dome of the Rock and Al-Aqsa are located. The Temple Mount is also holy to Muslims because, according to Islamic tradition, their prophet Muhammad ascended from the mount on his white stallion named Boraq.

Mount Moriah is important to Jews because of Abraham offering Isaac (Gen. 22:2) and because the two sacred Jewish temples—Solomon's temple and the rebuilt temple—once stood proudly on the mountain. This small yet holy site will one day become the powder keg that will ignite a global conflict.

HISTORICAL MOUNT MORIAH

The history of the mountain begins with the appearance of a mysterious king-priest named Melchizedek. He is identified in Jewish tradition as Shem, the righteous son of Noah. In Christian tradition, he is a picture of Christ, the future High Priest of heaven. In Genesis 14, Abraham offered a tithe to Melchizedek, and in Genesis 22 Abraham returned to the land of Moriah to present Isaac to God on an altar (Gen. 22:1–8).

In David's time, Mount Moriah was owned by a Jebusite, an early inhabitant of the area. King David purchased the hill and constructed a stone altar to stop a plague (2 Sam. 24; 1 Chron. 21). David's son Solomon erected the first Jewish temple on Mount Moriah after David's death (2 Chron. 3:1). The only historical and biblical record where the mountain was ever purchased was during the reign of King David. This purchase agreement more than three thousand years ago gives the Jews the legal right to claim the mountain as belonging to their descendants.

Contemporary Muslims completely reject the biblical account of Jewish ownership. Muslims claim that the most sacred site in the world is in Mecca, where the black stone called the Ka'ba is alleged to be the place where Abraham offered his son Ishmael. Muslims teach that Abraham was a Muslim and that the Jews changed the Bible to fit their own opinions. To Muslims, Jerusalem is the third most sacred site in the Islamic religion. Muslims do not accept the fact that a Jewish presence ever existed on the mountain.

When the second temple was destroyed in the year A.D. 70, the remains of the Jewish temple were plowed under and the ground sprinkled with salt in A.D. 71 by the Romans. Years later, a group of Jews attempted to rebuild a structure on the mountain but were stopped.

Presently, there is no Jewish temple or Jewish presence on the Temple Mount. The two Islamic mosques are the main religious buildings on the mountain. Muslims are very skeptical of any Jew who desires to enter the temple compound, and most religious Jews refuse to enter the area for fear of standing on the former holy of holies. In the 1980s, a large sign was posted at the entrance of the Mount, forbidding religious Jews from entering the compound.

THE DOME OF THE ROCK

In the year 638 the Muslims entered Jerusalem and occupied the city. During this early occupation, an Islamic mosque was constructed over the site where the Jewish temple had once sat. This structure, called the Dome of the Rock (the *Qubbat Al-Sakhra*), was built over a rock that some believe to be the holy of holies in the first and second Jewish temples. Since the construction of this Islamic mosque, it has been impossible for the Jews to lay any claim to the Temple Mount.

However, important historical research conducted by Ya'akov Ofir gives some "inside information" concerning the Dome of the Rock. In 691, years after the Muslims began their occupation of Jerusalem in 638, Abd el-Malik, an Islamic ruler from Damascus, built the Dome of the Rock. At that time the Umayyad group was headquartered in Damascus, and the Abbasids were headquartered in Iraq and Arabia. The groups were involved in conflict. According to Ofir, Malik was actually a follower of the Jewish faith.[2]

Malik's followers were told to pray facing Jerusalem instead of Mecca, a Jewish custom that was established by Solomon. His followers made pilgrimages to Jerusalem instead of Mecca. He gave Jews the rights for managing the Temple Mount and allowed Jews to light candles in the Dome of the Rock. Malik was called *The Righteous* by the Jews and an *infidale* by the Muslims. According to Ofir, the Muslims erased information about this man in their history.[3]

The Dome architecture was done by the Byzantines. No other mosque in the world has eight sides. The entrance is in a different area than normally used for a mosque. The builders did not place a *Michrab* in the building to show the direction of Mecca until 1947. This has caused some to suggest that the original building was actually a Jewish house of prayer.

Dr. Ben Tzion Dinur shows in history where the Jews had a house of prayer in the early days of the Arab occupation. Jews were later evicted from the area. Rabbi Avraham bar Chia Hanassi said: "The Ishmaelite kings had the good habit of allowing Israel to come to the Temple Mount and build there a house of prayer and Midrash." A famous Karaite, ben Yerucham, said: "After the Ishmaelites occupied Jerusalem they gave permission to Israel to enter the Temple Mount to live there. They gave them the courtyards of G-d and they prayed there for many years... Later they were evicted."[4]

Sibias, an Armenian, said, "After the Jews had for some time enjoyed the help of the Arabs, they decided to rebuild Solomon's Temple. They discovered the site of the Holy of Holies and they built a house of prayer for themselves on the foundation of the temple using the remains of the temple." Rambam (Maimonides) wrote that he visited Jerusalem in 1165 and "went up to the Temple Mount and prayed in the great, holy house on the place of the Holy of Holies."[5]

THE ISLAMIC CONTROVERSY

In Islam, once a mosque is constructed, both the mosque and the land become the permanent property of Islam for as long as human history exists. I have heard fascinating wild tales about how the mosque will be removed. One rumor circulated that the Saudis were going to pay to have the mosque moved to Arabia because they believe some radical Jew (or Christian) will eventually blow the building to pieces. This is unlikely and would be rejected by not only Muslims globally but also by Palestinians living in Israel, Gaza, and the West Bank.

There could be a solution through a peace process whereby the mountain would be shared by the three monotheistic religions—Islam, Judaism, and Christianity. Not only is there ample room for a Jewish temple, but there is also room for a large Christian church. The times of worship would vary, since the Muslims worship on Friday, the Jews on Saturday, and the Christians on Sunday. I was informed by an inside source that this possibility was secretly discussed at a meeting in the Vatican when Yasser Arafat was still living. Arafat rejected the idea, but some of the more moderates in the group believed a future peace could lead to the mountain being shared.

Muslims deny any Jewish presence on the Temple Mount. Archeology proves otherwise. In Nehemiah 3:26, the water gate is mentioned, which goes back to the tenth century B.C. Archeologists discovered forty jars in the area. *Bullas* (an amulet worn like a locket) have been discovered, and *mik'vots* (a bathing vessel used in purification practices) have been found at the base of the hills.

THE REJOICING STONE

In 1967, nineteen hundred years after the Roman Tenth Legion toppled the walls of Jerusalem and burned the sacred temple, archeologists were excavating near the Western Wall when they unearthed a section of the wall from the Roman period. As they cleared the surface of a particular stone, Hebrew letters became visible. Excitement swept the group, and soon it was apparent that someone centuries earlier carved a message of hope on the stone itself. The words were a portion of a passage from Isaiah 66:14 (KJV):

> When ye see this, your heart shall rejoice, and your bones shall flourish like an herb.

It was in 1967 that Israeli military forces captured the eastern section of the old city of Jerusalem and united the western section with the eastern half, thus reuniting the city of Jerusalem under Israeli control. This was the first time since the year A.D. 70 that the entire city had been in the hands of the Hebrew people.

A FUTURE JEWISH TEMPLE?

Prophetic scriptures indicate that a Jewish temple will exist on this mountain in the future. In 2 Thessalonians 2:4, Paul states that the future man of sin (the Antichrist) "sits as God in the temple of God, showing himself that he is God." When Paul wrote this passage, the Jewish temple still existed in Jerusalem. However, since this verse identifies the future Antichrist, and a Jewish temple no longer exists, some form of a "temple" must be reconstructed on the Temple Mount.

Another reference to the temple is in Revelation 11:1–2, where John is told: "Rise and measure the temple of God, the altar, and those who worship there. But leave out the court which is outside the temple, and do not measure it, for it has been given to the Gentiles. And they will tread the holy city underfoot for forty-two months." John was not viewing the temple in heaven but an earthly temple with an outer court area that was handed over to the Gentiles. Since most scholars agree that Revelation was written around A.D. 95, John's prophecy could not have been referring to the temple in Jerusalem, which had been destroyed twenty-five years earlier. John was peering into the future and saw a temple in Jerusalem. He understood that the Gentiles would once again seize the city for a final forty-two months, the last forty-two months of the seven-year Tribulation.

During my first tour of Israel in 1985, when I asked Jewish people about the rebuilding of their temple, most would respond, "The spirit of our nation is our temple." Most acknowledged they had no interest in rebuilding the temple, and a few others said, "Perhaps when the Messiah comes." But according to a recent poll conducted by Jews living in Israel, today a majority of Jews desire to see a temple in Jerusalem!

The main questions that arise are:

1. How could a Jewish temple ever be constructed on the Temple Mount when there are two Islamic mosques on the mountain—Al-Aqsa and the Dome of the Rock?

2. Who would build the temple?

3. How long would it take to complete the structure?

Under present conditions in Jerusalem, Israel, and the Middle East, most modern scholars conclude there is no need for a Jewish temple, especially since the Muslims would never allow a Jewish temple to be built on Islam's third most holy site, Mecca and Medina in Arabia being the chief sites.

Contemporary scholars and students of biblical prophecy have differing opinions as to the theory of a future Jewish temple being reconstructed on Jerusalem's Temple Mount. Some modern scholars have written off several New Testament prophecies as merely symbolic or allegorical, including the following:

1. Christ's prediction of the "abomination of desolation…in the holy place" (Matt. 24:15)

2. The warning of "the man of sin," who "sits as God in the temple of God" (2 Thess. 2:3–4)

3. John's instruction in the Apocalypse to "measure the temple…and those who worship there" (Rev. 11:1–2)

There is an undercurrent of fear flowing among some Muslims who believe that in the future, Muslims will lose control of the Al-Aqsa mosque in Jerusalem, and that zealous Jews or Christians will seize both mosques—the Dome of the Rock and the Al-Aqsa, either destroying or dismantling them. Several years ago the Temple Institute in Jerusalem took an aerial photo of the Temple Mount and replaced the Dome with an image of the second Jewish temple. This was a photo sold in their store to give tourists a visual example of what the Temple Mount would look like with the Jewish temple constructed on the site. This photograph caused a small ruckus when former PLO leader Yasser Arafat held up the picture during an Indonesian television interview, warning the world's largest Islamic nation of future Jewish plans to rebuild a Jewish temple in Jerusalem after removing the Dome of the Rock from its foundation.[6]

SO WHAT IS THE PLAN?

Is there or is there not to be a Jewish temple reconstructed in Jerusalem some time in the future?

First, it would not be credible biblical interpretation to say that the prophetic warnings of Matthew 24 (the future abomination), 2 Thessalonians 2 (the Antichrist sitting in the temple), and Revelation 11:1–2 (measuring the temple) were mere symbolism or allegory just because at the present a Jewish temple is not in Jerusalem.

Second, we must take into account the seven-year treaty that will be signed:

> And he shall enter into a strong and firm covenant with the many for one week [seven years]. And in the midst of the week he shall cause the sacrifice and offering to cease [for the remaining three and one-half years]; and upon the wing or pinnacle of abominations [shall come] one who makes desolate, until the full determined end is poured out on the desolator.
>
> —DANIEL 9:27, AMP

This agreement is signed with "many," alluding to many different nations. However, it will be the Antichrist who breaks the contract and invades Jerusalem, stopping the temple sacrifices in the middle of the seven-year treaty. Should Jewish leaders (such as the two witnesses of Revelation 11) erect a new Jewish temple on the Temple Mount, the invasion of the Antichrist will be for the purpose of *liberating* the sacred mountain from the presence of Jews and *infidels*.

It may be that the incidence of Jews offering a sacrifice in this temple would be the fuse on the powder keg, igniting the final war between the Muslims and the Jews, a war identified by the prophets as the "time of Jacob's trouble" (Jer. 30:7).

In Revelation 11:1, John was told to measure the (future) temple and them who worship, but he was told, "But leave out the court which is outside the temple, and do not measure it, for it has been given to the Gentiles. And they will tread the holy city underfoot for forty-two months" (v. 2). One group of Bible scholars called the *preterists* teach that John wrote the Book of Revelation in A.D. 66–68 and that he was speaking of measuring the temple in Jerusalem *before* it was destroyed by the Romans in A.D. 70. History does not bear out this theory. Saint Jerome wrote:

> In the 14th year then after Nero, Domitian having raised a second persecution, he was banished to the island of Patmos, and wrote the Apocalypse.... But Domitian having been put to death and his acts, on account of his excessive cruelty, having been annulled by the Senate, he returned to Ephesus...and continuing there until the time of the Emperor Trajan, founded and built churches throughout all Asia, and, worn out by old age, died in the sixty-eighth year after our Lord's passion and was buried near the same city.[7]

If Christ was crucified around A.D. 32, and John died sixty-eight years after the crucifixion on the Isle of Patmos, then he would have died around A.D. 100. Nero died in A.D. 68 by suicide, and John was banished to Patmos where he wrote the Book of Revelation (Rev 1:9) fourteen years after Nero's death, or A.D. 82. Thus, John wrote Revelation *after* the Jewish temple was destroyed. He was told to measure a temple that will exist in Jerusalem during the Tribulation!

Why is the "outer court" not measured in Revelation 11:2? Because it is possible that the Temple Mount could one day be shared by the three monotheistic religions. The Roman and Orthodox Church could build a large sanctuary in one section, a Jewish temple could be built in another, and the Islamic mosque would remain in the "outer court." Dividing the sacred compound into three sections is possible, since the entire area is approximately thirty-four acres.

FORTY-TWO MONTHS TO BUILD A TEMPLE?

In the early 1990s, my friend Pastor Mike Coleman met with one of the professors from the Hebrew University, Dr. Asher Kaufman, whose expertise included the Jewish temple and the history of the Temple Mount. Immediately after the Six-Day War in 1967, Kaufman personally toured the Temple Mount and snapped pictures of various

ruins dating back to the Roman period (Christ's time). He had pic-
torial evidence indicating there was once a Jewish temple on the
mount. After discovering there were photographs, Islamic sources
removed the stones and columns to erase all evidence of any Jewish
presence.

According to what Kaufman told Coleman, if the Jews were to
rebuild a temple, it would take approximately forty-two months—
not to construct the facility, but to offer certain prayers during new
moons, Sabbaths, and feast days. This is interesting information
when considering that from the beginning of the seven-year treaty
to the time of the invasion of the Antichrist is forty-two months, or
three and a half years. It is possible that the Antichrist will set out to
seize Jerusalem upon the completion of this temple, perhaps when it
is dedicated. What makes this a strong possibility is the fact that two
"witnesses" will minister in Jerusalem for the first forty-two months
of the Tribulation but will be slain by the Antichrist in the middle
of the Tribulation.

As to the location, Kaufman believes that the original temple sat
in a line behind Jerusalem's eastern gate, north of the Dome of the
Rock, and in a location where a small copula is erected called the
Dome of the Tablets (also called the *Dome of the Spirits*). His theory
is interesting, since there is about 150 feet of space between the
northern outside wall of the Dome of the Rock and the area where
the small Dome of the Tablets sits. This would allow for the creation
of coexistence between Jewish and Islamic worship sites. Since Muslims worship on Friday and Jews on Saturday, a wall or partition
could be placed between the two buildings, thus giving each group
their own territory on the sacred compound.

Presently, this sounds impossible. However, there will be a major
season of false peace, after which the peace is broken and destruction follows:

> For when they say, "Peace and safety!" then sudden
> destruction comes upon them, as labor pains upon a
> pregnant woman. And they shall not escape.
>
> —1 Thessalonians 5:3

On December 23, 2000, President Clinton presented the idea of dividing the Temple Mount from the top to the bottom. He suggested that Muslims keep sovereignty of the two mosques, and Jews maintain control of the Western Wall and the holy of holies.[8] When former PLO leader Yasser Arafat heard about Clinton's idea, he totally rejected it, saying the Muslims would never give up sovereignty.[9] However, the same idea was also presented to the Vatican in September 2007 by former Israeli Prime Minister Shimon Perez, with the idea of the Vatican overseeing the entire area and helping to maintain the peace.[10]

WHO WILL REBUILD THE TEMPLE?

There are numerous opinions as to who would actually rebuild the temple. The most common theory presented for many years is that a Jewish leader who becomes the Antichrist will be in charge of the construction of the temple when he is received and acknowledged by the religious Jews as their anticipated Messiah. This theory emphasizes that only a Jew would be permitted to initiate the construction process—thus the Antichrist must be Jewish.

This theory falls apart when recalling the history of previous Jewish temples. Both Solomon's temple and Herod's temple were built by Gentiles. During the building of the first temple, Solomon hired thousands of Gentiles out of Lebanon to work with Hebrew workers preparing timbers and erecting the greatest temple of all time. (See 1 Kings 5.) Nehemiah rebuilt the temple after the Babylonian captivity, but a Gentile named Herod the Great expanded the platform, extending the Temple Mount toward the south.

Gentiles can be involved in the building of a temple, because while the temple is being constructed, the workers are considered to be ceremonially unclean. Once the sacred edifice is completed, then the building and the furniture must be purified with the water of purification, which must be performed by the priesthood. (See Numbers 19.) Thus, it does not take an alleged Jewish Messiah to rebuild the temple in Jerusalem. Gentiles can be involved prior to the actual dedication of the building.

We have already shown you earlier the biblical indications that the Antichrist will be a *Gentile* and not a Jew. He will not be received as the Jewish Messiah. When he invades Jerusalem, he will set up an image of himself, causing many Jews to flee into the wilderness (Rev. 12:14).

Who, then, will lead the charge to initiate plans for a new Jewish temple during the first half of the Tribulation? After many years of reading commentaries, listening to arguments, and studying the Scriptures, I believe I can suggest the best possible candidate to participate in the future process. It will be the reappearing of the prophet Elijah.

THE TWO WITNESSES—ELIJAH AND ENOCH

In biblical history, two mortal men escaped death and were translated into heaven. The first was the seventh man from Adam, named Enoch, who was translated after living for 365 years (Gen. 5:23–24; Heb. 11:5). The second man was the prophet Elijah, who was transported directly to heaven in a chariot of fire (2 Kings 2). Malachi, the last Old Testament prophet in the English translation of the Bible, predicted that Elijah will again appear on Earth in the future:

> Behold, I will send you Elijah the prophet before the coming of the great and dreadful day of the LORD.
> —MALACHI 4:5

Malachi revealed that God has a future plan for Elijah. He will appear again on Earth before the "dreadful day of the LORD." The term "dreadful day" alludes to the final forty-two months of the Tribulation, called by Christ, "great tribulation" (Matt. 24:21). Elijah will come to "restore the hearts of the fathers to their children" (Mal. 4:6, NAS). Even Christ predicted that, "Elijah is coming first and will restore all things" (Matt. 17:11).

Thus, Elijah will reappear at the end of days and begin a restoration process that will include revealing to Jewish men the tribe from which they come and restoring access to the temple and temple worship. There is more biblical evidence of Elijah and his ministry in the future Tribulation found in the Apocalypse.

After the apostle John was instructed to measure the temple of God, the Almighty then revealed:

> "And I will give power to my two witnesses, and they will prophesy one thousand two hundred and sixty days, clothed in sackcloth." These are the two olive trees and the two lampstands standing before the God of the earth.
>
> —REVELATION 11:3–4

These "two witnesses" are two men who will prophesy for forty-two months in Jerusalem. They will be given great power over their enemies. Called "two olive trees and two lampstands," these two witnesses were first identified in Zechariah chapter 4, hundreds of years prior to John's vision:

> Then I answered and said to him, "What are these two olive trees—at the right of the lampstand and at its left?" And I further answered and said to him, "What are these two olive branches that drip into the receptacles of the two gold pipes from which the golden oil

drains?" Then he answered me and said, "Do you not know what these are?" And I said, "No, my lord." So he said, "These are the two anointed ones, who stand beside the Lord of the whole earth."

—ZECHARIAH 4:11–14

Both Zechariah and John paint the same imagery:

◆ Two witnesses or anointed ones

◆ Two olive trees

◆ Two (the right or left) lampstands

Who are these two anointed ones? It is clear they both are seen in the temple. During the Old Testament era, Zechariah saw them in heaven hundreds of years before John revealed their appearing during the Tribulation. These two prophets will witness to the Jews for forty-two months and then be killed by the Antichrist (Rev. 11:7). Since Elijah is predicted to appear before the terrible day of the Lord, he is certainly one of these two men.

Even today, observant Jews welcome Elijah during the celebration of the Passover Seder. Often a child is sent to the front door to see if Elijah is on the street. Jews are ready to welcome him into their homes, where they place a special cup on the table, prepared for Elijah to drink from as he announces the arrival of their Messiah and a world of peace. When the leader lifts the cup called the "Cup of Elijah," he waits for the door to open and says, "We open this door on Passover to welcome any guest who might stand outside. We wish that all the poor and hungry people might celebrate this Seder as we do. We welcome Elijah, for with your coming comes the time of peace and goodness on earth." Then the door is closed.[11] Thus, Elijah is one of the witnesses who will appear at the end of days.

Traditional scholars differ as to the identity of the second witness. Because the Bible teaches that the two Tribulation witnesses will "have power to shut heaven, so that no rain falls in the days of their prophecy; and they have power over waters to turn them to blood, and to strike the earth with all plagues, as often as they desire" (Rev. 11:6), some scholars believe these plagues are parallel to the plagues that struck Egypt in the time of Moses. Therefore, they believe that Moses is the second witness.

The biggest hindrance to this theory is the fact that Moses died prior to Israel entering the Promised Land, and God Himself buried him in an unmarked grave (Deut. 34:5–6). Just as it is impossible for Judas or Nero to be resurrected bodily and then die a second time ("It is appointed for men to die once"—Heb. 9:27), likewise Moses died thirty-five hundred years ago and will not be resurrected as a witness, then to die in Jerusalem forty-two months later a second time.

Others point out that during the transfiguration of Christ, both Elijah and Moses appeared and spoke to Christ concerning His sufferings (Matt. 17:3). This incident further adds fuel to the theory of Moses and Elijah being the two witnesses. However, there is only one other man outside of Elijah who has not died. He is the best candidate for the second witness. This is Enoch. This prophet predicted that the "Lord [would come] with ten thousands of His saints, to execute judgment" (Jude 14–15). Enoch was translated and has never died.

Since the two witnesses are prophets, both Elijah and Enoch fit the description. Elijah performed miracles, and Enoch was the first man to prophesy of Christ's return.

Several of the early fathers identify the coming two witnesses as Enoch and Elijah. One such example is as follows:

> And I say to you, O my brethren, that they also, Enoch and Elias [Elijah], must towards the end of time return into the world and die—in the day, namely of commotion, of terror, of perplexity, and affliction. For

Antichrist will slay four bodies, and will pour out their blood like water.[12]

The early father Tertullian (A.D. 145–220) wrote that Enoch and Elijah were the two witnesses: "Enoch was no doubt translated, and so was Elijah; nor did they experience death: it was postponed (and only postponed) most certainly: they are reserved for the suffering of death, that by their blood they may extinguish Antichrist."[13]

I believe the two witnesses are Elijah and Enoch for the following reasons:

♦ Both men have never died.

♦ Both men were taken to heaven.

♦ Both men were prophets.

♦ Both men were alive when Zechariah saw his vision.

♦ Enoch gave the first prophecy of Christ's return and the coming judgment (Jude 14–15).

♦ Both men must die to fulfill Hebrews 9:27.

♦ Elijah is predicted to return before the terrible day of the Lord (Mal. 4:5).

♦ Enoch was a Gentile, and Elijah was a Jew.

♦ Elijah will produce judgments against his enemies.

Muslims believe in the last days and God's judgment. When these two witnesses appear, they will exercise their authority by closing the heavens, thus preventing rain, and by calling down fire from heaven on their enemies (Rev. 11:5–6). In fact, I believe some of the trumpet judgments mentioned in Revelation 8 may actually be pronounced through the mouths of these two prophets.

Prior to John introducing these two men, he is told to measure the temple (Rev. 11:1–2). I was always curious as to why John mentioned the temple when it had been destroyed twenty-five years earlier in A.D. 70. Obviously, John was seeing the temple in Jerusalem that had been rebuilt during the first forty-two months. This is the same temple in which Christ said the abomination would appear (Matt. 24:15) and the temple where the man of sin would sit and proclaim himself god (2 Thess. 2:4). Who will rebuild this temple? May I suggest that Elijah will be linked to the rebuilding process.

Picture this. The two witnesses suddenly appear in Jerusalem. As they speak, amazing miracles of judgment occur against their enemies. Anyone who speaks against them or attempts to kill them is struck down by fire. No Muslim in the world would attempt to kill these two men as long as they have authority to induce judgment on their enemies. This one fact enables the two witnesses to take over a portion of the Temple Mount and to initiate a rebuilding process. No one will be willing to come against them. They will be protected supernaturally by God's power.

Since Passover is the first of seven feasts on Israel's calendar, any future Jewish temple would be dedicated at Passover. If, as Professor Asher Kaufman believes, it would take forty-two months to complete the building of a temple, then the process would begin in the fall and, forty-two months later, be dedicated at Passover.

THE MAIN ARGUMENT

One main argument arises when teaching how the Antichrist will "bring an end to sacrifice" (Dan. 9:27). The issue is "sacrifices." Since Christ has become the final sacrifice for sin, some Christian scholars teach that God would never allow a temple to be built that would reintroduce animal sacrifices. Christ is the final sacrifice for our sins.

But in Ezekiel 44 through 48, we read the prophet's description of a temple that will be built in Jerusalem during the millennial reign of the Messiah. Part of the process includes the sacrifices of certain animals (Ezek. 40:41). However, these sacrifices are not being offered for the removal of sin. They are gift offerings and memorial sacrifices. Religious Jews who study the Torah in Jerusalem would still allow for the sacrifices to resume, based upon the numerous commandments in the five books of Moses (the Torah). Thus, as the Jews are offering the sacrifices in the middle of the Tribulation, the Antichrist will seize control of Jerusalem, causing the sacrifice to cease.

If Muslims view the coming Antichrist as their Mahdi, then they will be thrilled to hear that their leader moves into Jerusalem and liberates the Temple Mount from the Jews, killing the two witnesses. In fact, the deaths of the two witnesses will be celebrated in nations throughout the world:

> Now when they finish their testimony, the beast that ascends out of the bottomless pit will make war against them, overcome them, and kill them. And their dead bodies will lie in the street of the great city which spiritually is called Sodom and Egypt, where also our Lord was crucified. Then those from the peoples, tribes, tongues, and nations will see their dead bodies three-and-a-half days, and not allow their dead bodies to be put into graves. And those who dwell on the earth will rejoice over them, make merry, and send gifts to one another, because these two prophets tormented those who dwell on the earth.
>
> —Revelation 11:7–10

When a Jew dies in Jerusalem, that person is buried the same day. When a Muslim dies, that person is also buried the same day. However, if a person who has blasphemed Islam is slain, often that person's body is laid in the streets and spat upon and kicked, and the corpse is publicly humiliated in various Islamic nations. This was witnessed in Iraq when a car with Americans was burned. Their scorched bodies hung from ropes and were abused for some time before being removed.

The death of these two men points to another interesting Islamic tradition concerning the *Dajjal*. The actual term is the *Masih ad-Dajjal,* meaning "the imposter messiah," who is an apocalyptic figure in Islamic eschatology.[14] This person will form an army and fight against Christ and the Mahdi. This "christ" may be the false prophet of Revelation 13:11 (the lamb with two horns), and the Mahdi appears to be the beast in Revelation 13:1–2. Therefore, two men are revealed in Revelation who will fight the two witnesses—the Antichrist and the false prophet. These two men are similar to the traditions of the Islamic Christ and Mahdi who will defeat the Dajjal.

Muhammad taught that there would be thirty Dajjals, each of whom would say: "I am a prophet." Ironically, Muslim tradition teaches that the final Dajjal at the end of days will be a king of the Jews.[15] This teaching is revealed in a series of statements recorded in the hadith, alleged statements made by Muhammad overheard by his family and closest friends. It is strange that according to some traditions the Dajjal appears in Iraq!

According to Islamic hadith, at the end of days the world will sink into utter confusion, spreading spiritual darkness to Arab nations. Men will wake up believers but become infidels by nightfall. Prior to the arrival of Al-Mahdi, the final Islamic savior, the Jewish king Dajjal will rise up from the valley between Iraq and Syria. His appearing will cause great fussing and fighting on the left and the right and in all directions.

It is interesting to note how Muslims (in the time of Muhammad) taught that the Jews were looking for a messiah to restore the kingdom of Israel to them. In Muhammad's time, Israel was in the hands of the Christians, and Jerusalem was under the control of the Byzantine

Empire. Many Jews and Christians were scattered throughout the Arabian Desert, living in small communities among groups of men and women of the same faith. Muhammad made an effort to convince the Christians and Jews that he was a true prophet. After his claims were rejected, Muhammad turned against the "people of the book," especially the Jews.

THE ONE-EYED MONSTER

The description of this future "Jewish king" is quite fanciful to say the least. He is said to be so large that his head will be above the clouds, and the deepest spot in the sea will not go to his heels. Some take this literally, but more contemporary Islamic scholars indicate this imagery is a symbolic view of Al-Dajjal's dominion over the air, land, and sea.

He is described as a man with curly hair and a blind eye: "Then I moved forward and cast a glance and there was a bulky man of red complexion with thick locks of hair on his head, blind of one eye as if his eye was a swollen grape. I asked: Who is he? They answered: He is Dajjal."[16] *Sahih Muslim* states that seventy thousand Jews will be his followers.[17] Other hadith state that before his appearance, the world will experience famine for three years, and no one will be able to wage war against him while he rules.[18]

In 1967, during the Six-Day War, the leading Israeli general was Moshe Dayan. Under his direction, the city of Jerusalem was liberated, and the Jews gained free access to the Western Wall. The Jewish general had one bad eye that was covered with a black patch that bulged out. Some uneducated Muslims feared that the general might be the Dajjal, since the Muslims had lost control of East Jerusalem to the hands of the Jews!

Although the Israeli military had seized control of the Islamic Dome of the Rock and the Temple Mount, General Moshe Dayan gave the land back into the hands of Islamic authorities. There was a fear among the Israeli military that taking possession of the Temple Mountain would cause a worldwide war between Muslims and Jews. The "one-eyed" general proved not to be the Jewish king of Islamic tradition.

THE LETTERS ON THE FOREHEAD

The teaching on Al-Dajjal states that all believers (Muslims) will see the letters KFR appear on the forehead of Dajjal, which signify *KaFiR*, or *infidel*. When these letters are seen, Muslims are instructed to enter the mosque and begin praying intently for protection from the Jewish king.

Most Muslims believe this strong tradition about the Dajjal and his appearing as the Jewish king as much as many Christians believe in the return of Christ. These traditions not only form the foundation of Islamic End Time teaching, but they also have an influence upon the way Muslims react to the West and to wars occurring in their own backyard.

It may be possible that fanatical Muslims will view the two witnesses as Jewish leaders linked to the Dajjal, or the "Islamic Antichrist." By killing these two men, the Antichrist will again fulfill Islamic traditions and expectations, freeing the Temple Mount from Jewish hands and influence.

Notice the comparison between the Islamic traditions of the Dajjal and the prophetic scriptures about the two witnesses in Revelation 11:

The Dajjal of Islam	The Two Witnesses of Revelation 11	Scripture References
Will be a leader of the Jews	Appear to the Jews in Israel	Revelation 11:1–6
Will have 70,000 followers	Will have 144,000 followers	Revelation 7:1–8
Will help restore Israel	Will restore "all things"	Mark 9:12

The Dajjal of Islam	The Two Witnesses of Revelation 11	Scripture References
Will take over the Temple Mount	Will help rebuild a Jewish temple	Revelation 11:1–2
Will come from the East	Arise from the East	Revelation 7:1–3
Will work miracles	Will work miracles	Revelation 11:5–6

When the Antichrist slays the two witnesses in Jerusalem, it is reasonable to believe that many Muslims who believe in the appearing of the Dajjal will believe that the two witnesses in the Apocalypse were Jewish enemies of Islam and that their deaths fulfill the expectations of the Islamic Mahdi, who defeats the Dajjal. The deaths of these two men (Enoch and Elijah) will thrill the world.

THE IMAGE OF THE BEAST

After seizing the temple area, the false prophet constructs an "image of the beast" and, through a satanic miracle, will make the image speak and live (Rev. 13:14–15). The word *image* in Greek is *eikon*. According to W. E. Vine, the word *eikon* is used in Scripture to indicate an image or a coin (Matt. 22:20) or a statue (Rom. 1:23). In English, we use the word *icon* as a representation or picture of a sacred or sanctified person venerated in the Eastern Church. In some European churches, there are alleged "miracles" of bleeding and crying icons, which often draw thousands of worshipers.

When I observe thousands of people gathered around a statue, picture, or a religious image that appears to be manifesting blood or water, I am reminded of how the false prophet will build an *icon* that will speak and live, deceiving the nations and causing all to worship the image. Paul described this moment:

> The coming of the lawless one is according to the working of Satan, with all power, signs, and lying wonders, and with all unrighteous deception among those

who perish, because they did not receive the love of the truth, that they might be saved. And for this reason God will send them strong delusion, that they should believe the lie, that they all may be condemned who did not believe the truth but had pleasure in unrighteousness.

—2 THESSALONIANS 2:9–12

Those who refuse to worship the image will be beheaded (Rev. 20:4). This is a clue to an Islamic link, since beheading is a distinctly Islamic form of execution. When this image begins to speak, the Jews will escape Jerusalem and the dangers of the Antichrist by fleeing to Jordan and settling in an area that many scholars believe will be the rose-colored city of Petra (Ps. 60:9; 108:10). The Antichrist will then set himself up as God in the temple:

...the man of sin is revealed, the son of perdition, who opposes and exalts himself above all that is called God or that is worshiped, so that he sits as God in the temple of God, showing himself that he is God.

—2 THESSALONIANS 2:3–4

For the final forty-two months of the Tribulation, Muslims will unite with a ten-nation coalition that will not only control Jerusalem but will also set out to slay all Jews and any convert of Christianity. All who refuse worship of the beast and his image will die by beheading. The Antichrist's economic system will control all buying and selling in that region of the world, using the ten kings and their kingdoms as pawns on a chessboard to put the world in checkmate, making all humanity follow the will of the Antichrist.

This time will be a "time of trouble, such as never was since there was a nation, even to that time" (Dan. 12:1). Deaths caused by famines, pestilences, war, and plagues will be so great that "unless those days were shortened, no flesh would be saved" (Matt. 24:22). However, at the conclusion of seven years, when all nations march toward Jerusalem, the mother of all battles will unfold in the valley of Megiddo in Israel. John saw this when he wrote:

> For they are spirits of demons, performing signs, which go out to the kings of the earth and of the whole world, to gather them to the battle of that great day of God Almighty.... And they gathered them together to the place called in Hebrew, Armageddon.
>
> —REVELATION 16:14, 16

This valley has been host to famous battles throughout history. These battles include the Assyrians, Canaanites, Philistines, Egyptians, Greeks, Israelites, Persians, and Romans. This valley is located fifteen miles from the Mediterranean coast, and Jerusalem is about fifty-five miles as a bird flies from the ancient mount of Megiddo. Prior to the annihilation of mankind, Christ and the armies of heaven (Rev. 19:14) will interrupt the battle and destroy His enemies with the brightness of His coming (2 Thess. 2:8). Immediately, the false prophet and Antichrist will be physically removed and placed in a prison in the abyss, along with the adversary called Satan (Rev. 19:20; 20:1–3). This day initiates the beginning of the thousand-year reign of Christ (v. 4).

THE CONCLUSION OF THE MATTER

Both the Book of Daniel and the Apocalypse present the same climax to their visions of the time of the end. The kingdom of the beast is defeated and destroyed by the return of the Messiah, Jesus Christ, identified as the "King of kings and Lord of lords" (Rev. 19:16).

I believe you can see that we are certainly in the time of the end. The nations of prophecy are aligning in position for the great battles of prophecy. While there will be differences of opinion concerning certain parts of this teaching, I believe we have given a large-scale picture of what will occur and how recent events come into play. We have gone backstage to see what is going to happen.

Now let's get ready for the opening scene in the last-day drama. The curtain is about to rise. The action is about to start, and the actors are taking their position on stage. It is about to become interesting. But at least you know the outcome, and, for believers, it is going to be a great day when Messiah returns.

APPENDIX

THE SEVEN-PHASE MANIFESTO
OF THE ANTICHRIST

MANIFESTO PHASE 1:
TO TAKE CONTROL OF ISRAEL

It is a necessity for the Palestinians to defeat the Jewish state and seize possession of the ancient high places (the West Bank), Judea, and Samaria.

The prophecy:

> And he shall plant the tents of his palace between the seas and the glorious holy mountain; yet he shall come to his end, and no one will help him.
> —DANIEL 11:45

MANIFESTO PHASE 2:
TO TAKE CONTROL OVER JERUSALEM

Since the destruction of the Jewish temple and Jerusalem in A.D. 70, Jerusalem has changed hands among Gentile empires. From the Romans, to the Byzantines, to the Muslims, to the Crusaders, to the Turks, to the British, and finally to the Jews, Jerusalem has been occupied for more than nineteen hundred years. Prophecy indicates the Gentiles will take possession of Jerusalem one more time.

The prophecy:

> And they will fall by the edge of the sword, and be led away captive into all nations. And Jerusalem will be trampled by Gentiles until the times of the Gentiles are fulfilled.
>
> —Luke 21:24

Manifesto Phase 3: To Convert the World to His Own Religion

For centuries Europe and the Middle East were hotbeds for forced "conversions." During the times when the Roman Church leaders ruled, Spanish Jews were forced to convert or face expulsion and, in some instances, death. When radical Islamic forces ruled, then Jews faced terrorism and Christians faced martyrdom. Forced conversion will again become common, and those who refuse will face the final solution—death.

The prophecy:

> So they worshiped the dragon who gave authority to the beast; and they worshiped the beast, saying, "Who is like the beast? Who is able to make war with him?"
>
> —Revelation 13:4

Manifesto Phase 4: To Destroy All Opposition to His Control

The Antichrist will show no mercy to those who oppose his rule and his religion. The avenue of punishment will be to behead those who resist him. In anger and wrath he will take lives. In the beginning, he will make a peace treaty with many (Dan. 9:27), and at the end of his rule he will go forth to destroy many. The blood of Christian martyrs will become the seed that will bring the wrath of God upon the earth and eventually bring destruction to the beast's kingdom.

The prophecy:

> But news from the east and the north shall trouble him; therefore he shall go out with great fury to destroy and annihilate many.
>
> —DANIEL 11:44

> And I saw thrones, and they sat on them, and judgment was committed to them. Then I saw the souls of those who had been beheaded for their witness to Jesus and for the word of God.
>
> —REVELATION 20:4

MANIFESTO PHASE 5: TO CONTROL ALL BUYING AND SELLING

Prophecy indicates an extensive famine will occur during the final seven years prior to Christ's return (Rev. 6:5–6). This famine will impact entire nations and continents, thus creating the need for food rationing (v. 6). Forty-two months into the Tribulation, a controlled system of buying and selling will be introduced by a religious leader identified as the false prophet (Rev. 13:11; 19:20). A mysterious religious mark will be etched on the right hand or on the forehead of those following the Antichrist and the false prophet. Those rejecting this new system of economic control will be subject to martyrdom.

The prophecy:

> He causes all, both small and great, rich and poor, free and slave, to receive a mark on their right hand or on

their foreheads, and that no one may buy or sell except one who has the mark or the name of the beast, or the number of his name.

—REVELATION 13:16–17

MANIFESTO PHASE 6:
TO CONTROL THE TEMPLE MOUNT IN JERUSALEM

The temple John was told to measure was not a temple in heaven but a future temple that will be erected in Jerusalem during the first forty-two months of the Tribulation. The only place the Jews would construct a temple would be on the site of the previous two temples, the Temple Mount in Jerusalem.

Islam will not permit a Jewish house of worship without a war. The Antichrist will be restrained from his unbridled authority and his desire for invasion during the first half of the Tribulation, giving the two witnesses time to minister to a Jewish remnant.

After God's supernatural restraining power is removed, this "man of sin and son of perdition" will be unleashed upon the nations. His main assignment will be to free the Temple Mount from the hands of the infidel Jews. After his invasion, the holy city (Jerusalem) will be trodden down by the Antichrist's armies for forty-two months.

The prophecy:

> Then I was given a reed like a measuring rod. And the angel stood, saying, "Rise and measure the temple of God, the altar, and those who worship there. But leave out the court which is outside the temple, and do not measure it, for it has been given to the Gentiles. And they will tread the holy city underfoot for forty-two months."
>
> —REVELATION 11:1–2

Manifesto Phase 7: To Be Worshiped as a God

Why would so many people desire to "worship" a man? Today there are imams, Hindu holy men, and gurus who are literally worshiped as though they were gods. One such Islamic man is from France where twenty million Shi'ite followers claim him to be the incarnation of God.

The fact that the Antichrist will be a military warrior and no one will be able to make war with him will cause his followers to treat him as a god.

The prophecy:

> Who opposes and exalts himself above all that is called God or that is worshiped, so that he sits as God in the temple of God, showing himself that he is God.
>
> —2 Thessalonians 2:4

> So they worshiped the dragon who gave authority to the beast; and they worshiped the beast, saying, "Who is like the beast? Who is able to make war with him?"
>
> —Revelation 13:4

Quotes From the Quran

> Fighting is prescribed for you, and you dislike it. But it is possible that you dislike a thing which is good for you, and that you love a thing which is bad for you. But Allah knows, and you know not.
>
> —Surah 2:216

> Let the People of the Gospel judge by what Allah has revealed therein. If any do fail to judge by (the light of)

what Allah has revealed, they are (no better than) those who rebel.

—SURAH 5:47

O you who believe! take not the Jews and the Christians for your friends and protectors: they are but friends and protectors to each other. And he amongst you that turns to them (for friendship) is of them. Verily Allah guides not a people unjust.

—SURAH 5:51

O You who believe! take not for friends and protectors those who take your religion for a mockery or sport, whether among those who received the Scripture before you, or among those who reject Faith; but you should fear Allah, if you have Faith (indeed).

—SURAH 5:57

NOTES

CHAPTER 1
THE EVIDENCE IS IN—WE ARE IN THE TIME OF THE END

1. Flavius Josephus, *War of the Jews*, book 7, chapter 3, http://bible
.crosswalk.com/HISTORY/BC/FLAVIUSJOSEPHUS/?book=War_7&cha
pter=3 (accessed December 2, 2008).

2. W. E. Vine, *W. E. Vine's Expository Dictionary of Old and New
Testament Words* (Nashville, TN: Thomas Nelson Publishers, 1997), 357.

3. Biblesoft, *Thayer's Greek Lexicon* (Seattle, WA: Biblesoft, 1994), licensed
and used by permission of Institute of Creation Research.

4. Notes in Finis Dake, *Dake's Annotated Reference Bible* (Laurens, SC:
Dake Bible Sales, 1963), s.v. "Revelation 10."

5. Paul said that the "man of sin" (the Antichrist) would not be revealed until
a restrainer was taken out of the way, and once the restrainer was removed, then
this man of sin would be revealed. Once the restrainer is removed, then time is
no longer delayed and all prophetic events will accelerate.

6. A. B. Simpson, *The Coming One* (New York: Christian Alliance
Publishing Company, 1912).

7. Harry Rimmer, *The Coming War and the Rise of Russia* (Grand
Rapids, MI: Wm. B. Eerdmans, 1940).

8. Dake, *Dake's Annotated Reference Bible*, s.v. "Isaiah 35."

9. Jerusalemites.org, "14-May-48: The Proclamation of 'Israel's
Independence,'" http://www.jerusalemites.org/facts_documents/proclamation
.htm (accessed October 20, 2008).

10. Benny Morris, *1948: The First Arab-Israeli War* (New Haven, CT: Yale
University Press, 2008).

11. Joan Comay, *Ben-Gurion and the Birth of Israel* (New York: Random
House, 1967), 136.

12. For more information about drip irrigation methods as developed by
Israel, see: "Israeli Water Technologies for Agriculture," *Agrotechnology*,
http://www.export.gov.il/Eng/_Articles/Articles.asp?CategoryID=1005&Sourc
eCategoryID=1005 (accessed December 2, 2008).

13. Jewish Virtual Library, "The 1967 Six-Day War," http://www.jewish
virtuallibrary.org/jsource/History/1967toc.html (accessed October 21, 2008).

14. The Scripture references predicting the last-day return of the Jews are
found in Isaiah 11:11–14; 43:5–6; 49:8–12; Jeremiah 16:13–16; Zechariah 8:7–8;
and others.

CHAPTER 2
SEVEN DOWN AND ONE MORE TO GO

1. Several classical prophetic books are available that detail the ten groups listed here. One of these is: Roy Allan Anderson, *Unfolding Daniel's Prophecies* (Nampa, ID: Pacific Press Publishing Association, 1975).

2. Gudrun Krämer and Graham Harman, *A History of Palestine: From the Ottoman Conquest to the Founding of the State of Israel* (Princeton, NJ: Princeton University Press, 2008).

CHAPTER 3
THE MAN WHO WOULD BE THE BEAST

1. Vine, W. E. *Vine's Expository Dictionary of Old and New Testament Words*, 53–43.

2. Greek Interlinear Translation of the New Testament.

3. Vine, W. E. *Vine's Expository Dictionary of Old and New Testament Words*, 94–95.

4. Commodianus, *Ante-Nicene Fathers*, "XLI.—Of the Time of Antichrist," http://bible.crosswalk.com/History/AD/EarlyChurchFathers/Ante-Nicene/Commodianus/view.cgi?file=anf04-38.htm&size=20&start=21852 (accessed December 3, 2008).

5. Ibid.

6. Katherine E. Welch, *The Roman Amphitheatre: From Its Origins to the Colosseum* (New York: Cambridge University Press, 2007), 157.

7. Lactantius, *Ante-Nicene Fathers*, "Chapter XVII.—Of the False Prophet, and the Hardships of the Righteous, and His Destruction," http://bible.crosswalk.com/History/AD/EarlyChurchFathers/Ante-Nicene/Lactantius/view.cgi?file=anf07-10.htm&size=20&start=106384 (accessed December 3, 2008).

8. Christian Classics Ethereal Library, "ANFO7: Fathers of the Third and Fourth Centuries: Lactantius, Venantius, Asterius, Victorinus, Dionysius, Apostolic Teaching and Constitutions, Homily," Chapter XIX, http://www.ccel.org/ccel/schaff/anf07.iii.ii.vii.xix.html (accessed December 3, 2008).

9. Christian Classics Ethereal Library, "ANFO5: Fathers of the Third Century: Hippolytus, Cyprian, Caius, Novatian, Appendix," III. Scholia on Daniel, http://www.ccel.org/ccel/schaff/anf05.iii.iv.i.x.iii.html (accessed December 3, 2008).

10. Hippolytus, "On the End of the World," *New Advent*, http://www.newadvent.org/fathers/0504.htm (accessed October 31, 2008).

CHAPTER 4
TWO FEET, TEN TOES, AND A LITTLE HORN WITH A BIG MOUTH

1. An anonymous, medieval manual for the afterlife, *The Book of the States of the Resurrection,* numbers seven levels, cited in Francis E. Peters, *Islam, a Guide for Jews and Christians* (New York: Princeton University Press, 2003), 259.

2. Hesiod, *Works and Days,* Evelyn White, trans., About.com: Ancient/Classical History, http://ancienthistory.about.com/library/bl/bl_text_hesiod_worksanddays.htm (accessed October 22, 2008).

3. Hippolytus, "On Christ and Antichrist," NewAdvent.org, http://www.newadvent.org/fathers/0516.htm (accessed December 4, 2008).

4. For a full description of Hippolytus's explanation of the vision of the four beasts, see: "Ante-Nicene Fathers/Volume V/Hippolytus/The Extant Works and Fragments of Hippolytus/Exegetical/On Daniel/Part 3," http://en.wikisource.org/wiki/Ante-Nicene_Fathers/Volume_V/Hippolytus/The_Extant_Works_and_Fragments_of_Hippolytus/Exegetical/On_Daniel/Part_3 (accessed October 22, 2008).

5. Dake, *Dake's Annotated Reference Bible,* O.T. notes, page 918.

6. Francis Brown, S. Driver, and C. Briggs, *Brown-Driver-Briggs Hebrew and English Lexicon* (N.p.: Hendrickson Publishers, 1996).

CHAPTER 5
ISLAM 101—WHAT YOU SHOULD KNOW

1. Jack Fairweather, "Bloody Ritual, Modern Meaning," WashingtonPost.com, January 30, 2008, http://newsweek.washingtonpost.com/postglobal/islamsadvance/2008/01/ashura.html (accessed October 28, 2008).

2. SeattleTimes.com, "Sunni Muslims, Shiite Muslims," http://seattletimes.nwsource.com/art/news/nation_world/sept_11/understandingthecrisis/islammap.pdf (accessed December 4, 2008).

3. Adherents.com, "The Largest Shi'ite Communities," http://www.adherents.com/largecom/com_shiite.html (accessed October 28, 2008).

CHAPTER 6
ISLAM AND THE LAST DAYS

1. This story was related to my father in the early 1970s when he pastored in Arlington, Virginia.

2. Shahabuddin, "The Coming of Mystery Imam al-Mahdi."

3. Patrick Jackson, "Who Are Iraq's Mehdi Army?" *BBC News,* http://news.bbc.co.uk/2/hi/middle_east/3604393.stm (accessed October 27, 2008).

4. Alkhilafah.net, "Black Banners From Khurasan (Afghanistan) to Jerusalem," http://alkhilafah.net/victoriousarmy.html (accessed October 27, 2008).

5. Abu Nu'aym and As-Suyuti, related by Thawban, as quoted by Izzat and Arif, p. 44, cited in Joel Richardson, "The Mahdi: Islam's Awaited Messiah," *Will Islam Be Our Future?* Answering-Islam.org, http://www.answering-islam.org/Authors/JR/Future/ch04_the_mahdi.htm (accessed December 5, 2008).

6. HP-Time.com, "Sacrilege in Mecca," *TIME*, December 3, 1979, http://www.time.com/time/magazine/article/0,9171,948637-1,00.html (accessed October 27, 2008).

7. Thomas Hegghammer and Stephane Lacroix, "Rejectionist Islamism in Saudi Arabia: The Story of Juhayman al-'Utaybi Revisited," http://moyen -orient.sciences-po.fr/articles_pour_revue_en_ligne/17042007%20Hegg hammer%20%20Lacroix%20-%20Juhayman%20-%20Website%20version.pdf (accessed October 27, 2008).

8. LookLex Encyclopaedia, "Samarra," http://lexicorient.com/e.o/samarra .htm (accessed October 27, 2008).

CHAPTER 7
A CRESCENT REVOLUTION RISES OVER THE MIDDLE EAST

1. Huda, "The Crescent Moon," About.com, http://islam.about.com/od/ history/a/crescent_moon.htm (accessed June 16, 2011).

2. Talmud-Mas Sukkah 29a.

3. Naseema Noor, "Tunisia: The Revolution That Started It All," *International Affairs Review*, January 31, 2011, http://www.iar-gwu.org/ node/257 (accessed June 16, 2011).

4. Abigail Hauslohner and Yasmine El Rashidi, "The 18-Day Miracle: Egyptian People Power Ousts Hosni Mubarak," Time.com, February 11, 2011, http://www.time.com/time/world/article/0,8599,2048575,00.html (accessed June 16, 2011).

5. Reuters.com, "Timeline—Libya's Uprising Against Muammar Gaddafi," May 31, 2011, http://www.reuters.com/article/2011/05/31/libya-events-idUSLDE 74O1KJ20110531 (accessed June 16, 2011).

6. Richard Spencer, "Libya: Col Gaddafi Plots Retaliatory Strikes If Forced From Leadership," *The Telegraph*, June 1, 2011, http://www.telegraph.co.uk/ news/worldnews/africaandindianocean/libya/8548392/Libya-Col-Gaddafi -plots-retaliatory-strikes-if-forced-from-leadership.html (accessed June 16, 2011).

7. Alexander Roberts and James Donaldson, eds., *The Ante-Nicene Fathers*, vol. 5 (New York: Charles Scribner's Sons, 1903), 190. Viewed at http://books.google.com.

8. Herman Cain, "Egypt Crisis and Oil," *American Spectator*, February 1, 2011, http://spectator.org/archives/2011/02/01/egypt-crisis-and-oil# (accessed June 16, 2011).

9. Nayla Razzouk and Ola Galal, "Egyptian Gas to Israel, Jordan May Halt for Two Weeks," Bloomberg.com, February 6, 2011, http://www.bloomberg.com/news/2011-02-05/egypt-gas-pipeline-feeding-israel-explodes-in-sinai-desert -arabiya-says.html (accessed June 16, 2011).

10. *Barnes' Notes*, electronic database, copyright © 1997 by Biblesoft, s.v. "Daniel 11:43."

11. *Maritime Sun News*, "Hostage-Taking at Sea Rises to Record Levels, Says IMB," January 19, 2011, http://www.maritimesun.com/news/hostage -taking-at-sea-rises-to-record-levels-says-imb (accessed June 17, 2011).

12. Ibid.

13. HistoryGuy.com, "Arab-Israeli Wars (1948–Present)," http://www .historyguy.com/arab_israeli_wars.html (accessed June 17, 2011).

14. Central Intelligence Agency, "Egypt," *The World Factbook*, https:// www.cia.gov/library/publications/the-world-factbook/geos/eg.html (accessed June 17, 2011).

15. Egypt.com, "Experts: Egypt's Tourism Feels the Pinch of Bin Laden Slaying," *Egypt News*, May 3, 2011, http://news.egypt.com/en/2011050314526/ news/-egypt-news/experts-egypt-s-tourism-feels-the-pinch-of-bin-laden -slaying.html (accessed June 17, 2011).

16. Reuters.com, "Factbox: The Strait of Hormuz, Key Oil Shipping Route," January 7, 2010, http://www.reuters.com/article/2010/01/07/us-iran-hormuz -factbox-idUSTRE6062OG20100107 (accessed June 17, 2011).

17. Central Intelligence Agency, "Iran," *The World Factbook*, https://www .cia.gov/library/publications/the-world-factbook/geos/ir.html (accessed June 17, 2011).

CHAPTER 8
THE OSAMA FACTOR AND AMERICA

1. Shahabuddin, "The Coming of Mystery Imam al-Mahdi," *The Sunday Times* (Colombo, Sri Lanka), November 18, 1990, http://kataragama.org/ al-mahdi.htm (accessed July 20, 2011).

2. Al-Qiyamah.org, "The End Times and the Emergence of the Mahdi," http://www.al-qiyamah.org/_/end_times_and_the_emergence_of_the_mahdi .htm (accessed July 20, 2011).

3. Harvard-Smithsonian Center for Astrophysics, "Press Information Sheet: Comet C/1995 01 (Hale-Bopp)," October 20, 2000, http://www.cfa.harvard.edu/ iau/pressinfo/HaleBopp.html (accessed July 20, 2011).

4. Lawrence Auster, "How Many Radical Muslims Are There in the World?", View From the Right, May 9, 2008, http://www.amnation.com/vfr/archives/010556.html (accessed July 20, 2011).

5. This story was related directly to the author by the pastor of the church where the martial arts expert attends and was related to him by the man himself.

6. For the protection of my Pakistani friend, I will not reveal his name or the city where he lives in California, as this story was related directly to me from him.

7. Sehar Sabir, "Census Statistics for Muslims in America," Islamic Information Center, http://www.islamicinformationcenter.org/interfaith-center/interfaith-center/census-statistics-for-muslims-in-america.html (accessed July 20, 2011).

8. "Culture of Afghanistan," Afghanistan, http://afghanistan.saarctourism.org/culture.html (accessed July 20, 2011).

9. *Daily Mail Reporter*, "Will Bin Laden's Sea Burial Backfire? Radical Muslims Already Name Location 'Martyr's Sea,'" May 5, 2011, http://www.dailymail.co.uk/news/article-1383698/Osama-Bin-Laden-dead-Radical-Muslims-burial-location-Martyrs-Sea.html (accessed July 21, 2011).

10. Ibid.

11. Patrik Jonsson, "Fort Hood Suspect: Portrait of a Terrorist?", *Christian Science Monitor*, November 10, 2009, http://www.csmonitor.com/USA/2009/1110/p02s15-usgn.html (accessed July 20, 2011).

CHAPTER 9
THE BIBLE AND THE QURAN—ISLAMIC
AND CHRISTIAN PROPHECIES

1. Muhammad ibn Izzat and Muhammad 'Arif, *Al Mahdi and the End of Time* (London: Dar Al-Taqwa, 1997), 33.

2. Ibid., 32.

3. Mufti A.H. Elias and Mohammad Ali ibn Zubair Ali, "Imam Mahdi (Descendent of Prophet Muhammad PBUH)," http://www.islam.tc/prophecies/imam.html (accessed December 5, 2008).

4. IslamicWeb.com, "Who Is Imam Al-Mahdi?", http://islamicweb.com/?folder=history&file=Mahdi (accessed December 5, 2008).

5. Iqra.net, "His Prophecies," Iqra Islamic Publications, http://www.iqra.net/Hadith/Prophecies.htm (accessed December 5, 2008).

6. SearchforTruth.com, "8. Al-Anfal [75]," http://www.searchfortruth.com/chapter_display.php?chapter=8&translator=3 (accessed December 5, 2008).

7. See individual stories of persecution around the world, including these cited in Indonesia, at the Voice of the Martyrs website at http://www .persecution.com/.

8. Mervyn Bendle, "How to Be a Useful Idiot: Saudi Funding in Australia," ABC.net.au, October 13, 2008, http://www.abc.net.au/unleashed/stories/ s2389000.htm (accessed December 5, 2008).

9. Dr. Liyakat Takim, "Apostasy (*Irtidad*) in Islam," http://www.al-islam .org/organizations/AalimNetwork/msg00228.html (accessed November 14, 2008).

CHAPTER 10
IRAQ—THE FUTURE HEADQUARTERS
OF THE COMING ANTICHRIST

1. For more information on Saddam Hussein's extensive building plans, see: Matt Viser, "Design for a Dictator," Boston.com, March 13, 2005, http:// www.boston.com/news/local/articles/2005/03/13/design_for_a_dictator/ (accessed October 28, 2008).

2. Josephus, *Antiquities of the Jews*, book 1, chapter 4, section 3, http:// www .ccel.org/ccel/josephus/works/files/ant-1.htm (accessed December 5, 2008).

3. John F. Burns, "Mideast Tensions; New Babylon Is Stalled By a Modern Upheaval," *New York Times*, October 11, 1990, http://query.nytimes.com/gst/ fullpage.html?res=9C0CE0D71E3CF932A25753C1A966958260&sec=&spon= &pagewanted=1 (accessed October 28, 2008).

4. Ibid.

5. Paul Lewis, "Babylon Journal; Ancient King's Instructions to Iraq: Fix My Palace," *New York Times*, April 19, 1989, http://query.nytimes.com/gst/ fullpage.html?res=950DE2DF1738F93AA25757C0A96F948260 (accessed October 28, 2008).

6. PBS.org, "Transcript: The Mind of Hussein," February 26, 1991, http:// www.pbs.org/wgbh/pages/frontline/shows/longroad/etc/mind.html (accessed December 5, 2008).

7. NationMaster.com, "Project Babylon," http://www.nationmaster.com/ encyclopedia/Project-Babylon (accessed October 28, 2008).

CHAPTER 11
THE MARK OF THE BEAST AND THE ISLAMIC LINK

1. J. N. Darby, *Notes on the Apocalypse* (N.p.: n.d.), 68, quoted in John F. Walvoord, "13. The Beasts and the False Prophet," http://www.bible.org/page .php?page_id=5681#P1252_547338 (accessed March 30, 2009).

2. Ibson T. Beckwith, *The Apocalypse of John* (Eugene, OR: Wipf and Stock Publishers, 2001), 403.

3. Matthew Henry, *Matthew Henry's Commentary on the Whole Bible,* electronic database, PC Study Bible V3.2F (www.biblesoft.com: BibleSoft, 1998, s.v. "Revelation 13:11).

4. Answers.com, "Gematria," http://www.answers.com/topic/gematria (accessed October 28, 2008).

5. Christian Apologetics and Research Ministry, "Gematria," http://www .carm.org/kabbalah/gematria.htm (accessed February 5, 2009).

6. *Barnes' Notes,* electronic database, PC Study Bible V3.2F (www.biblesoft .com: BibleSoft, 1998, s.v. "Revelation 13:18."

7. E. W. Bullinger, *Number in Scripture* (Whitefish, MT: Kessinger Publishing, 2003), 283.

CHAPTER 12
FANATICAL ISLAM'S PLAN TO CONTROL THE WORLD

1. Hal Lindsey, *The Final Battle* (Los Angeles, CA: Western Front Ltd., 1995), 187.

2. Irshad.org, "Identification of the Prophesied Imam Mahdi," http://www .irshad.org/islam/prophecy/mahdi.htm (accessed October 29, 2008).

3. Elias and Ali, "Imam Mahdi (Descendent of Prophet Muhammad PBUH)."

CHAPTER 13
THE (ISLAMIC) SUN WILL RISE IN THE WEST

1. *Sahih Bukhari,* vol. 9, bk. 88, no. 237, narrated Abu Huraira, http:// www .usc.edu/schools/college/crcc/engagement/resources/texts/muslim/hadith/ bukhari/088.sbt.html (accessed December 9, 2008).

2. Daniel Pipes, "How Many U.S. Muslims?" *New York Post,* October 29, 2001, http://www.danielpipes.org/article/76 (accessed November 14, 2008).

3. Aaron Klein, "Election 2008: Nation of Islam Activists on Obama Camp Payroll," WorldNetDaily.com, June 3, 2008, http://www.worldnetdaily.com/ index.php?fa=PAGE.view&pageId=66167 (accessed January 21, 2009).

4. Ryan Lizza, "The Agitator," *The New Republic,* March 19, 2007, http:// www.tnr.com/politics/story.html?id=a74fca23-f6ac-4736-9c78-f4163d 4f25c7&p=8 (accessed January 26, 2009).

5. Nicole Neroulias, "American Muslims Relieved, Hopeful at Obama's Election," USAToday.com, November 7, 2008, http://www.usatoday.com/news/ religion/2008-11-06-obama-muslims_n.htm (accessed January 26, 2009).

6. Bud Simmons, "A New Seal Debuted on Obama's Podium Friday, Sporting Iconography Used in the U.S. Presidential Seal," Associated Press, June 20, 2008, http://bsimmons.wordpress.com/2008/06/20/a-new-seal-debuted-on-obamas-podium-friday-sporting-iconography-used-in-the-us-presidential-seal/ (accessed October 29, 2008).

7. RushLimbaugh.com, "Farrakhan Calls Obama 'Messiah,'" October 10, 2008, http://www.rushlimbaugh.com/home/daily/site_101008/content/01125108.guest.html (accessed January 26, 2009).

8. Klein, "Election 2008: Nation of Islam Activists on Obama Camp Payroll."

9. Dale Hurd, "Imam Wants Islamic State of North America by 2050," CBNnews.com, November 9, 2007, http://www.cbn.com/CBNnews/267338.aspx (accessed October 29, 2008).

10. JihadWatch.org, "Did CAIR Founder Say Islam to Rule America?" December 11, 2006, http://jihadwatch.org/archives/014370.php (accessed October 29, 2008).

11. Daniel Pipes, "The Danger Within: Militant Islam in America," *Commentary*, November 2001, http://www.danielpipes.org/article/77 (accessed December 9, 2008).

12. Ibid.

13. Lisa Gardiner, "American Muslim Leader Urges Faithful to Spread Islam's Message," *San Ramon Valley Herald*, July 4, 1998, as referenced in Daniel Pipes, "CAIR: 'Moderate' Friends of Terror," *New York Post*, April 22, 2002, http://www.danielpipes.org/article/394 (accessed January 26, 2009).

14. Stacey Johnson, "Number of People in a Family," Hypertextbook.com, http://hypertextbook.com/facts/2006/StaceyJohnson.shtml (accessed January 28, 2009).

15. CIA Boy, "Will Britain Convert to Islam?" reader comment on article "The Islamic States of America," October 24, 2005, http://www.danielpipes.org/comments/27273 (accessed January 26, 2009).

16. IslamUnveiled.info, "The Nation of Islam," http://islamunveiled.info/nation.html (accessed January 26, 2009).

17. *Sahih Bukhari*, vol. 1, bk. 3, no. 63, narrated Anas bin Malik, http://www.usc.edu/schools/college/crcc/engagement/resources/texts/muslim/hadith/bukhari/003.sbt.html (accessed December 9, 2008).

18. *Sahih Bukhari*, vol. 4, bk. 56, no. 744, narrated Isma'il bin Abi Khalid, http://www.usc.edu/schools/college/crcc/engagement/resources/texts/muslim/hadith/bukhari/056.sbt.html (accessed December 9, 2008).

19. *Sahih Muslim*, book 004, number 1951, http://abdurrahman.org/sunnah/sahihMuslim/004.smt.html (accessed December 9, 2008).

20. *Sahih Bukhari*, vol. 8, bk. 73, no. 182, narrated Anas bin Malik, http://www.usc.edu/schools/college/crcc/engagement/resources/texts/muslim/hadith/bukhari/073.sbt.html (accessed December 9, 2008).

21. *Sahih Bukhari*, vol. 2, bk. 15, no. 103, narrated 'Urwa on the authority of 'Aisha, http://www.usc.edu/schools/college/crcc/engagement/resources/texts/muslim/hadith/bukhari/015.sbt.html (accessed December 9, 2008).

22. *Sunan Abu-Dawud*, book, number 4458, http://www.usc.edu/schools/college/crcc/engagement/resources/texts/muslim/hadith/abudawud/038.sat.html (accessed December 9, 2008).

23. *Sahih Bukhari*, vol. 1, bk. 11, no. 662, narrated Anas, http://www.usc.edu/schools/college/crcc/engagement/resources/texts/muslim/hadith/bukhari/011.sbt.html (accessed December 10, 2008). Also, *Sahih Bukhari*, vol. 9, bk. 89, no. 256, narrated Anas bin Malik, http://www.usc.edu/schools/college/crcc/engagement/resources/texts/muslim/hadith/bukhari/089.sbt.html (accessed December 10, 2008).

24. *Newsweek*, "Slavery," May 4, 1992, 30, cited in Craig Keener, "Christianity, Islam and Slavery," http://www.answering-islam.org/ReachOut/ckeener.html (accessed October 29, 2008).

CHAPTER 14
THE OIL BEAST RISING OUT OF THE SEA

1. Sacred-Destinations.com, "The Prophet's Mosque: Medina," accessed at http://www.sacred-destinations.com/saudi-arabia/medina-prophets-mosque.htm (accessed October 30, 2008).

2. I was given this information about Osama bin Laden by a Palestinian Christian during a conversation.

3. This story came to me from an Ohio bishop, who heard it from an Orthodox bishop in Iraq.

4. Raja Menon, *Weapons of Mass Destruction: Options for India* (Thousand Oaks, CA: Sage, 2004), 172.

5. Oliver Burkeman, "Bin Laden 'Asked Scientist to Build N-bomb,'" Guardian.co.uk, December 30, 2002, http://www.guardian.co.uk/world/2002/dec/30/alqaida.pakistan (accessed October 30, 2008).

6. *Compendium of Muslim Texts*, "Signs of the Last Hour," http://www.usc.edu/dept/MSA/fundamentals/pillars/signsofthelasthour.html (accessed November 14, 2008).

7. TheLampholder.org, "Islamic Eschatology, End Times Prophecy, Imam al-Mahdi," http://www.lampholderpub.com/Islamic_Prophecy.htm (accessed November 14, 2008).

8. JihadWatch.org, "Terror Attack Against the U.S. With 100,000 Deaths Is Imminent," November 13, 2003, http://jihadwatch.org/archives/2003_11.php (accessed October 30, 2008).

9. Verity Murphy, "Mecca Cola Challenges US Rival," *BBC News, World Edition*, January 8, 2003, http://news.bbc.co.uk/2/hi/middle_east/2640259. stm (accessed October 30, 2008).

10. IslamicMint.com, "Introducing the Islamic Dinar and Dirham," http://www.islamicmint.com/islamicdinar/ (accessed December 10, 2008).

11. Bill Sardi, "How the Islamic World Plans to Beat the West: A Gold Coin," LewRockwell.com http://www.lewrockwell.com/sardi/sardi20.html (accessed October 30, 2008).

12. Roland Watson, "The Great Silver Spike of 1980," *The Silver Analyst*, May 10, 2006, http://www.safehaven.com/article-5133.htm (accessed October 30, 2008); Roland Watson, "Silver and Gold Stocks Revisited," *SilverSeeker. com*, March 28, 2008, http://news.silverseek.com/SilverSeek/1206684000.php (accessed October 30, 2008).

CHAPTER 15
THE CONTROVERSIAL DOME OF THE ROCK

1. NobleSanctuary.com, "Al-Aqsa Mosque," http://www.noblesanctuary. com/AQSAMosque.html (accessed November 12, 2008).

2. TempleMountFaithful.org, "The Riddle of the Dome of the Rock: Was it Built as a Jewish Place of Prayer?" Summer 2001, http://www.templemount faithful.org/Newsletters/2001/5761-11.htm (accessed October 30, 2008).

3. Ibid.

4. Ibid.

5. Ibid.

6. Palestinian National Authority Ministry of Foreign Affairs, "National and Regional Responses to the Recent Israeli Threats to Harm Al-Aqsa Holy Mosque," July 27, 2004, http://www.mofa.gov.ps/day.php?m=7&y=2004&d=27 (accessed November 12, 2008).

7. Quoted from Jerome's *Lives of Illustrious Men*, in R. Alan Culpepper, *John, the Son of Zebedee* (New York: Continuum International Publishing Group, 2000), 162.

8. Jewish Virtual Library, "The Clinton Peace Plan," December 23, 2000, http://www.jewishvirtuallibrary.org/jsource/Peace/clinton_plan.html (accessed November 12, 2008).

9. Andrew Hammond, "Anticipating New U.S. Administration, Egypt Backs Arafat's Rejection of Final Clinton 'Peace Proposal,'" *Washington Report on Middle East Affairs*, March 2001, http://www.washington-report .org/archives/march01/0103027.html (accessed November 12, 2008).

10. FreeRepublic.com, "Peres on Sept 5th Goes to the Vatican to See If Catholic Church Will Oversee Temple Mount," August 27, 2007, http://www .freerepublic.com/focus/f-news/1887526/posts (accessed December 10, 2008).

11. Maraz Studios, "Passover 2008," www.marazstudios.com/ Passover_2008.html (accessed November 12, 2008).

12. *The Ante-Nicene Fathers*, volume 8 (Grand Rapids, MI: Wm. B. Eerdmans Publishing Company, 1951), 394.

13. *The Ante-Nicene Fathers*, volume 2 (Grand Rapids, MI: Wm. B. Eerdmans Publishing Company, 1951), 141.

14. Mohammed Ali Ibn Zubair Ali, "Who Is the Evil Dajjal (the 'anti-Christ')?" http://www.islam.tc/prophecies/masdaj.html (accessed January 8, 2009).

15. Ibid.

16. *Sahih Muslim*, book 001, number 0327, http://www.usc.edu/schools/ college/crcc/engagement/resources/texts/muslim/hadith/muslim/001.smt.html (accessed March 10, 2009).

17. *Sahih Muslim*, book 041, number 6979, http://www.usc.edu/schools/ college/crcc/engagement/resources/texts/muslim/hadith/muslim/041.smt.html (accessed March 10, 2009).

18. MissionIslam.com, "Signs of the Appearance of the Dajjal and His Destruction," http://www.missionislam.com/nwo/signsdajjal.htm (accessed March 10, 2009).

FREE NEWSLETTERS
TO HELP EMPOWER YOUR LIFE

Why subscribe today?

❑ **DELIVERED DIRECTLY TO YOU.** All you have to do is open your inbox and read.

❑ **EXCLUSIVE CONTENT.** We cover the news overlooked by the mainstream press.

❑ **STAY CURRENT.** Find the latest court rulings, revivals, and cultural trends.

❑ **UPDATE OTHERS.** Easy to forward to friends and family with the click of your mouse.

CHOOSE THE E-NEWSLETTER THAT INTERESTS YOU MOST:

- Christian news
- Daily devotionals
- Spiritual empowerment
- And much, much more

SIGN UP AT: **http://freenewsletters.charismamag.com**

8178